DENNIS HOPELESS
SERG ACUÑA
DOUG GARBARK

THE SAMI & KEVIN SHOW

BOOM!
STUDIOS

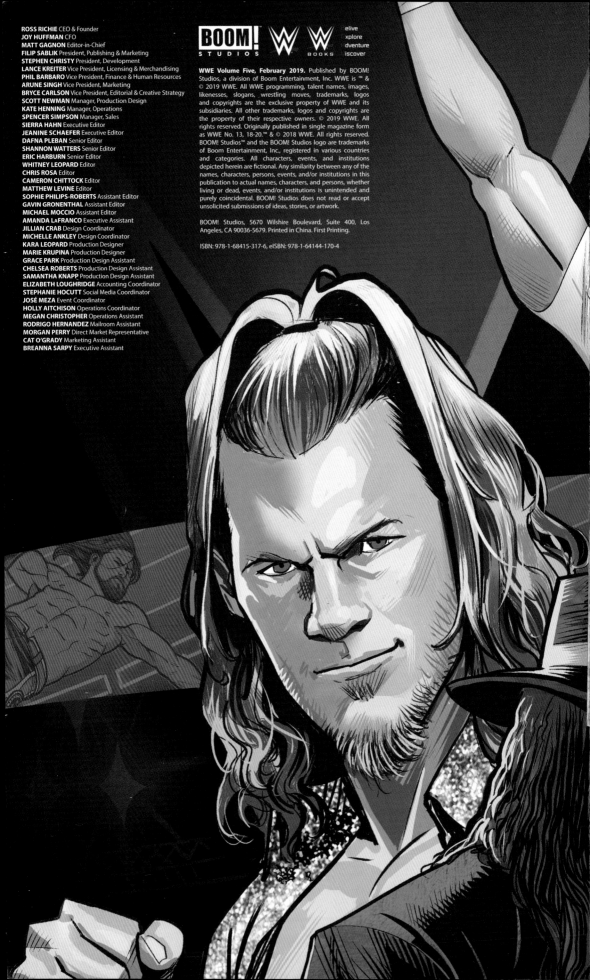

BOOM! STUDIOS   WWE   WWE BOOKS
elive
xplore
dventure
iscover

WWE Volume Five, February 2019. Published by BOOM!
Studios, a division of Boom Entertainment, Inc. WWE is ™ &
© 2019 WWE. All WWE programming, talent names, images,
likenesses, slogans, wrestling moves, trademarks, logos
and copyrights are the exclusive property of WWE and its
subsidiaries. All other trademarks, logos and copyrights are
the property of their respective owners. © 2019 WWE. All
rights reserved. Originally published in single magazine form
as WWE No. 13, 18-20.™ & © 2018 WWE. All rights reserved.
BOOM! Studios™ and the BOOM! Studios logo are trademarks
of Boom Entertainment, Inc., registered in various countries
and categories. All characters, events, and institutions
depicted herein are fictional. Any similarity between any of the
names, characters, persons, events, and/or institutions in this
publication to actual names, characters, and persons, whether
living or dead, events, and/or institutions is unintended and
purely coincidental. BOOM! Studios does not read or accept
unsolicited submissions of ideas, stories, or artwork.

BOOM! Studios, 5670 Wilshire Boulevard, Suite 400, Los
Angeles, CA 90036-5679. Printed in China. First Printing.

ISBN: 978-1-68415-317-6, eISBN: 978-1-64144-170-4

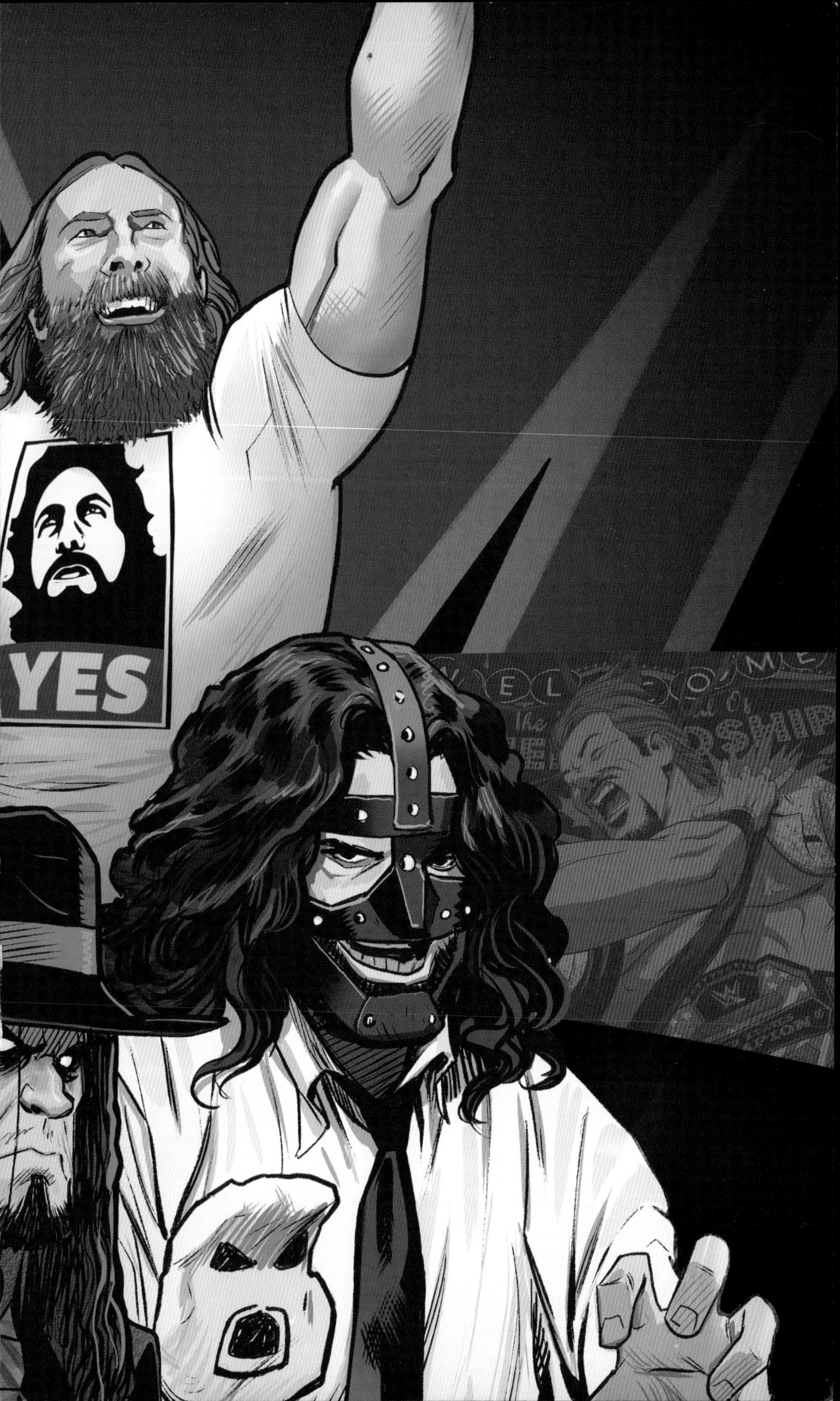
YES

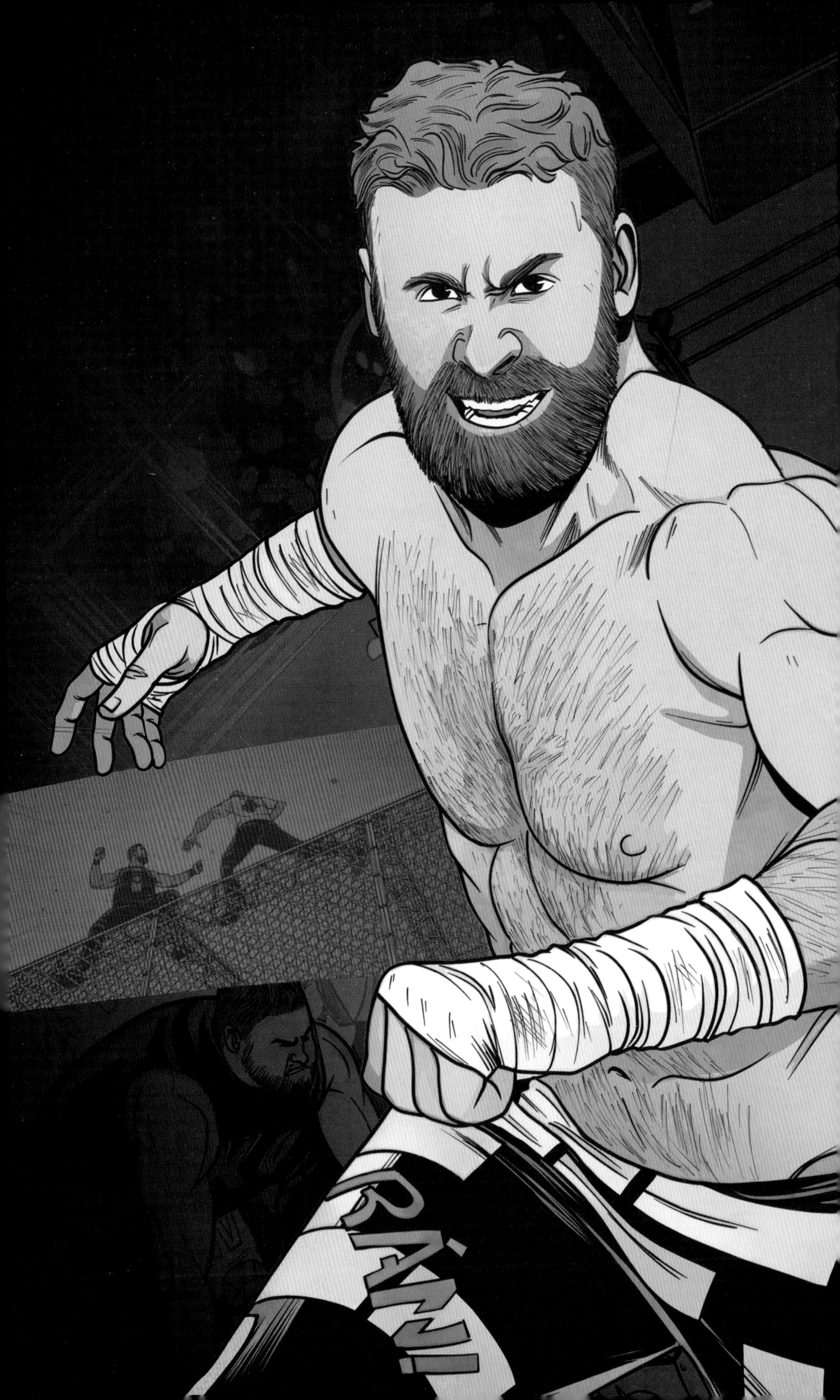
BAM!

UNDRAFTED
WRITTEN BY
SAMOA JOE & MICHAEL KINGSTON
ILLUSTRATED BY
MICHEL MULIPOLA
COLORED BY
DOUG GARBARK

THE YES! MOVEMENT
WRITTEN BY
JULIAN MAY
ILLUSTRATED BY
RODRIGO LORENZO
COLORED BY
DOUG GARBARK

UNBROKEN
WRITTEN BY
LAN PITTS
ILLUSTRATED BY
KENDALL GOODE

FEST PREP
WRITTEN BY
KEVIN PANETTA
ILLUSTRATED BY
DANIEL BAYLISS

THE SAMI & KEVIN SHOW

WRITTEN BY
DENNIS HOPELESS

ILLUSTRATED BY
SERG ACUÑA

COLORED BY
DOUG GARBARK

LETTERED BY
JIM CAMPBELL

COVER BY
DAN MORA

SERIES DESIGNER
GRACE PARK

COLLECTION DESIGNER
JILLIAN CRAB

ASSISTANT EDITOR
GAVIN GRONENTHAL

EDITOR
CHRIS ROSA

SPECIAL THANKS TO
STEVE PANTALEO
CHAD BARBASH
BEN MAYER
JOHN JONES
STAN STANSKI
LAUREN DIENES-MIDDLEN
AND EVERYONE AT **WWE**

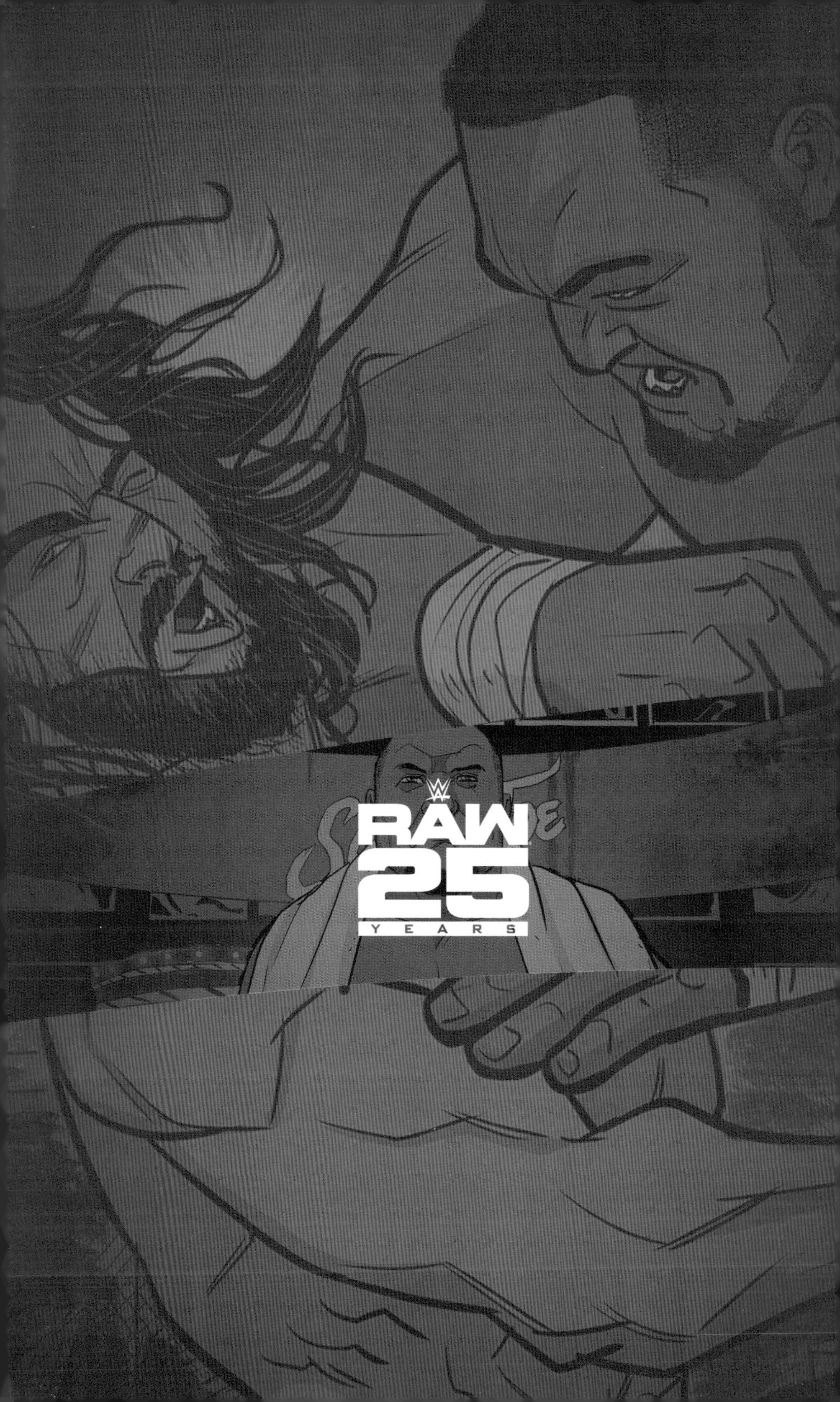
RAW
25
YEARS

IF YOU'LL EXCUSE ME, I HAVE TO TAKE THIS.

Mick Foley

JOE? MICK FOLEY. I'M HERE IN THE **MONDAY NIGHT RAW** DRAFT ROOM.

WE'RE LOOKING AT BRINGING IN SOME FRESH TALENT TO REALLY KICK OFF THE NEW ERA OF MONDAY NIGHT RAW WITH A BANG.

I'M LISTENING...

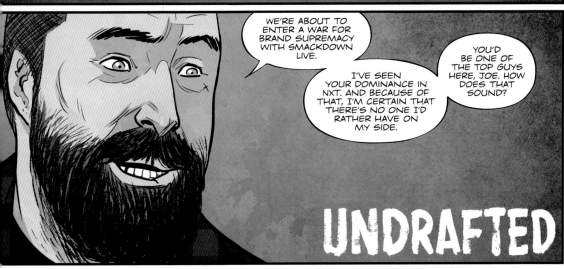

WE'RE ABOUT TO ENTER A WAR FOR BRAND SUPREMACY WITH SMACKDOWN LIVE.

I'VE SEEN YOUR DOMINANCE IN NXT. AND BECAUSE OF THAT, I'M CERTAIN THAT THERE'S NO ONE I'D RATHER HAVE ON MY SIDE.

YOU'D BE ONE OF THE TOP GUYS HERE, JOE. HOW DOES THAT SOUND?

UNDRAFTED

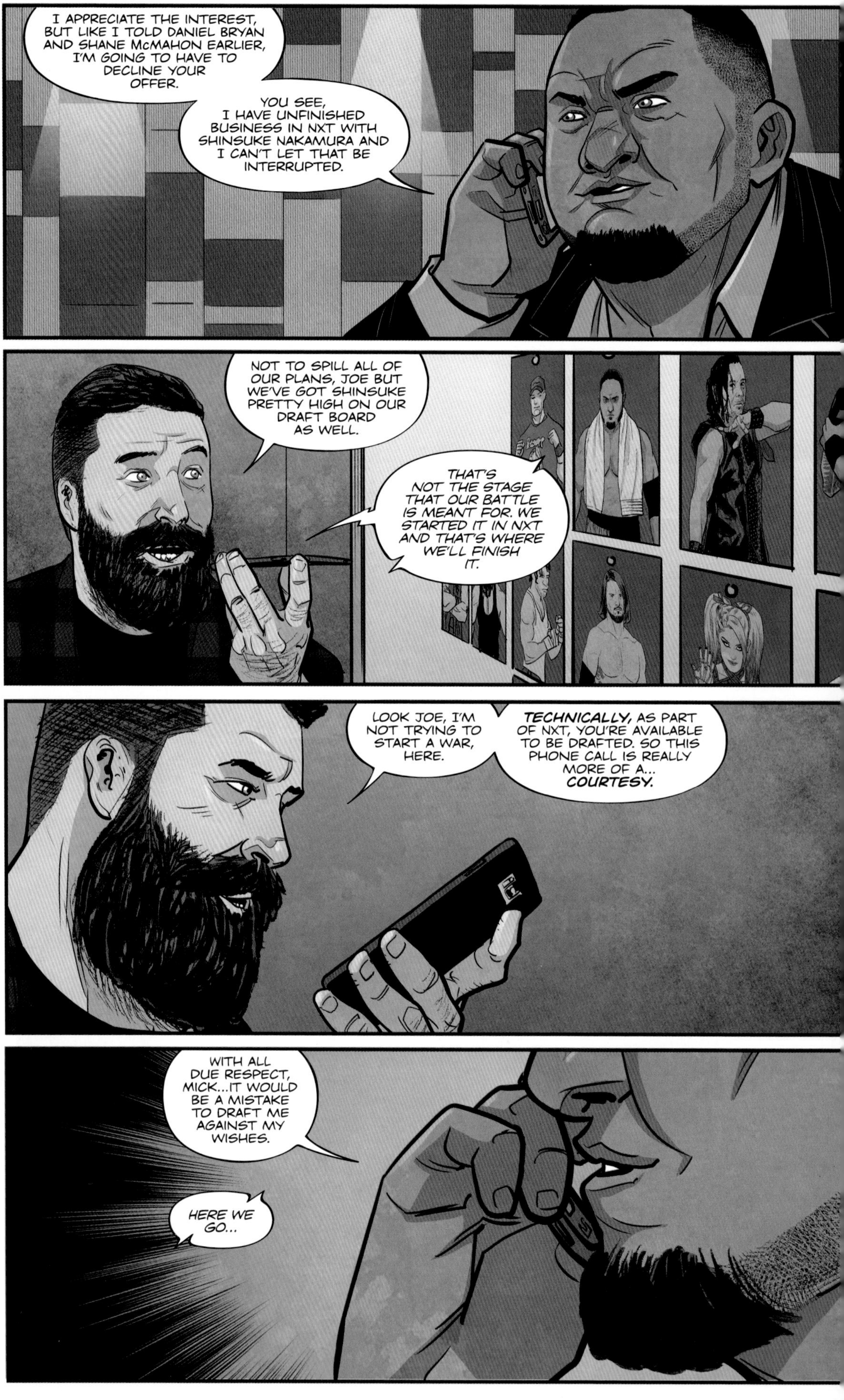
I APPRECIATE THE INTEREST, BUT LIKE I TOLD DANIEL BRYAN AND SHANE McMAHON EARLIER, I'M GOING TO HAVE TO DECLINE YOUR OFFER.
YOU SEE, I HAVE UNFINISHED BUSINESS IN NXT WITH SHINSUKE NAKAMURA AND I CAN'T LET THAT BE INTERRUPTED.
NOT TO SPILL ALL OF OUR PLANS, JOE BUT WE'VE GOT SHINSUKE PRETTY HIGH ON OUR DRAFT BOARD AS WELL.
THAT'S NOT THE STAGE THAT OUR BATTLE IS MEANT FOR. WE STARTED IT IN NXT AND THAT'S WHERE WE'LL FINISH IT.
LOOK JOE, I'M NOT TRYING TO START A WAR, HERE.
TECHNICALLY, AS PART OF NXT, YOU'RE AVAILABLE TO BE DRAFTED. SO THIS PHONE CALL IS REALLY MORE OF A... COURTESY.
WITH ALL DUE RESPECT, MICK...IT WOULD BE A MISTAKE TO DRAFT ME AGAINST MY WISHES.
HERE WE GO...

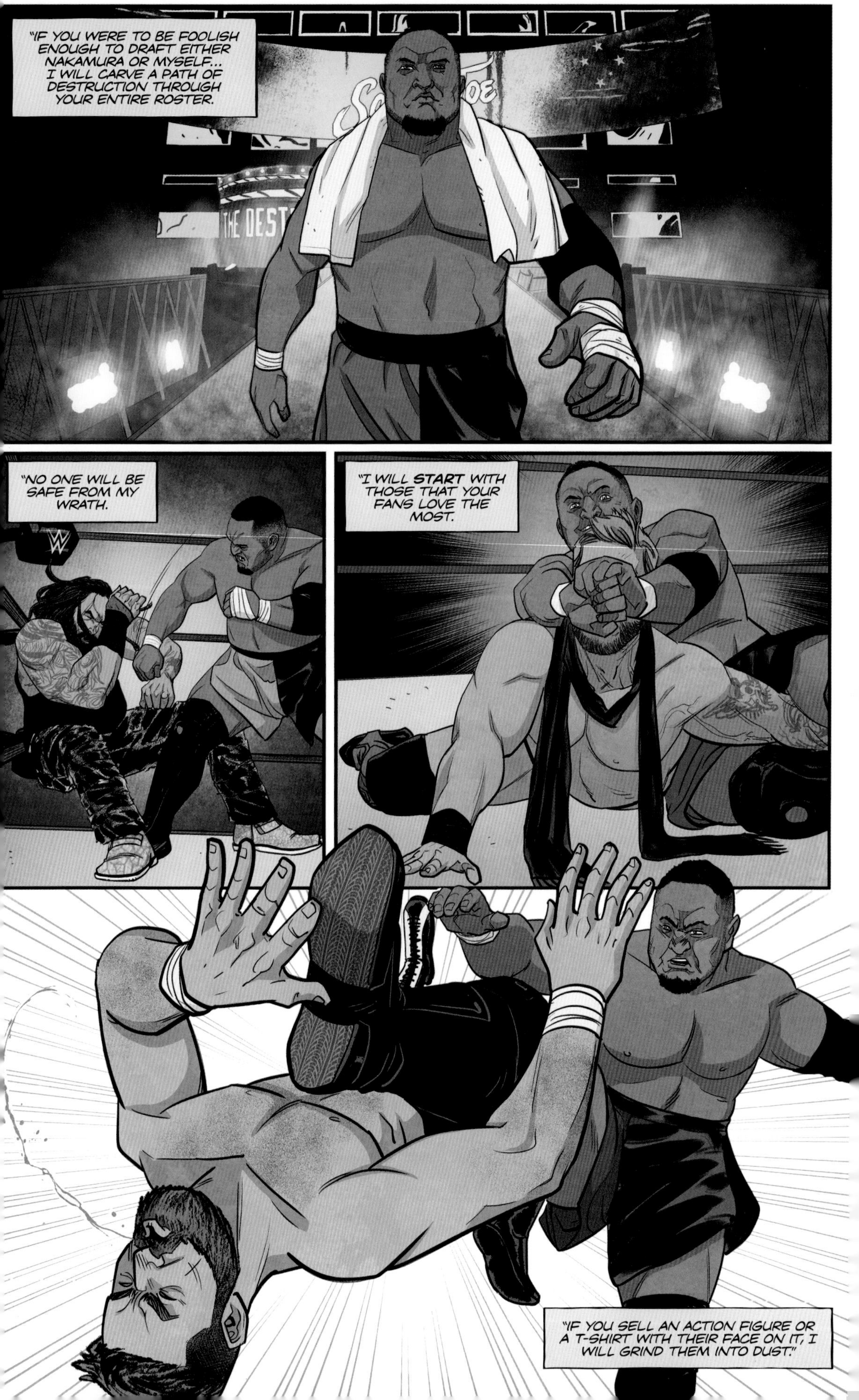
"IF YOU WERE TO BE FOOLISH ENOUGH TO DRAFT EITHER NAKAMURA OR MYSELF... I WILL CARVE A PATH OF DESTRUCTION THROUGH YOUR ENTIRE ROSTER.
THE DEST
"NO ONE WILL BE SAFE FROM MY WRATH.
"I WILL START WITH THOSE THAT YOUR FANS LOVE THE MOST.
"IF YOU SELL AN ACTION FIGURE OR A T-SHIRT WITH THEIR FACE ON IT, I WILL GRIND THEM INTO DUST."

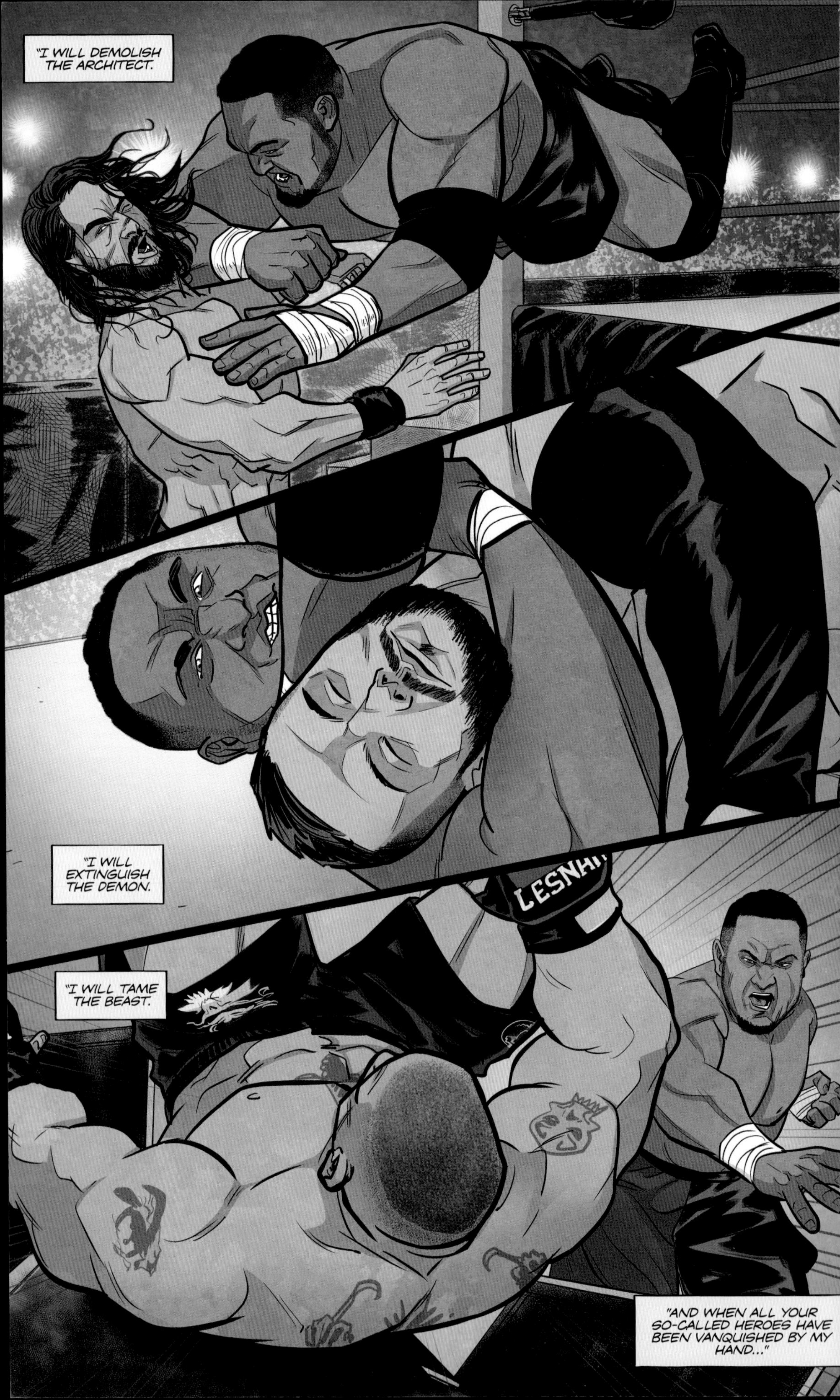
"I WILL DEMOLISH THE ARCHITECT.
"I WILL EXTINGUISH THE DEMON.
LESNAR
"I WILL TAME THE BEAST.
"AND WHEN ALL YOUR SO-CALLED HEROES HAVE BEEN VANQUISHED BY MY HAND..."

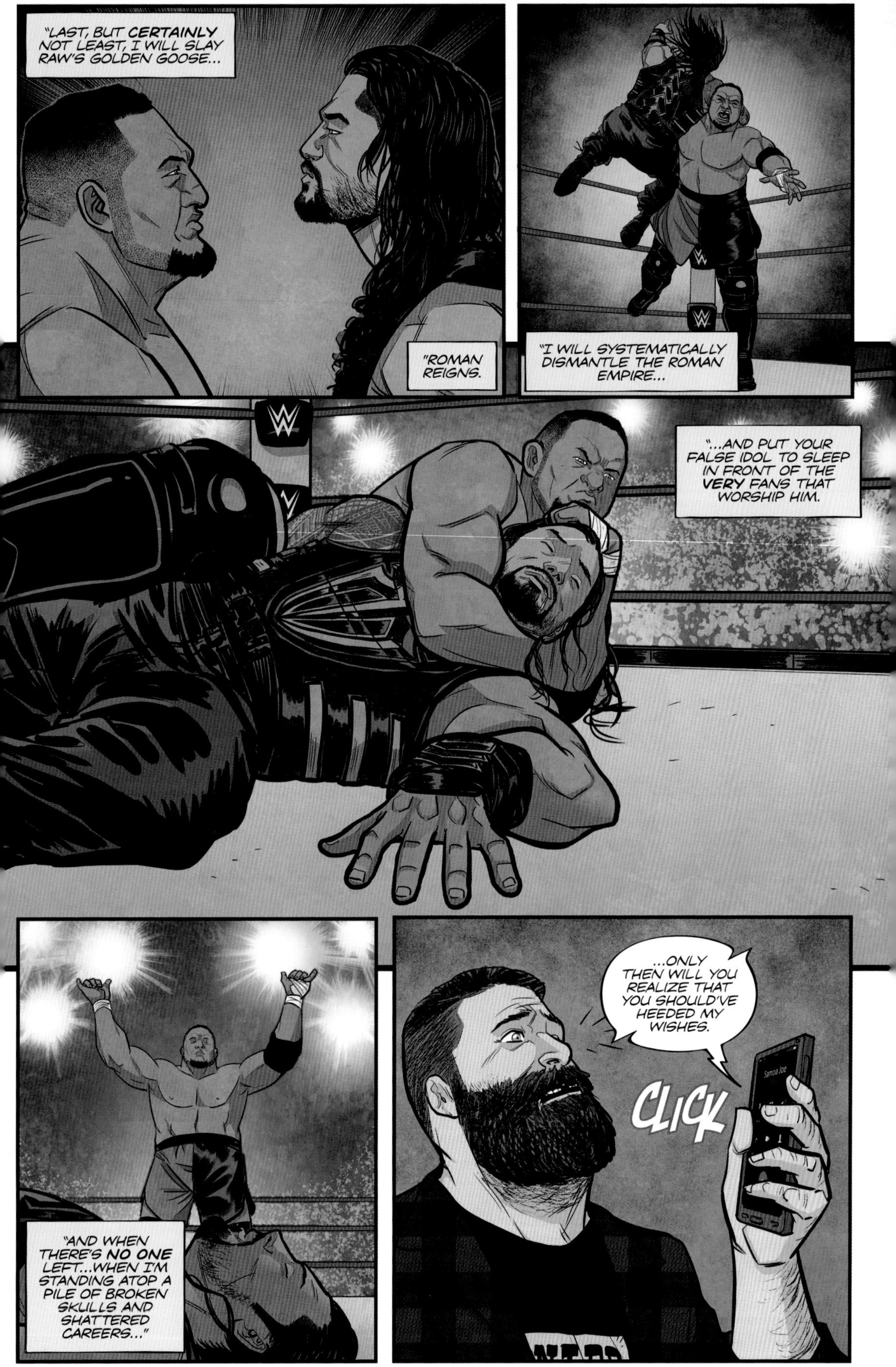
"LAST, BUT CERTAINLY NOT LEAST, I WILL SLAY RAW'S GOLDEN GOOSE...
"ROMAN REIGNS.
"I WILL SYSTEMATICALLY DISMANTLE THE ROMAN EMPIRE...
"...AND PUT YOUR FALSE IDOL TO SLEEP IN FRONT OF THE VERY FANS THAT WORSHIP HIM.
"AND WHEN THERE'S NO ONE LEFT...WHEN I'M STANDING ATOP A PILE OF BROKEN SKULLS AND SHATTERED CAREERS..."
...ONLY THEN WILL YOU REALIZE THAT YOU SHOULD'VE HEEDED MY WISHES.
Samoa Joe
CLICK

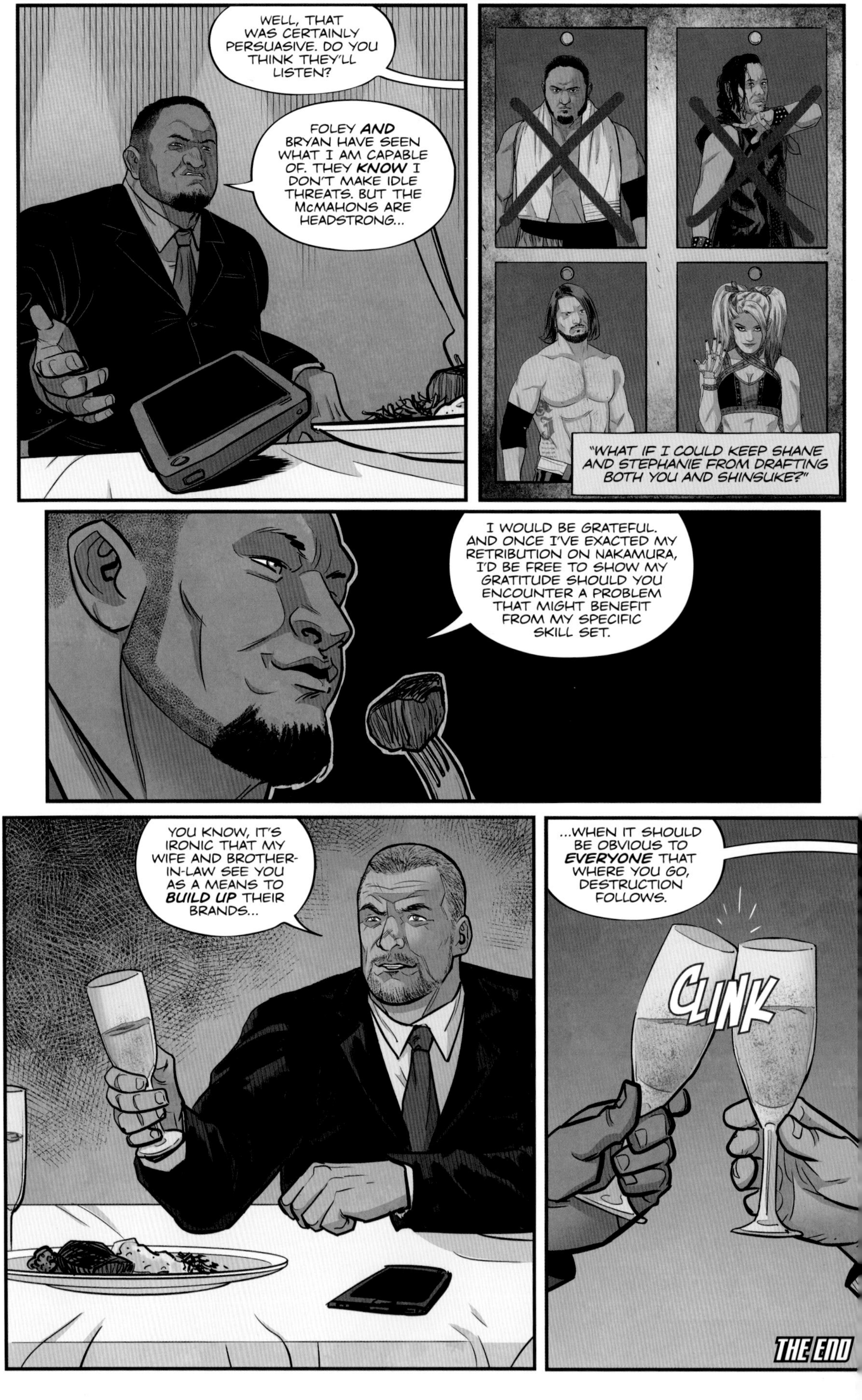
WELL, THAT WAS CERTAINLY PERSUASIVE. DO YOU THINK THEY'LL LISTEN?
FOLEY AND BRYAN HAVE SEEN WHAT I AM CAPABLE OF. THEY KNOW I DON'T MAKE IDLE THREATS. BUT THE McMAHONS ARE HEADSTRONG...
"WHAT IF I COULD KEEP SHANE AND STEPHANIE FROM DRAFTING BOTH YOU AND SHINSUKE?"
I WOULD BE GRATEFUL. AND ONCE I'VE EXACTED MY RETRIBUTION ON NAKAMURA, I'D BE FREE TO SHOW MY GRATITUDE SHOULD YOU ENCOUNTER A PROBLEM THAT MIGHT BENEFIT FROM MY SPECIFIC SKILL SET.
YOU KNOW, IT'S IRONIC THAT MY WIFE AND BROTHER-IN-LAW SEE YOU AS A MEANS TO BUILD UP THEIR BRANDS...
...WHEN IT SHOULD BE OBVIOUS TO EVERYONE THAT WHERE YOU GO, DESTRUCTION FOLLOWS.
CLINK
THE END

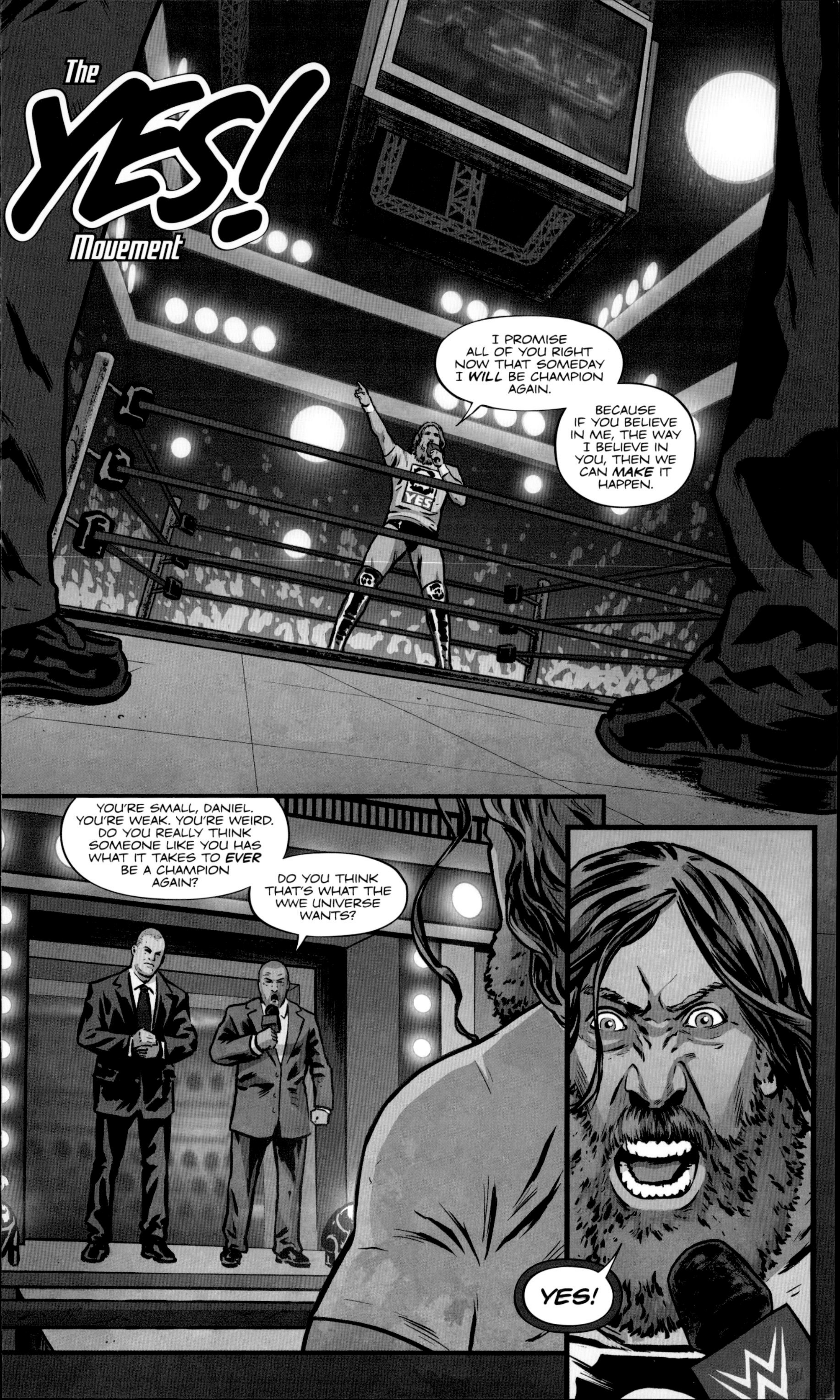
The YES! Movement
I PROMISE ALL OF YOU RIGHT NOW THAT SOMEDAY I WILL BE CHAMPION AGAIN.
BECAUSE IF YOU BELIEVE IN ME, THE WAY I BELIEVE IN YOU, THEN WE CAN MAKE IT HAPPEN.
YES
YOU'RE SMALL, DANIEL. YOU'RE WEAK. YOU'RE WEIRD. DO YOU REALLY THINK SOMEONE LIKE YOU HAS WHAT IT TAKES TO EVER BE A CHAMPION AGAIN?
DO YOU THINK THAT'S WHAT THE WWE UNIVERSE WANTS?
YES!

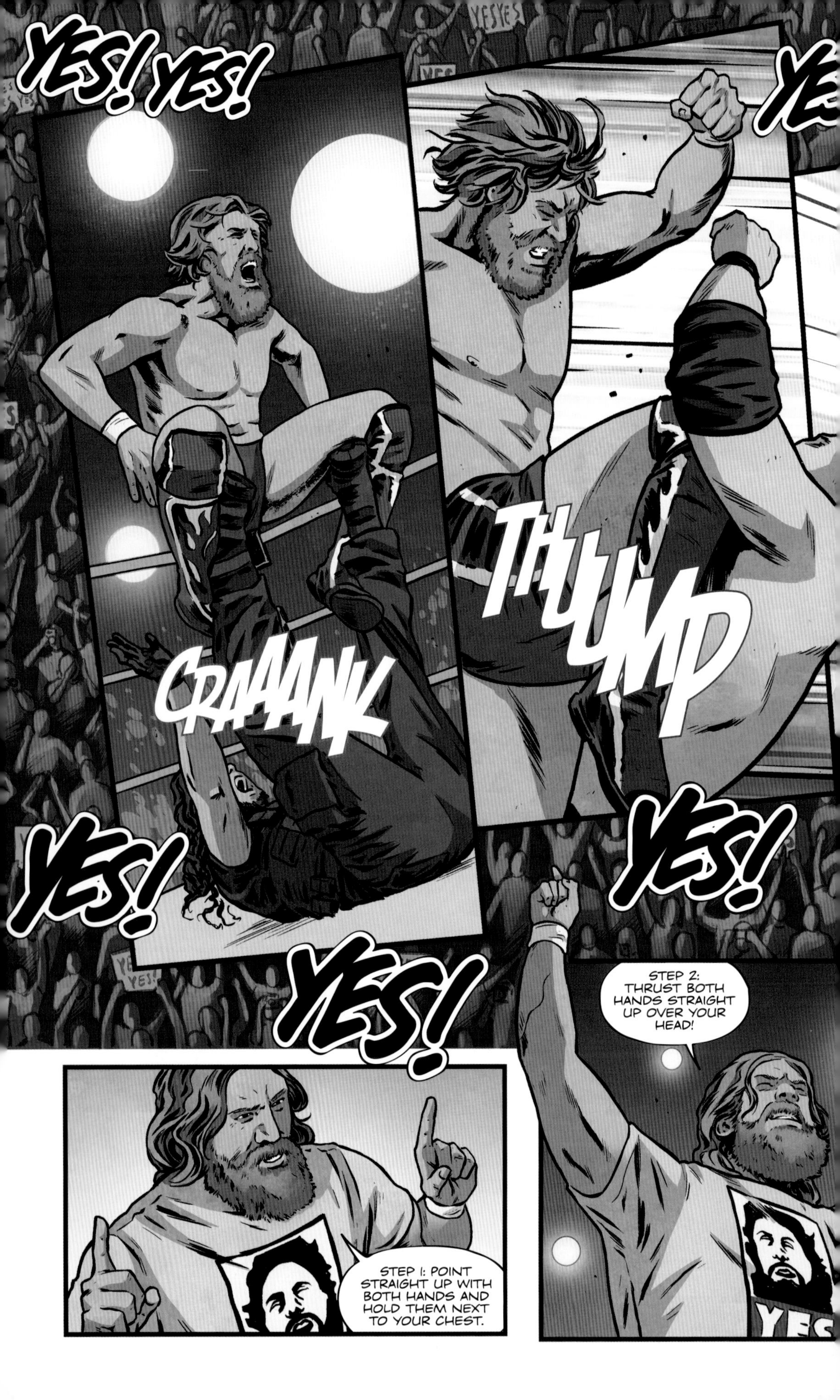
YES! YES!
YES
CRAAAANK
THUUMP
YES!
YES!
YES!
STEP 1: POINT STRAIGHT UP WITH BOTH HANDS AND HOLD THEM NEXT TO YOUR CHEST.
STEP 2: THRUST BOTH HANDS STRAIGHT UP OVER YOUR HEAD!

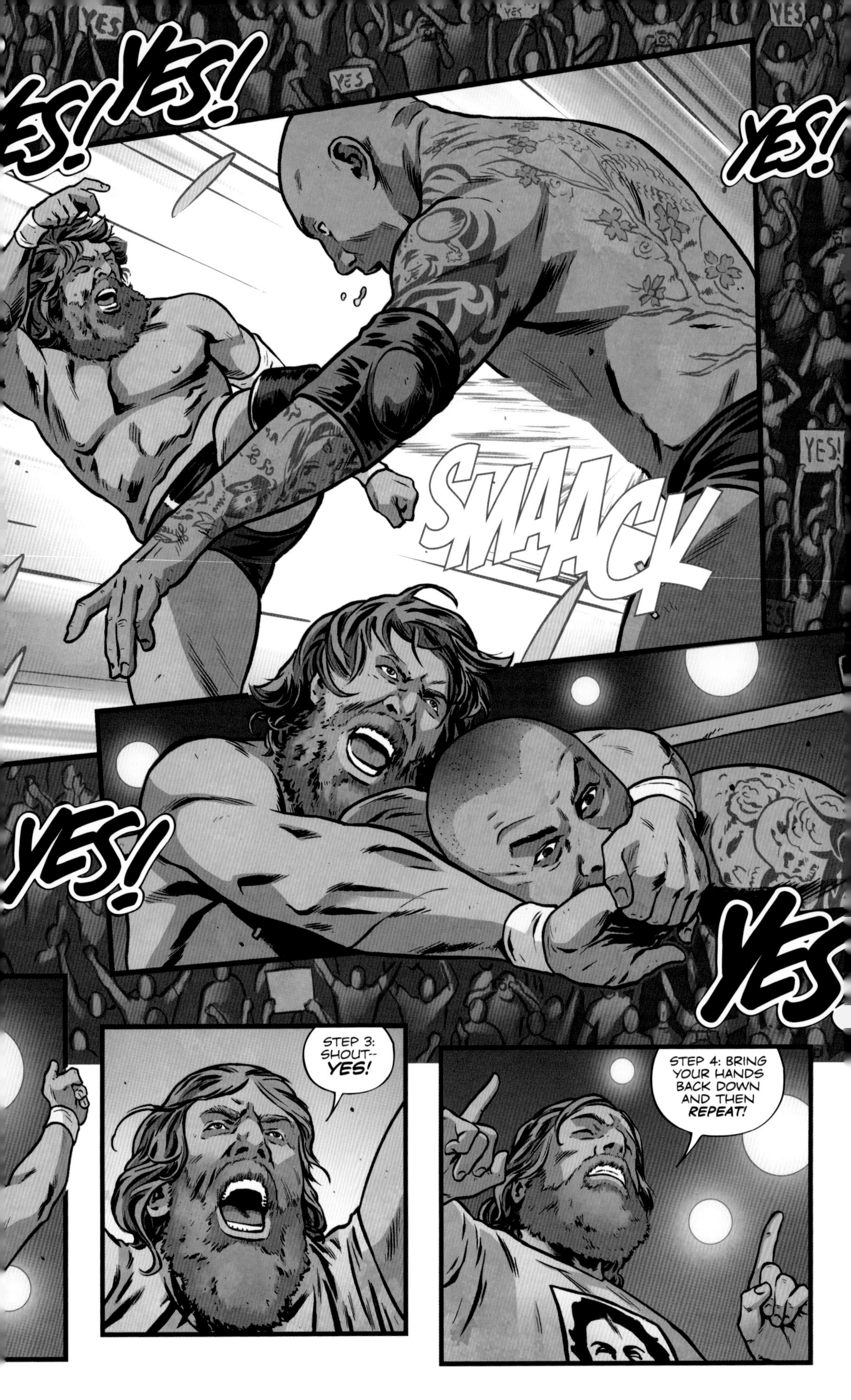

YES! YES!
YES!
SMAAACK
YES!
YES!
STEP 3: SHOUT-- YES!
STEP 4: BRING YOUR HANDS BACK DOWN AND THEN REPEAT!

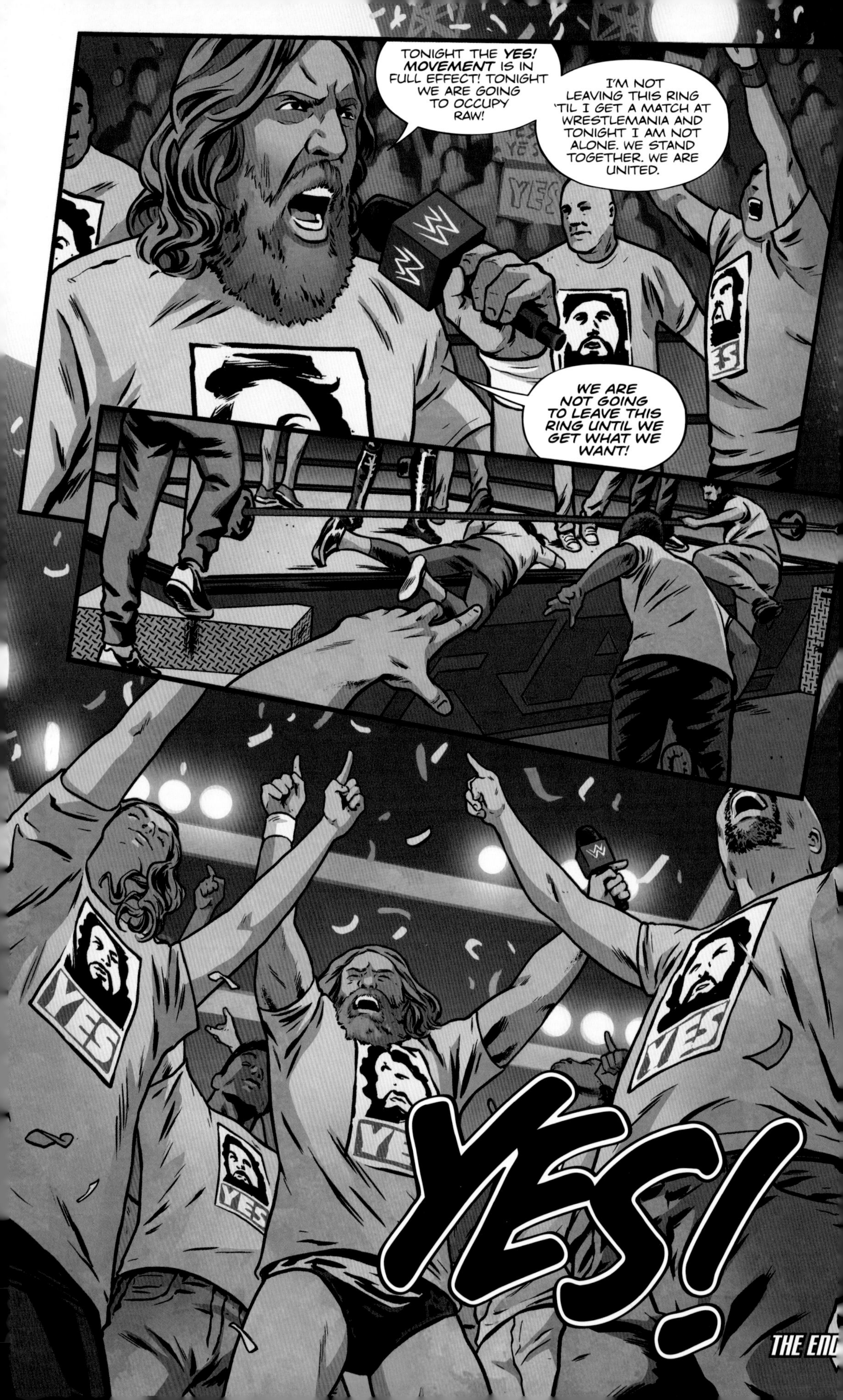

TONIGHT THE YES! MOVEMENT IS IN FULL EFFECT! TONIGHT WE ARE GOING TO OCCUPY RAW!
I'M NOT LEAVING THIS RING 'TIL I GET A MATCH AT WRESTLEMANIA AND TONIGHT I AM NOT ALONE. WE STAND TOGETHER. WE ARE UNITED.
WE ARE NOT GOING TO LEAVE THIS RING UNTIL WE GET WHAT WE WANT!
YES!
THE END

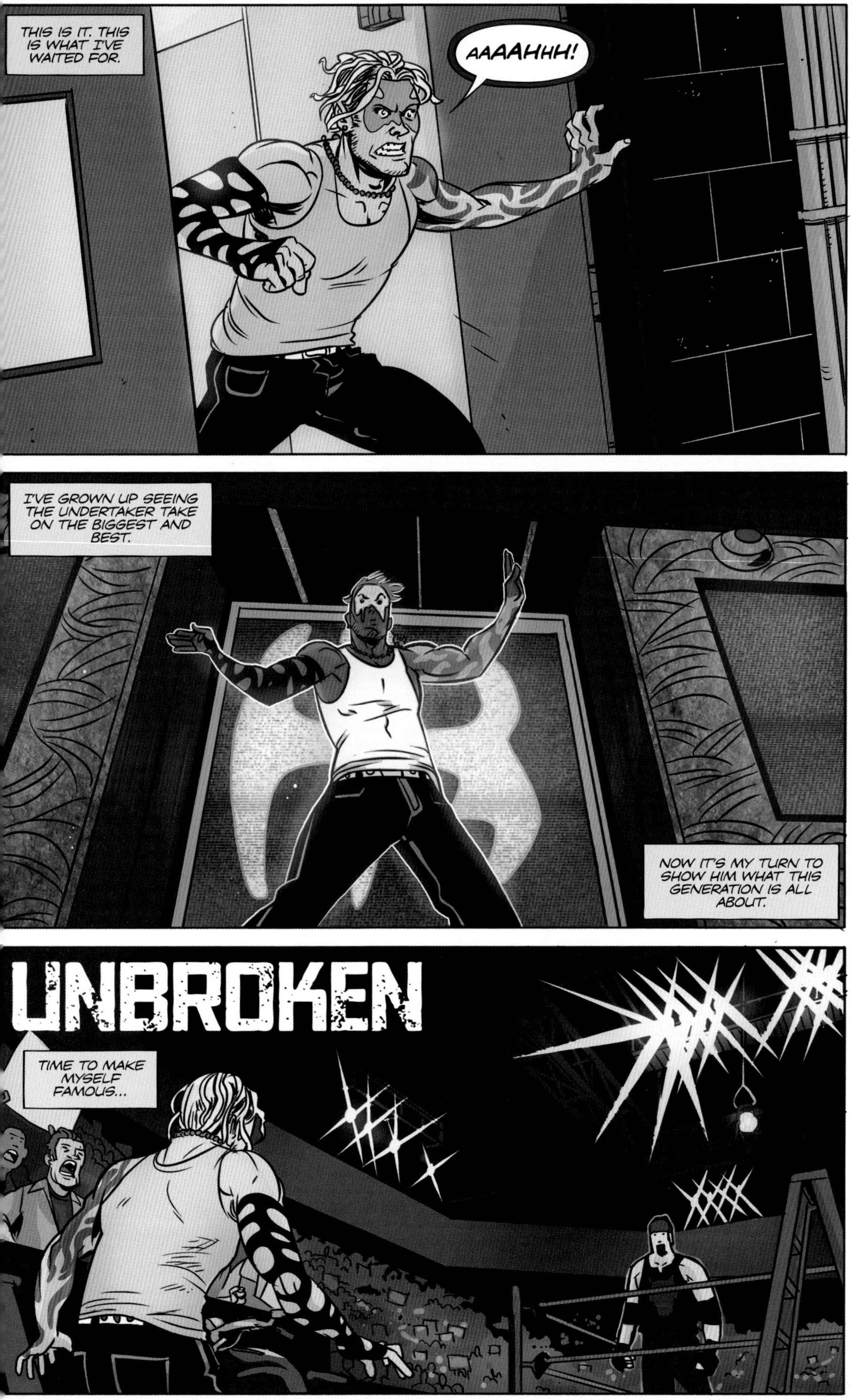
THIS IS IT. THIS IS WHAT I'VE WAITED FOR.
AAAAHHH!
I'VE GROWN UP SEEING THE UNDERTAKER TAKE ON THE BIGGEST AND BEST.
NOW IT'S MY TURN TO SHOW HIM WHAT THIS GENERATION IS ALL ABOUT.
UNBROKEN
TIME TO MAKE MYSELF FAMOUS...

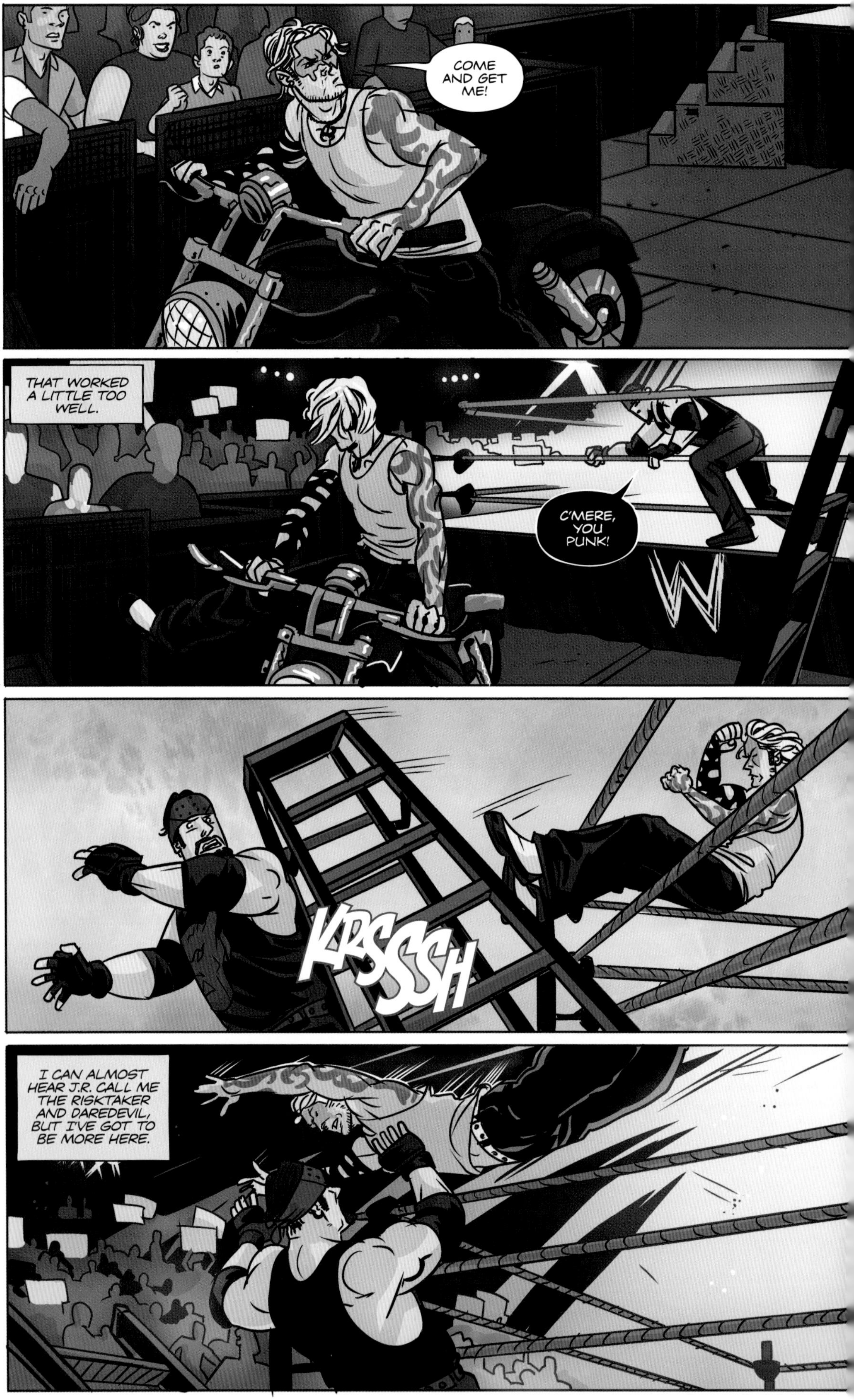
COME AND GET ME!
THAT WORKED A LITTLE TOO WELL.
C'MERE, YOU PUNK!
KRSSSH
I CAN ALMOST HEAR J.R. CALL ME THE RISKTAKER AND DAREDEVIL, BUT I'VE GOT TO BE MORE HERE.

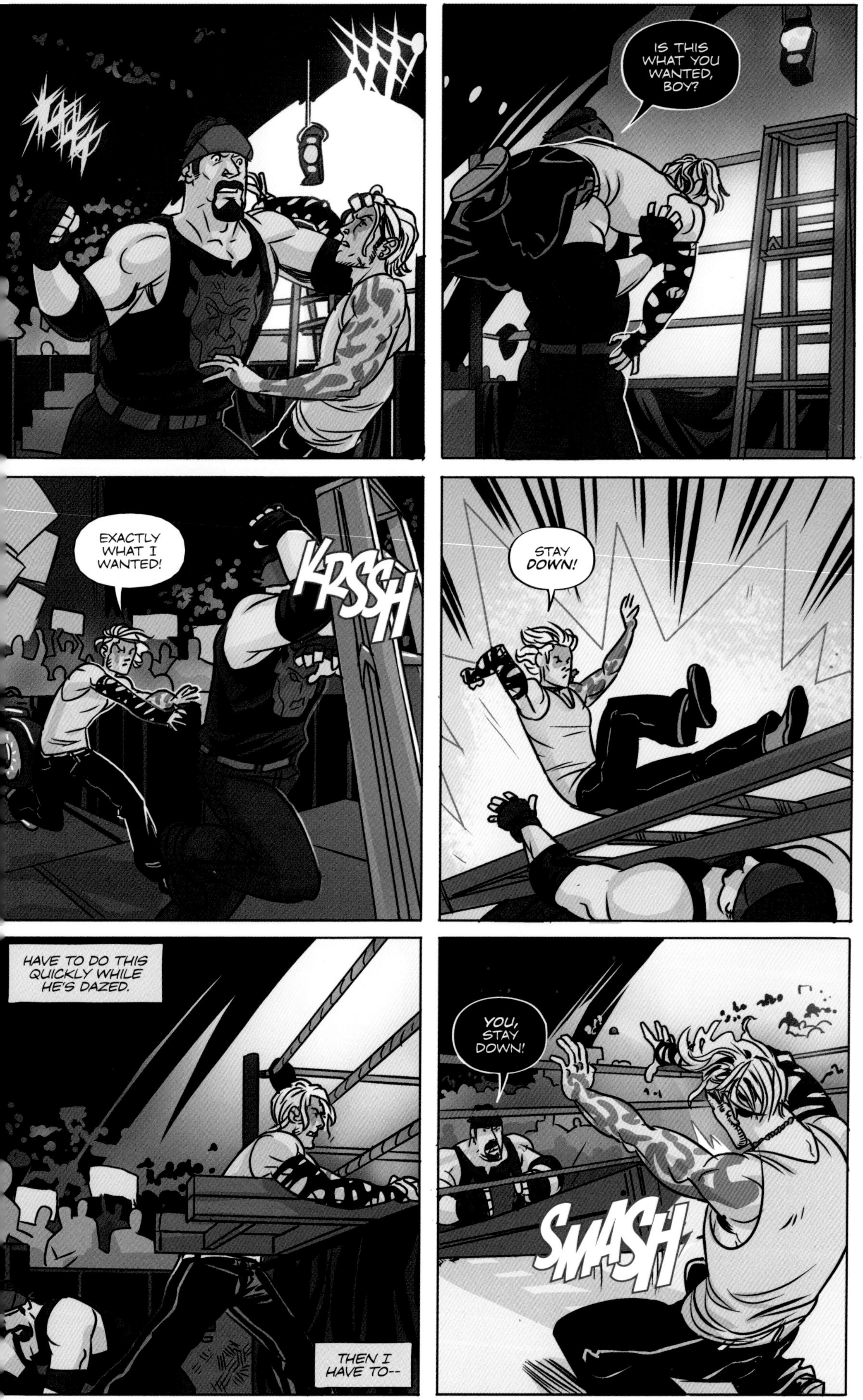
IS THIS WHAT YOU WANTED, BOY?
EXACTLY WHAT I WANTED!
KRSSH
STAY DOWN!
HAVE TO DO THIS QUICKLY WHILE HE'S DAZED.
THEN I HAVE TO--
YOU, STAY DOWN!
SMASH

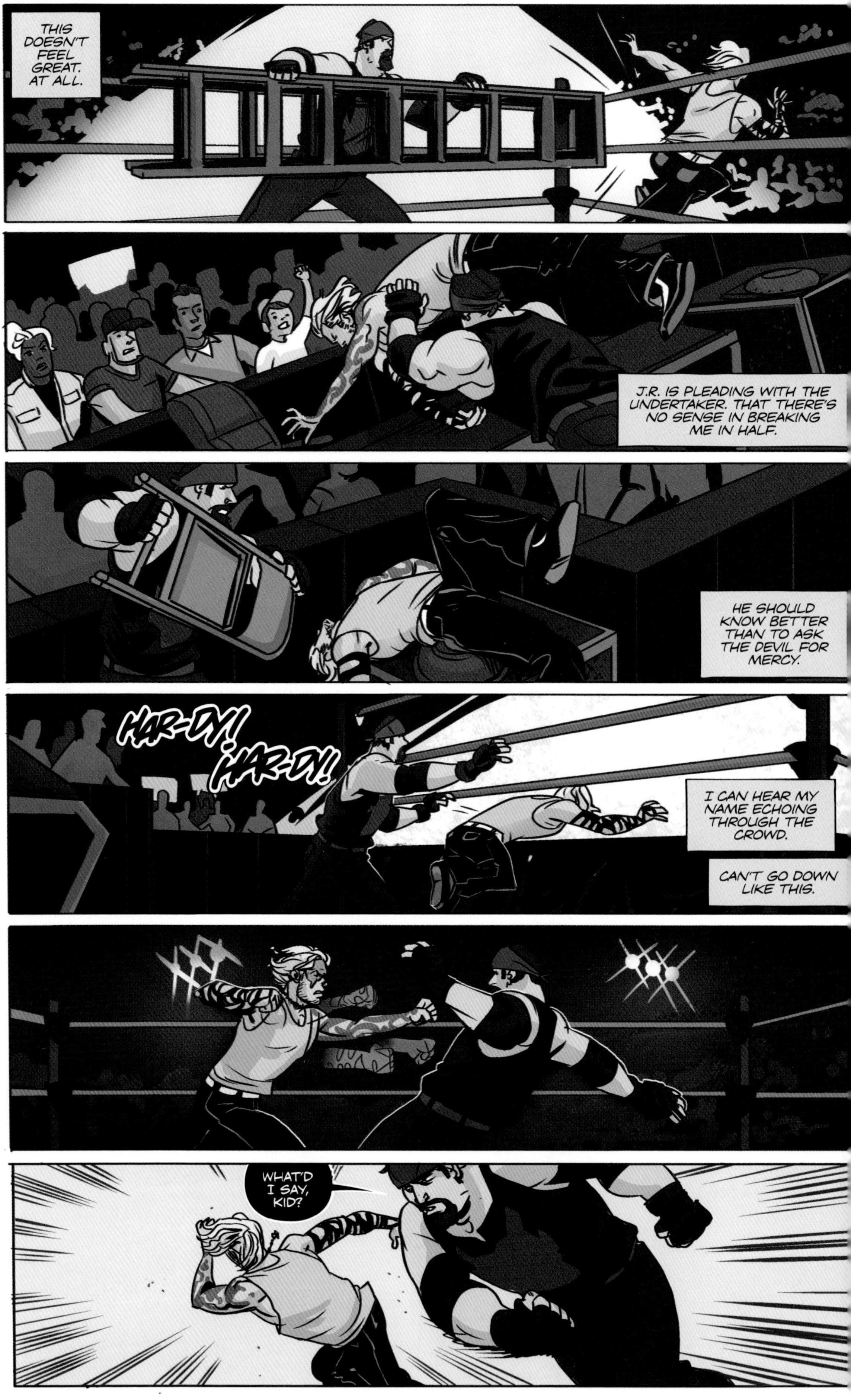
THIS DOESN'T FEEL GREAT. AT ALL.
J.R. IS PLEADING WITH THE UNDERTAKER. THAT THERE'S NO SENSE IN BREAKING ME IN HALF.
HE SHOULD KNOW BETTER THAN TO ASK THE DEVIL FOR MERCY.
HAR-DY! HAR-DY!
I CAN HEAR MY NAME ECHOING THROUGH THE CROWD.
CAN'T GO DOWN LIKE THIS.
WHAT'D I SAY, KID?

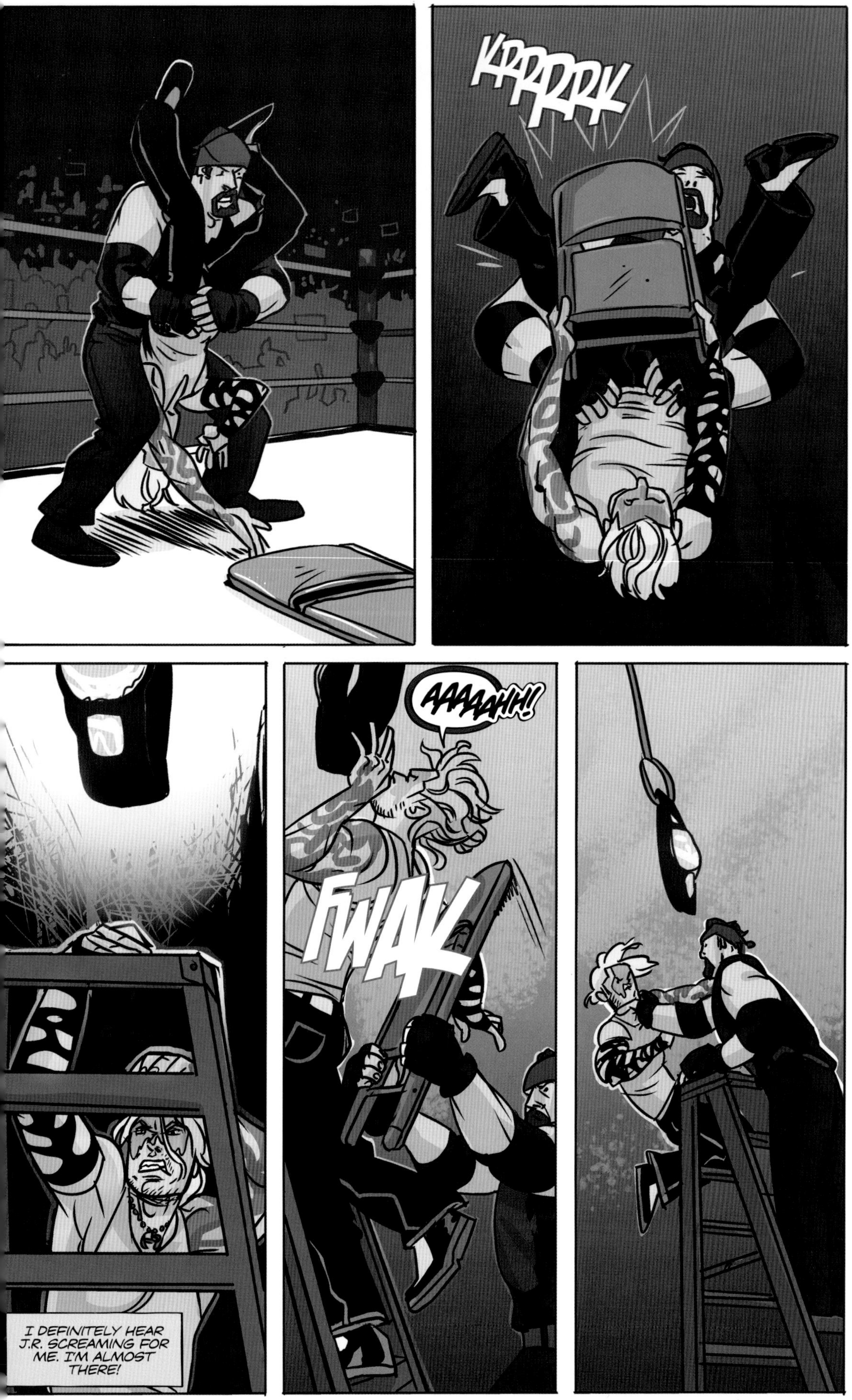
KRRRRK
I DEFINITELY HEAR J.R. SCREAMING FOR ME. I'M ALMOST THERE!
AAAAAHH!
FWAK

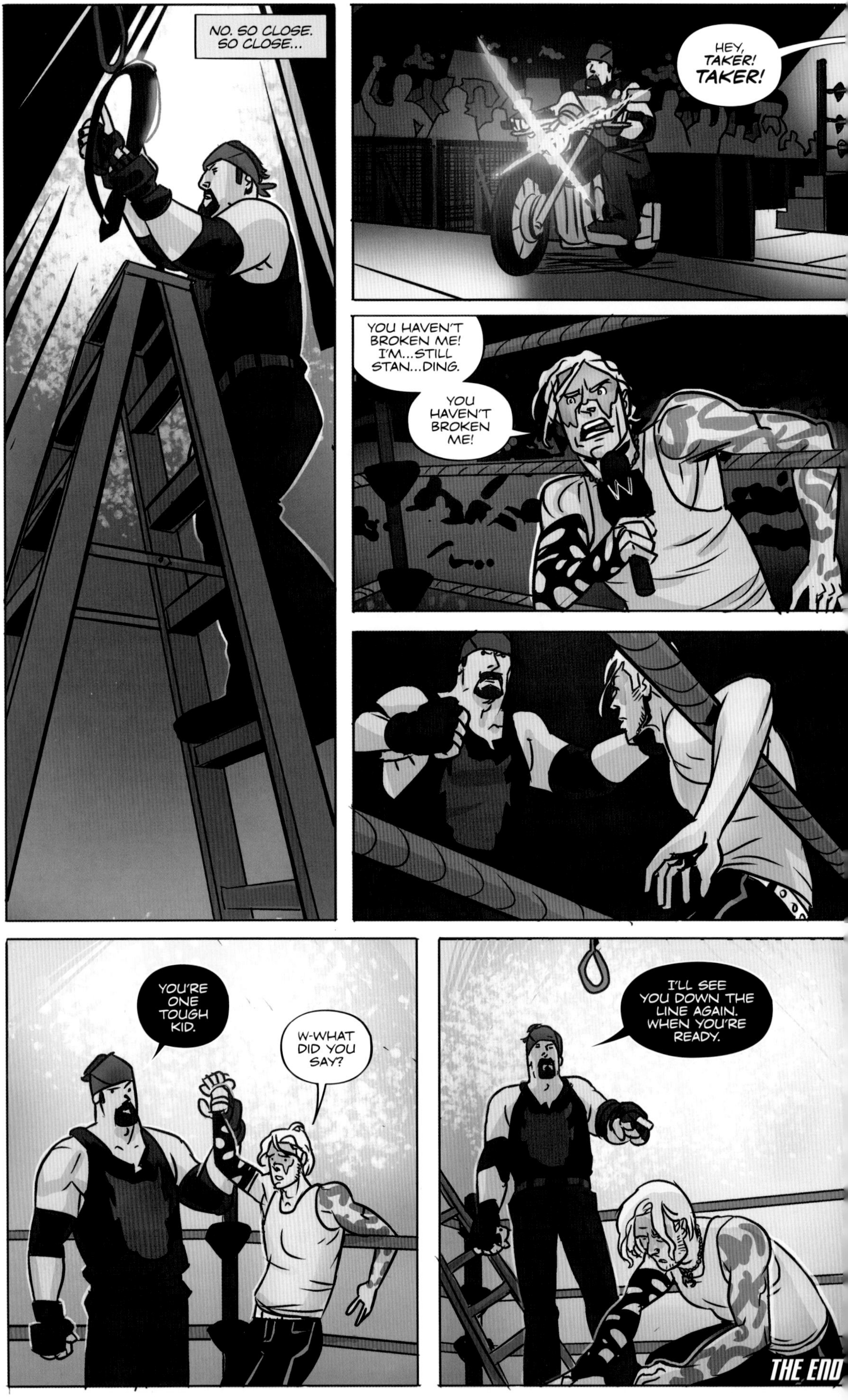

NO. SO CLOSE. SO CLOSE...
HEY, TAKER! TAKER!
YOU HAVEN'T BROKEN ME! I'M...STILL STAN...DING.
YOU HAVEN'T BROKEN ME!
YOU'RE ONE TOUGH KID.
W-WHAT DID YOU SAY?
I'LL SEE YOU DOWN THE LINE AGAIN. WHEN YOU'RE READY.
THE END

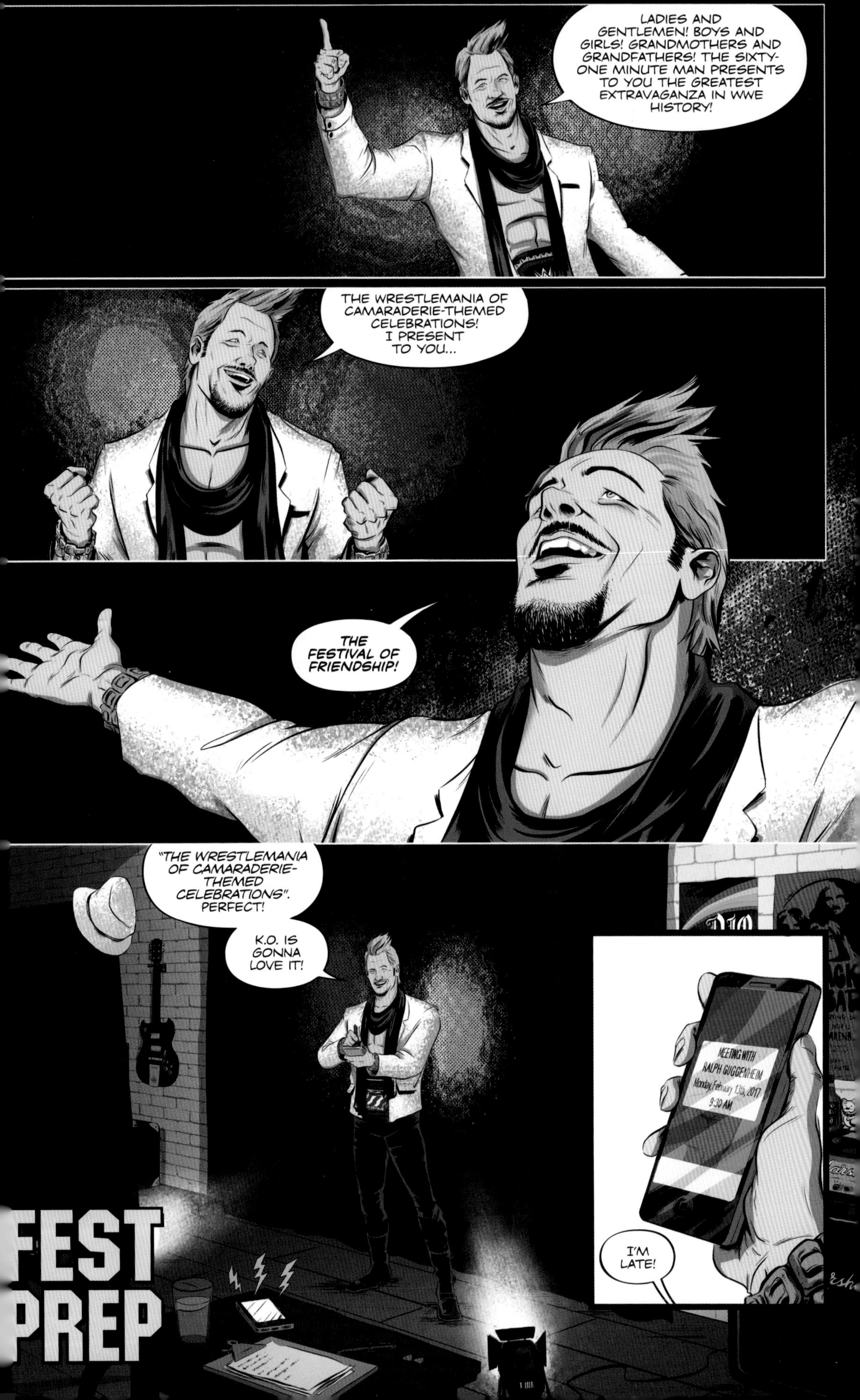
LADIES AND GENTLEMEN! BOYS AND GIRLS! GRANDMOTHERS AND GRANDFATHERS! THE SIXTY-ONE MINUTE MAN PRESENTS TO YOU THE GREATEST EXTRAVAGANZA IN WWE HISTORY!
THE WRESTLEMANIA OF CAMARADERIE-THEMED CELEBRATIONS! I PRESENT TO YOU...
THE FESTIVAL OF FRIENDSHIP!
"THE WRESTLEMANIA OF CAMARADERIE-THEMED CELEBRATIONS". PERFECT!
K.O. IS GONNA LOVE IT!
MEETING WITH RALPH GUGGENHEIM
Monday, February 13th, 2017
9:30 AM
I'M LATE!
FEST PREP

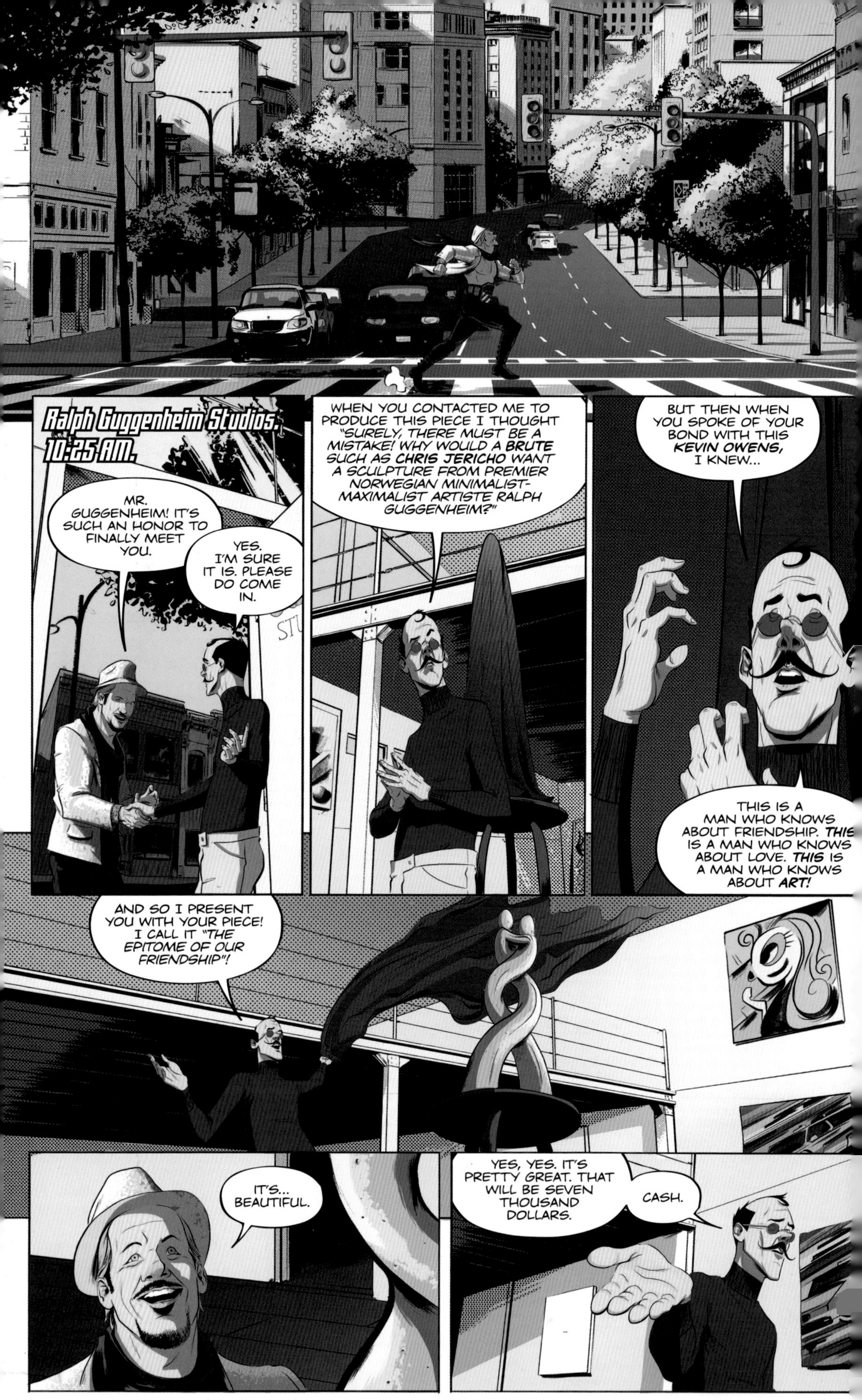

Ralph Guggenheim Studios. 10:25 AM.
MR. GUGGENHEIM! IT'S SUCH AN HONOR TO FINALLY MEET YOU.
YES. I'M SURE IT IS. PLEASE DO COME IN.
WHEN YOU CONTACTED ME TO PRODUCE THIS PIECE I THOUGHT "SURELY, THERE MUST BE A MISTAKE! WHY WOULD A BRUTE SUCH AS CHRIS JERICHO WANT A SCULPTURE FROM PREMIER NORWEGIAN MINIMALIST-MAXIMALIST ARTISTE RALPH GUGGENHEIM?"
BUT THEN WHEN YOU SPOKE OF YOUR BOND WITH THIS KEVIN OWENS, I KNEW...
THIS IS A MAN WHO KNOWS ABOUT FRIENDSHIP. THIS IS A MAN WHO KNOWS ABOUT LOVE. THIS IS A MAN WHO KNOWS ABOUT ART!
AND SO I PRESENT YOU WITH YOUR PIECE! I CALL IT "THE EPITOME OF OUR FRIENDSHIP"!
IT'S... BEAUTIFUL.
YES, YES. IT'S PRETTY GREAT. THAT WILL BE SEVEN THOUSAND DOLLARS.
CASH.

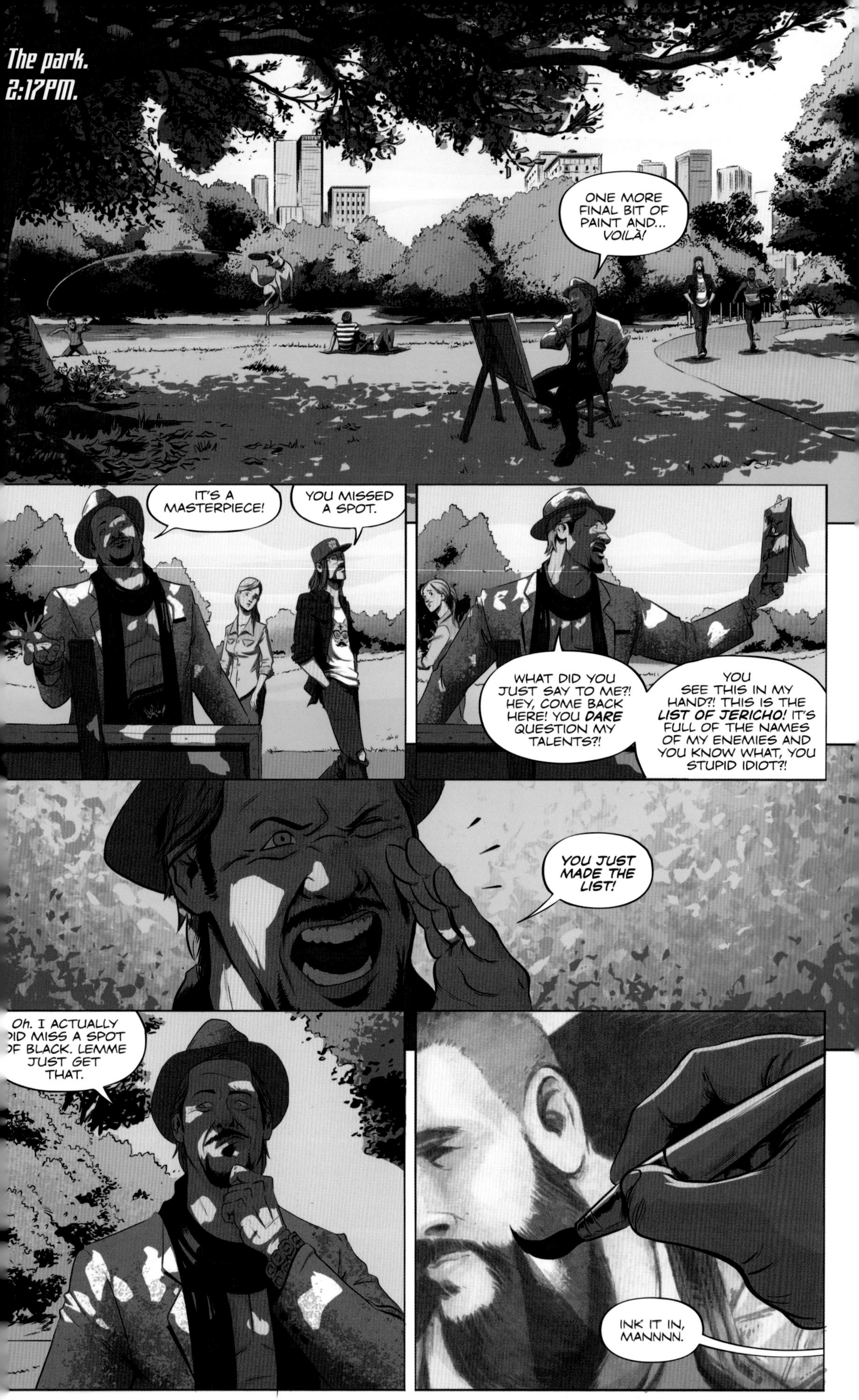

The park.
2:17PM.
ONE MORE FINAL BIT OF PAINT AND... VOILÀ!
IT'S A MASTERPIECE!
YOU MISSED A SPOT.
WHAT DID YOU JUST SAY TO ME?! HEY, COME BACK HERE! YOU DARE QUESTION MY TALENTS?!
YOU SEE THIS IN MY HAND?! THIS IS THE LIST OF JERICHO! IT'S FULL OF THE NAMES OF MY ENEMIES AND YOU KNOW WHAT, YOU STUPID IDIOT?!
YOU JUST MADE THE LIST!
Oh. I ACTUALLY DID MISS A SPOT OF BLACK. LEMME JUST GET THAT.
INK IT IN, MANNNN.

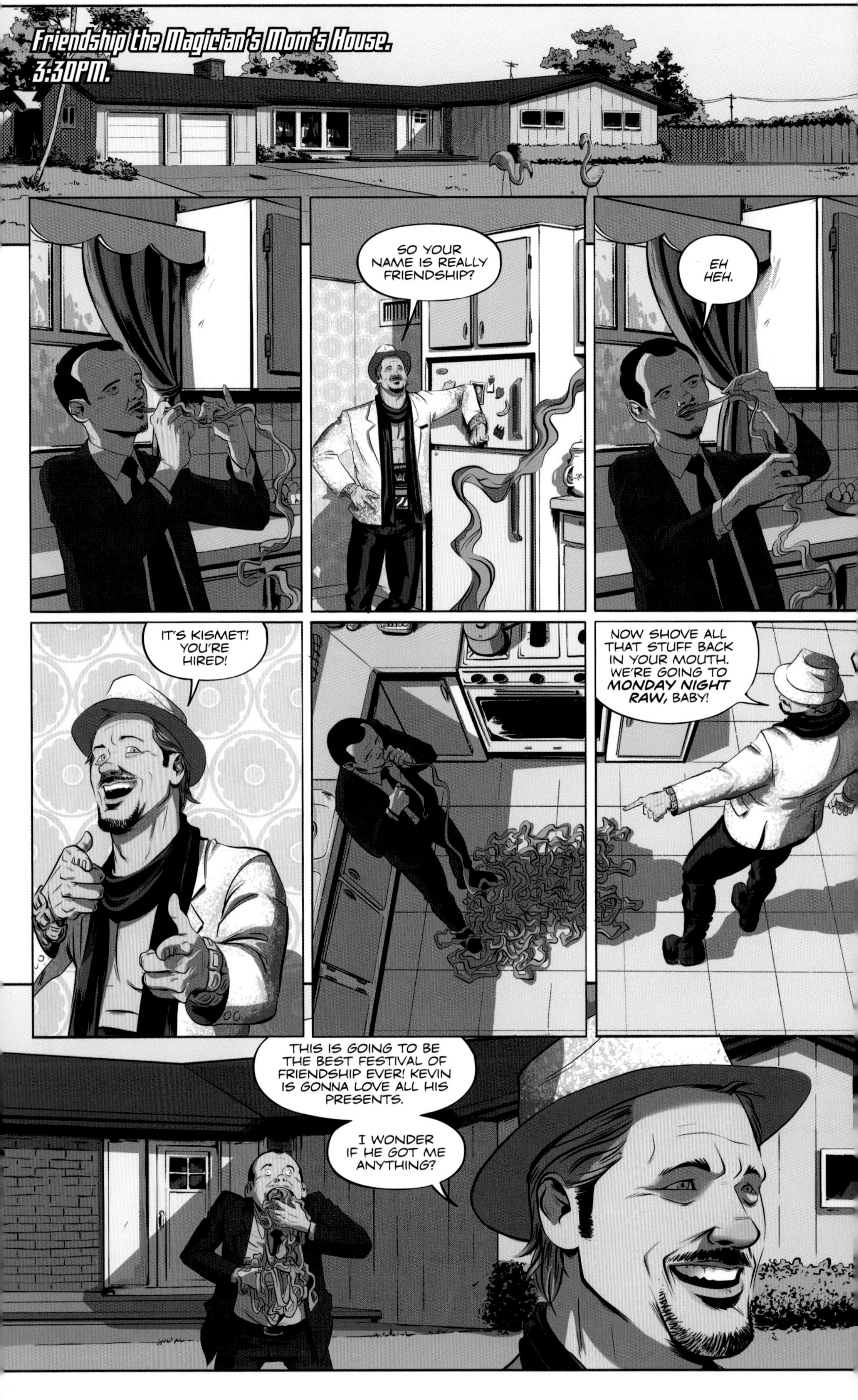

Friendship the Magician's Mom's House.
3:30PM.
SO YOUR NAME IS REALLY FRIENDSHIP?
EH HEH.
IT'S KISMET! YOU'RE HIRED!
NOW SHOVE ALL THAT STUFF BACK IN YOUR MOUTH. WE'RE GOING TO MONDAY NIGHT RAW, BABY!
THIS IS GOING TO BE THE BEST FESTIVAL OF FRIENDSHIP EVER! KEVIN IS GONNA LOVE ALL HIS PRESENTS.
I WONDER IF HE GOT ME ANYTHING?

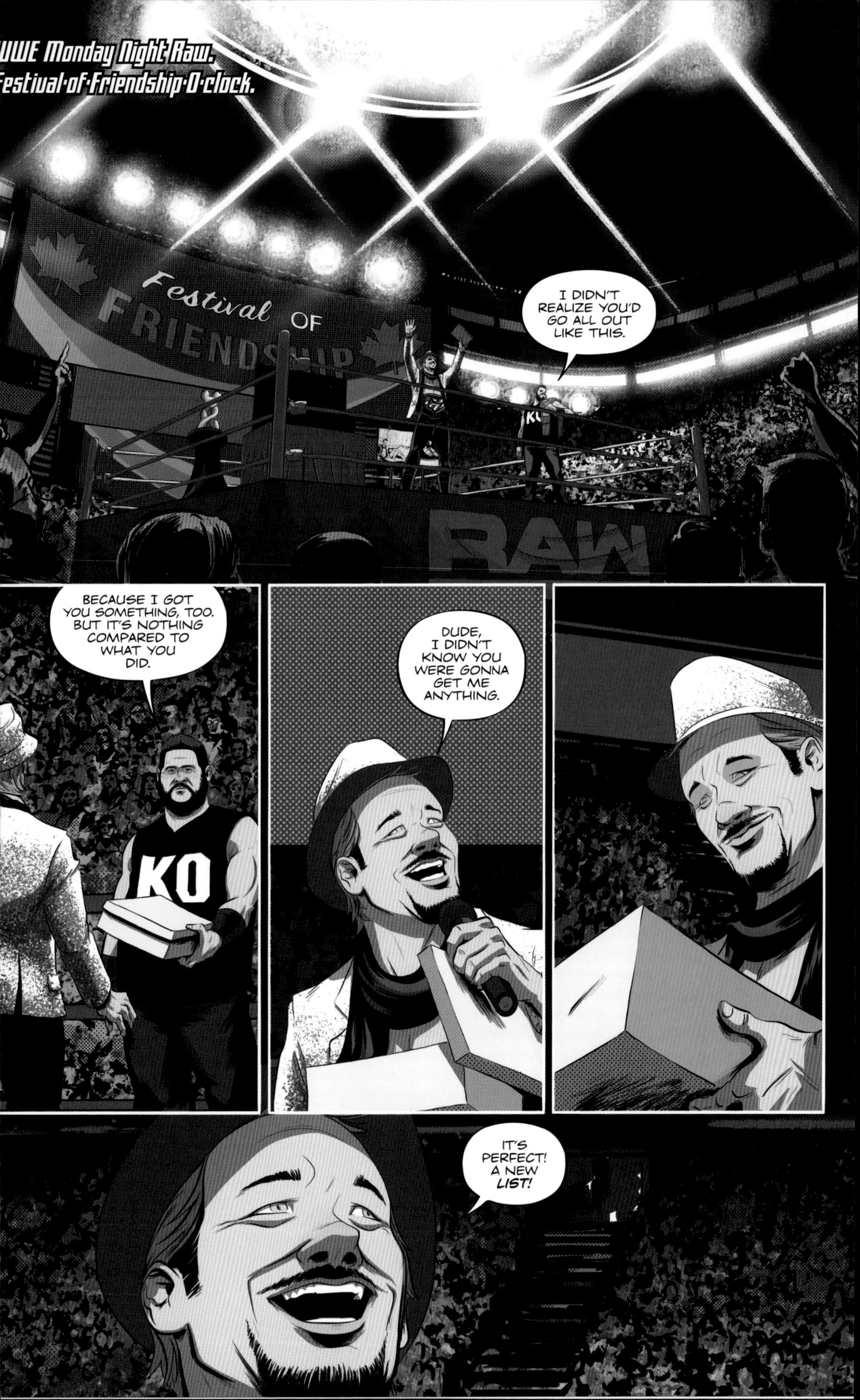
WWE Monday Night Raw.
Festival-of-Friendship-O-clock.
Festival of FRIENDSHIP
I DIDN'T REALIZE YOU'D GO ALL OUT LIKE THIS.
KO
RAW
BECAUSE I GOT YOU SOMETHING, TOO. BUT IT'S NOTHING COMPARED TO WHAT YOU DID.
KO
DUDE, I DIDN'T KNOW YOU WERE GONNA GET ME ANYTHING.
IT'S PERFECT! A NEW LIST!

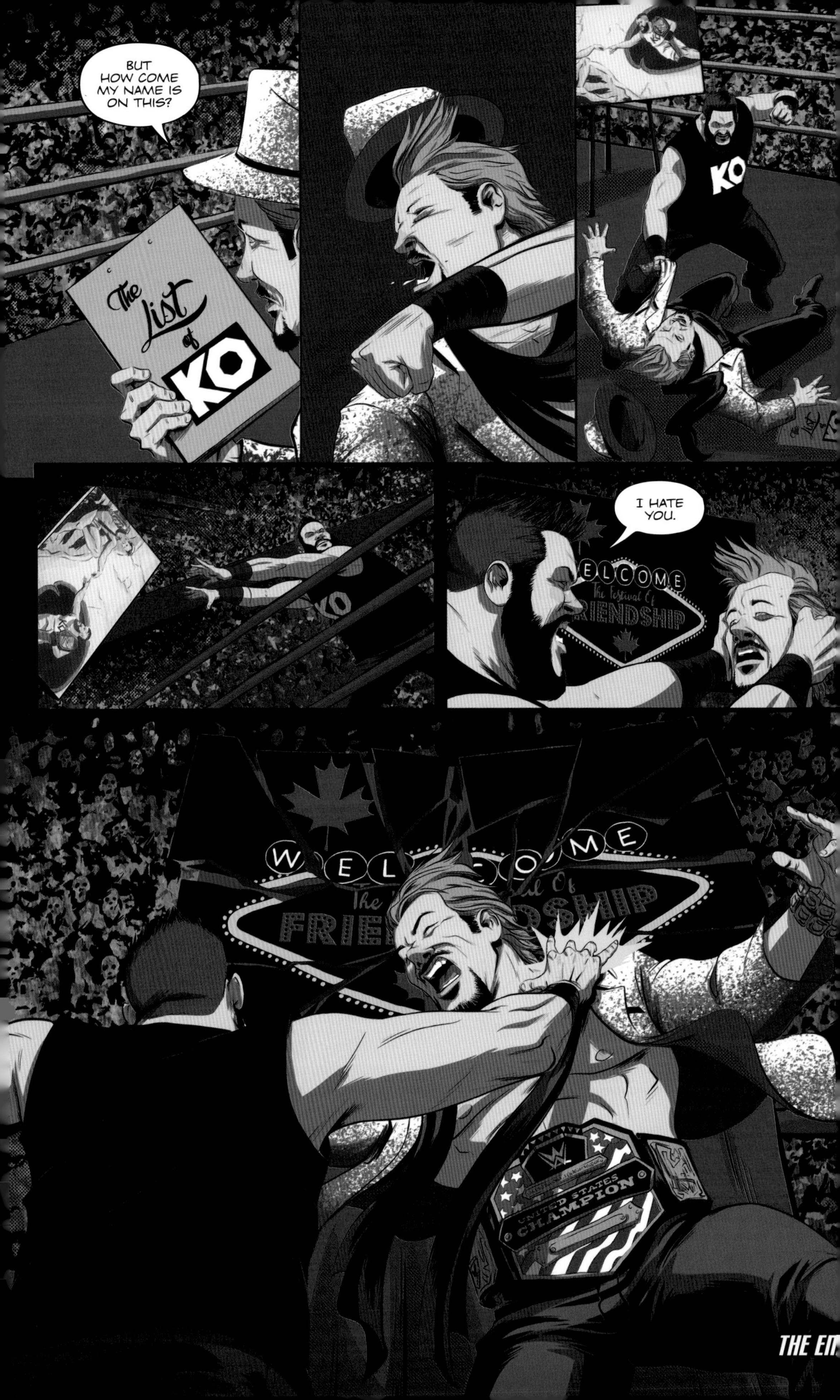
BUT HOW COME MY NAME IS ON THIS?
The List of KO
KO
I HATE YOU.
WELCOME The Festival Of FRIENDSHIP
UNITED STATES CHAMPION
THE EN

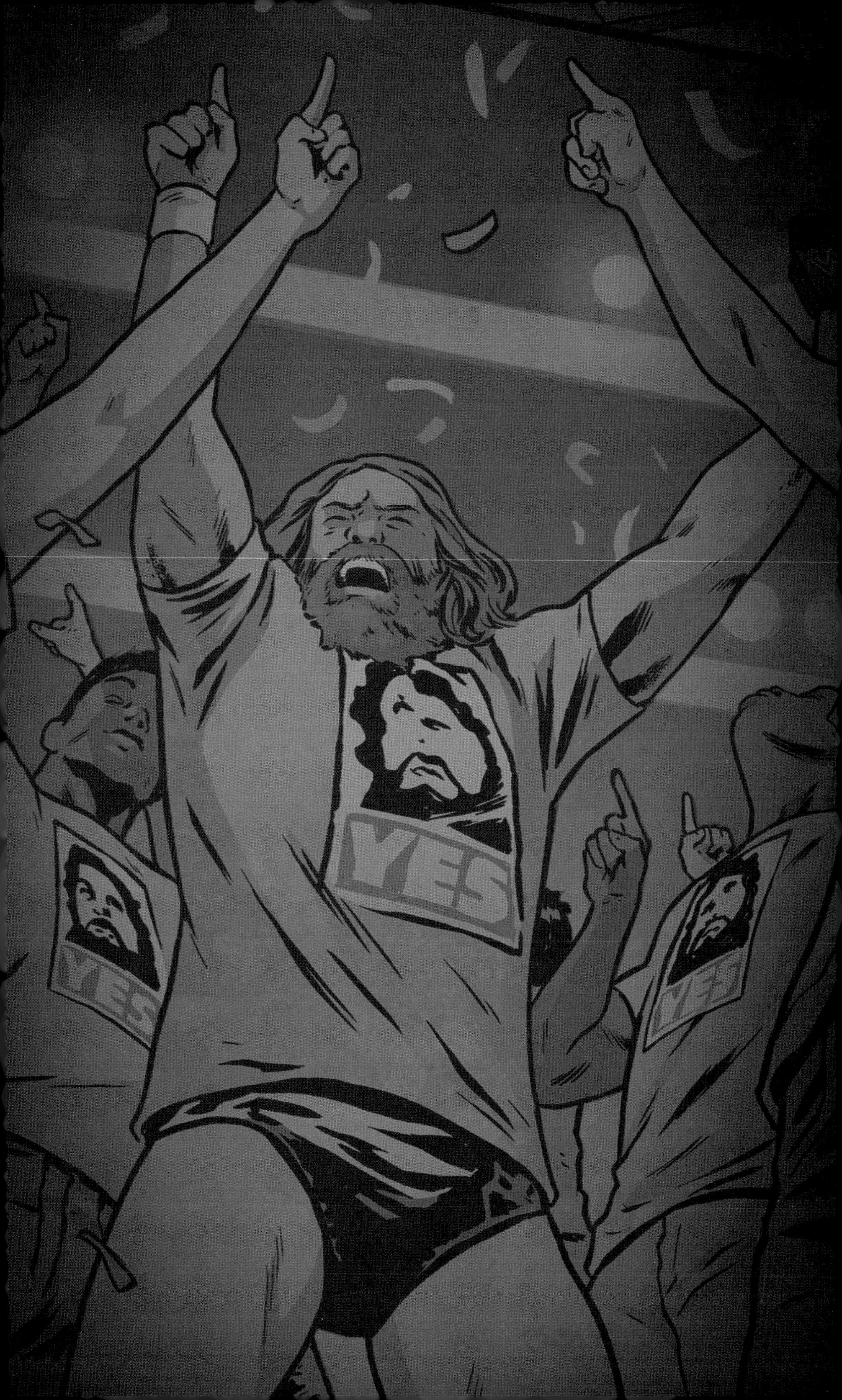
YES
YES
YES

THE SAMI & KEVIN SHOW

CHAPTER ONE

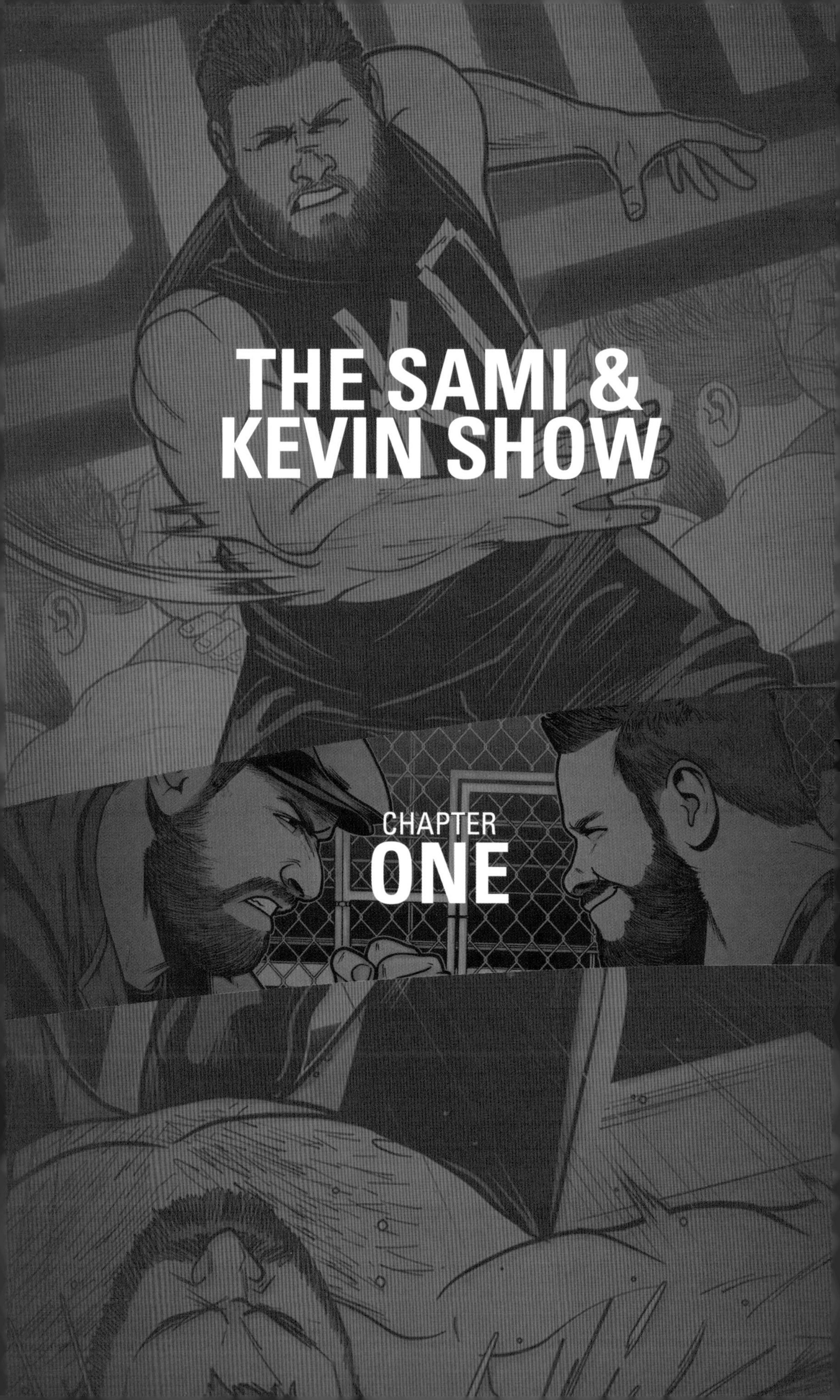

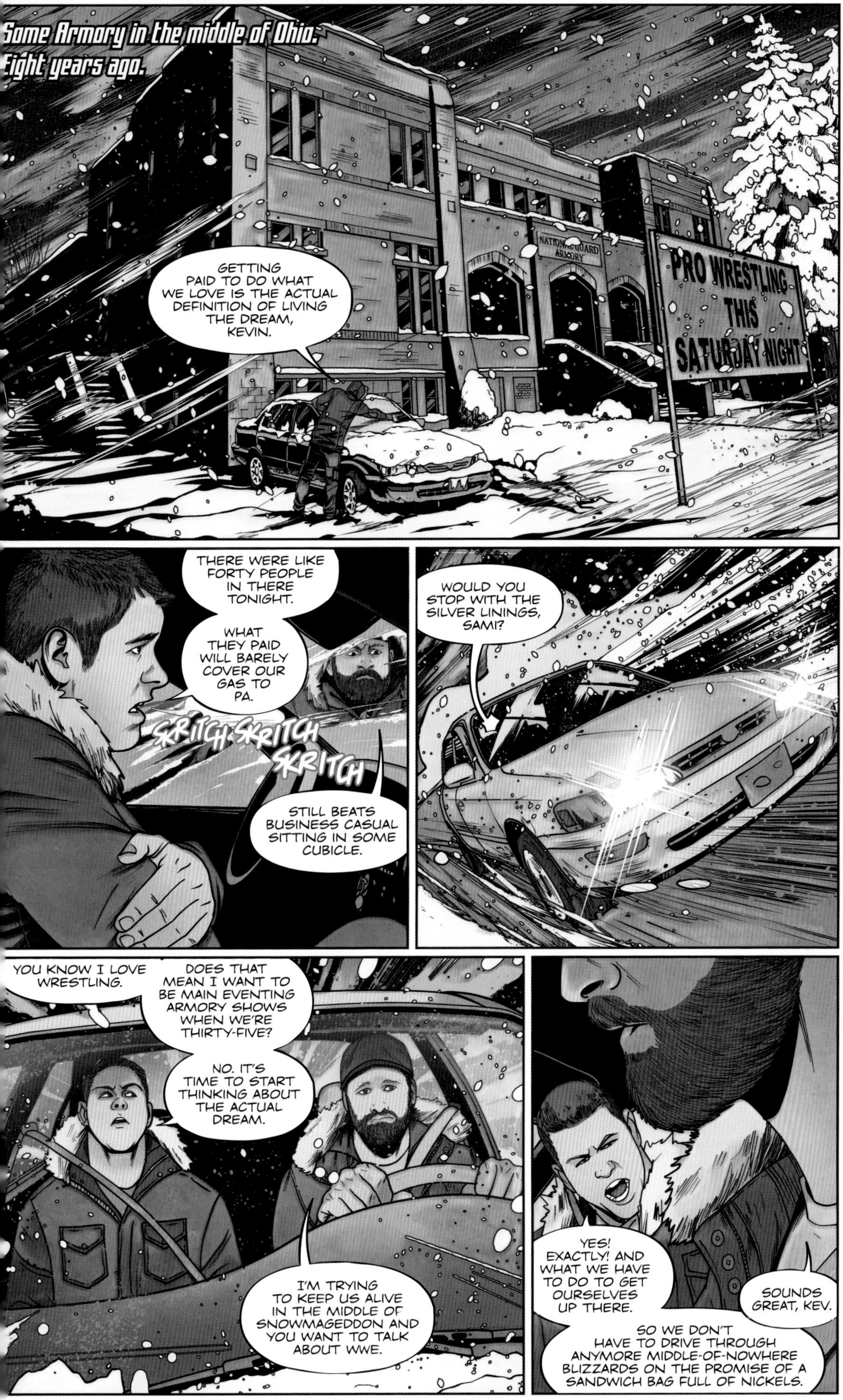
Some Armory in the middle of Ohio.
Fight years ago.
NATIONAL GUARD ARMORY
PRO WRESTLING THIS SATURDAY NIGHT
GETTING PAID TO DO WHAT WE LOVE IS THE ACTUAL DEFINITION OF LIVING THE DREAM, KEVIN.
THERE WERE LIKE FORTY PEOPLE IN THERE TONIGHT.
WHAT THEY PAID WILL BARELY COVER OUR GAS TO PA.
SKRITCH SKRITCH SKRITCH
STILL BEATS BUSINESS CASUAL SITTING IN SOME CUBICLE.
WOULD YOU STOP WITH THE SILVER LININGS, SAMI?
YOU KNOW I LOVE WRESTLING.
DOES THAT MEAN I WANT TO BE MAIN EVENTING ARMORY SHOWS WHEN WE'RE THIRTY-FIVE?
NO. IT'S TIME TO START THINKING ABOUT THE ACTUAL DREAM.
I'M TRYING TO KEEP US ALIVE IN THE MIDDLE OF SNOWMAGEDDON AND YOU WANT TO TALK ABOUT WWE.
YES! EXACTLY! AND WHAT WE HAVE TO DO TO GET OURSELVES UP THERE.
SOUNDS GREAT, KEV.
SO WE DON'T HAVE TO DRIVE THROUGH ANYMORE MIDDLE-OF-NOWHERE BLIZZARDS ON THE PROMISE OF A SANDWICH BAG FULL OF NICKELS.

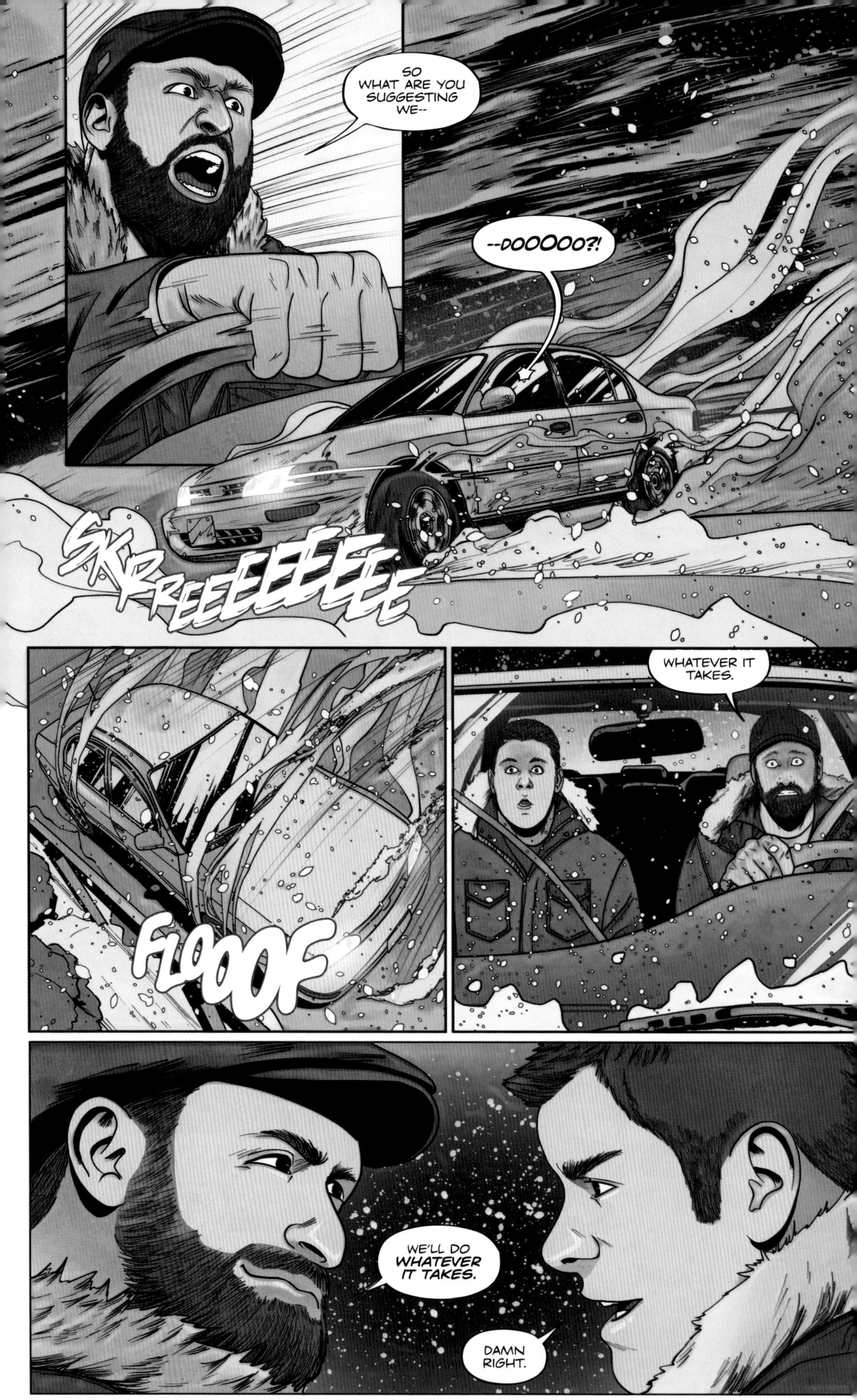

SO WHAT ARE YOU SUGGESTING WE--
--DOOOOO?!
SKREEEEEEEEE
FLOOOF
WHATEVER IT TAKES.
WE'LL DO *WHATEVER IT TAKES.*
DAMN RIGHT.

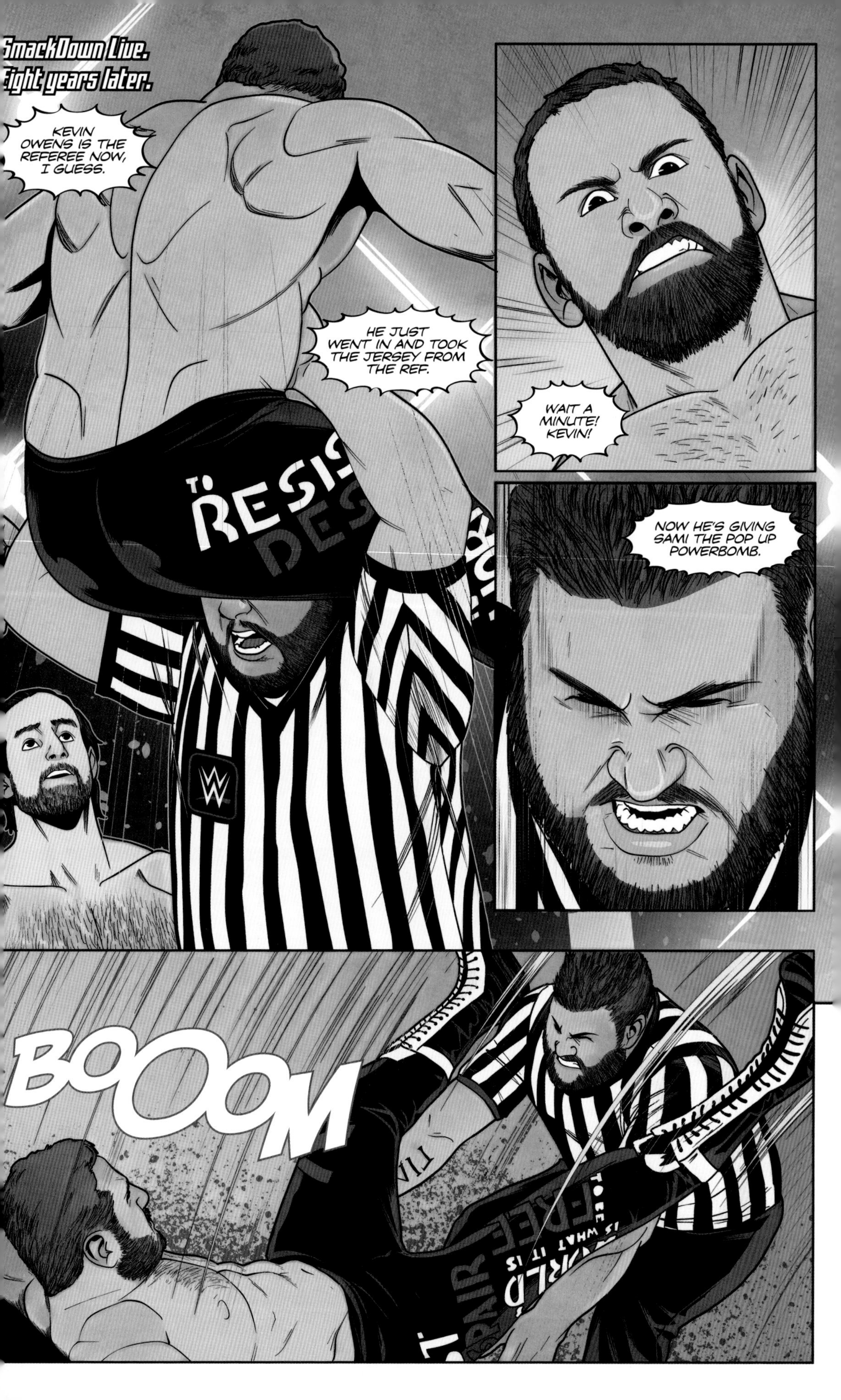
SmackDown Live.
Eight years later.
KEVIN OWENS IS THE REFEREE NOW, I GUESS.
HE JUST WENT IN AND TOOK THE JERSEY FROM THE REF.
WAIT A MINUTE! KEVIN!
NOW HE'S GIVING SAMI THE POP UP POWERBOMB.
BOOOOM

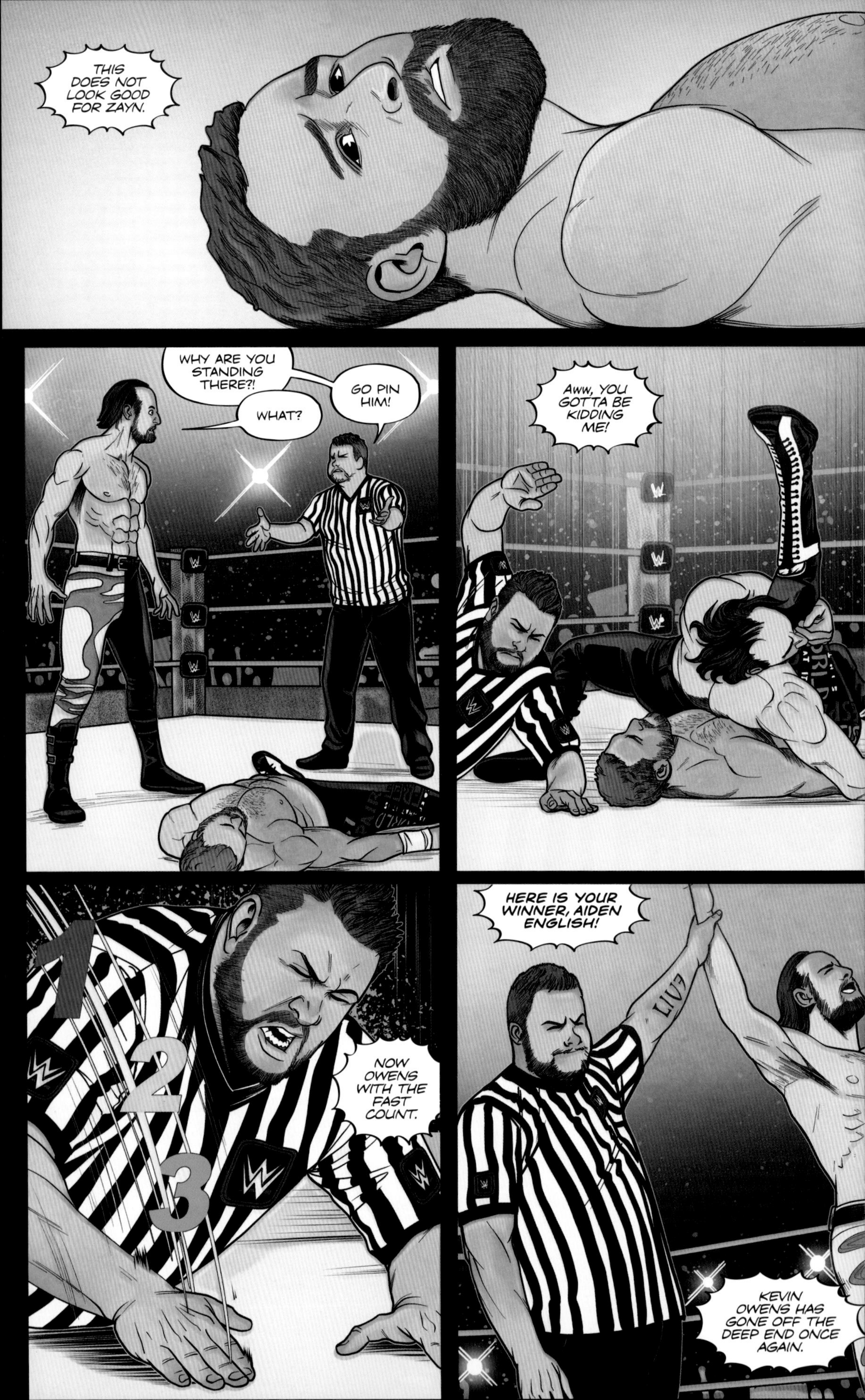
THIS DOES NOT LOOK GOOD FOR ZAYN.
WHY ARE YOU STANDING THERE?!
WHAT?
GO PIN HIM!
Aww, YOU GOTTA BE KIDDING ME!
1
2
3
NOW OWENS WITH THE FAST COUNT.
HERE IS YOUR WINNER, AIDEN ENGLISH!
KEVIN OWENS HAS GONE OFF THE DEEP END ONCE AGAIN.

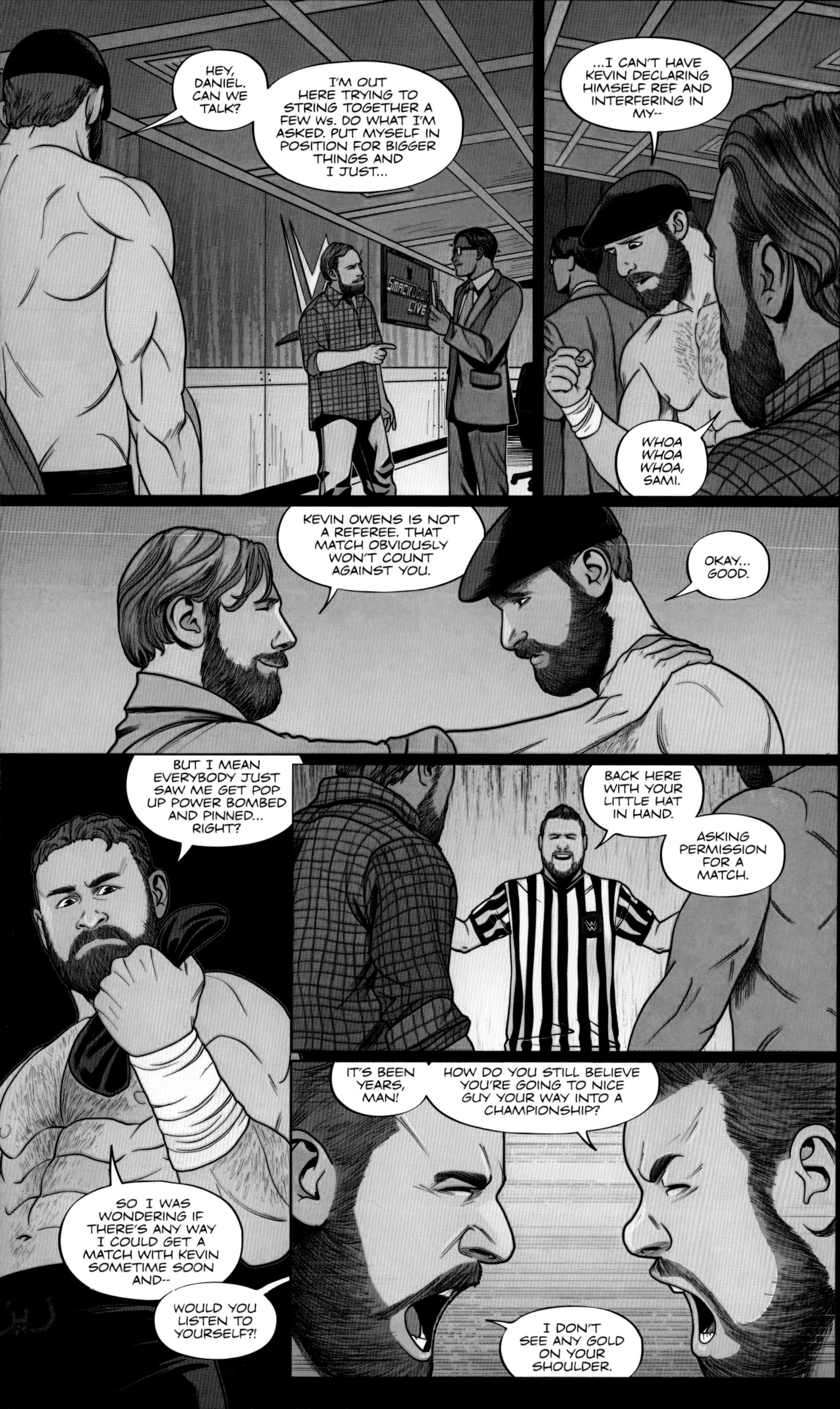

HEY, DANIEL. CAN WE TALK?
I'M OUT HERE TRYING TO STRING TOGETHER A FEW Ws. DO WHAT I'M ASKED. PUT MYSELF IN POSITION FOR BIGGER THINGS AND I JUST...
SMACKDOWN LIVE
...I CAN'T HAVE KEVIN DECLARING HIMSELF REF AND INTERFERING IN MY--
WHOA WHOA WHOA, SAMI.
KEVIN OWENS IS NOT A REFEREE. THAT MATCH OBVIOUSLY WON'T COUNT AGAINST YOU.
OKAY... GOOD.
BUT I MEAN EVERYBODY JUST SAW ME GET POP UP POWER BOMBED AND PINNED... RIGHT?
SO I WAS WONDERING IF THERE'S ANY WAY I COULD GET A MATCH WITH KEVIN SOMETIME SOON AND--
WOULD YOU LISTEN TO YOURSELF?!
BACK HERE WITH YOUR LITTLE HAT IN HAND.
ASKING PERMISSION FOR A MATCH.
IT'S BEEN YEARS, MAN!
HOW DO YOU STILL BELIEVE YOU'RE GOING TO NICE GUY YOUR WAY INTO A CHAMPIONSHIP?
I DON'T SEE ANY GOLD ON YOUR SHOULDER.

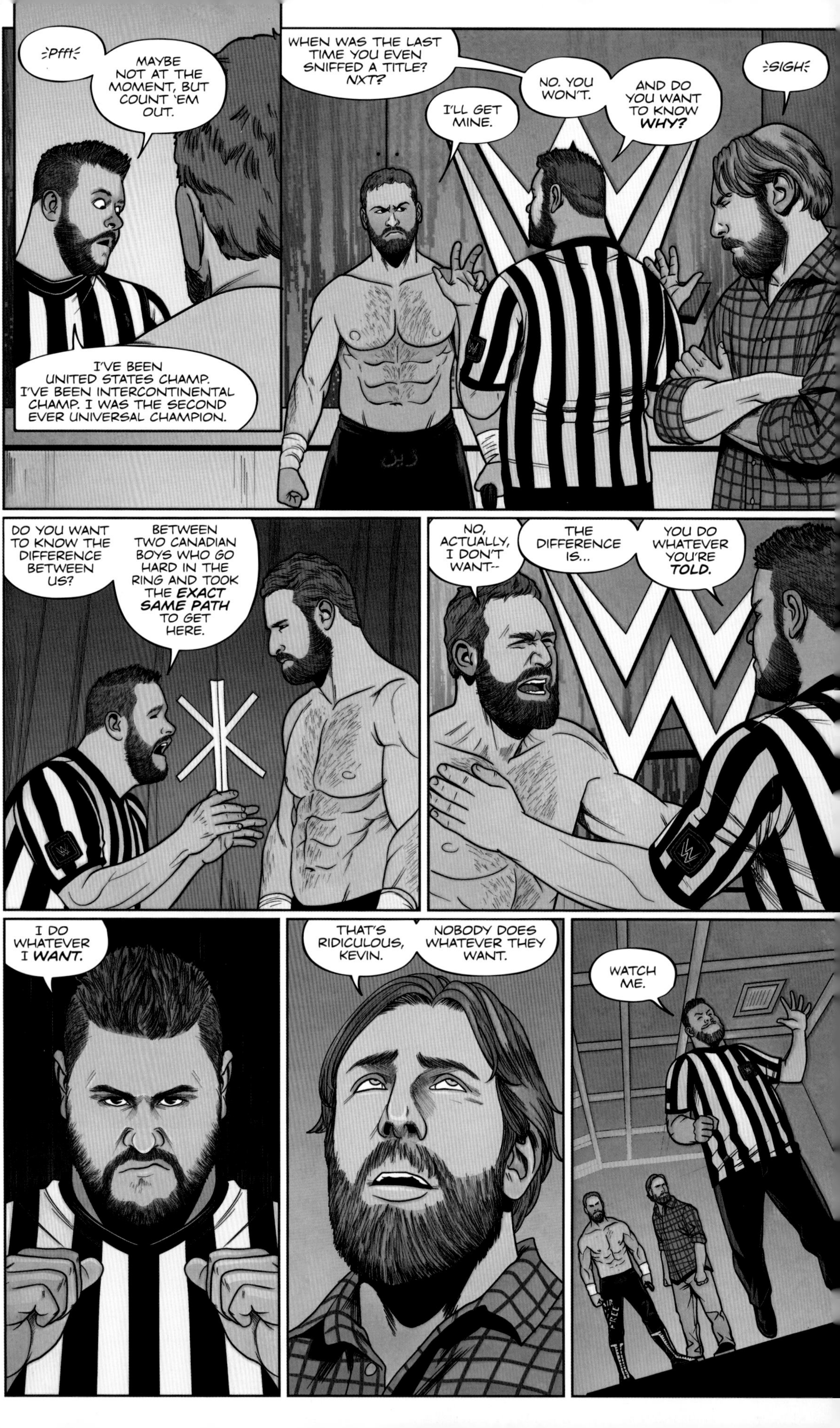

PFFT
MAYBE NOT AT THE MOMENT, BUT COUNT 'EM OUT.
I'VE BEEN UNITED STATES CHAMP. I'VE BEEN INTERCONTINENTAL CHAMP. I WAS THE SECOND EVER UNIVERSAL CHAMPION.
WHEN WAS THE LAST TIME YOU EVEN SNIFFED A TITLE? NXT?
I'LL GET MINE.
NO. YOU WON'T.
AND DO YOU WANT TO KNOW WHY?
SIGH
DO YOU WANT TO KNOW THE DIFFERENCE BETWEEN US?
BETWEEN TWO CANADIAN BOYS WHO GO HARD IN THE RING AND TOOK THE EXACT SAME PATH TO GET HERE.
NO, ACTUALLY, I DON'T WANT--
THE DIFFERENCE IS...
YOU DO WHATEVER YOU'RE TOLD.
I DO WHATEVER I WANT.
THAT'S RIDICULOUS, KEVIN.
NOBODY DOES WHATEVER THEY WANT.
WATCH ME.

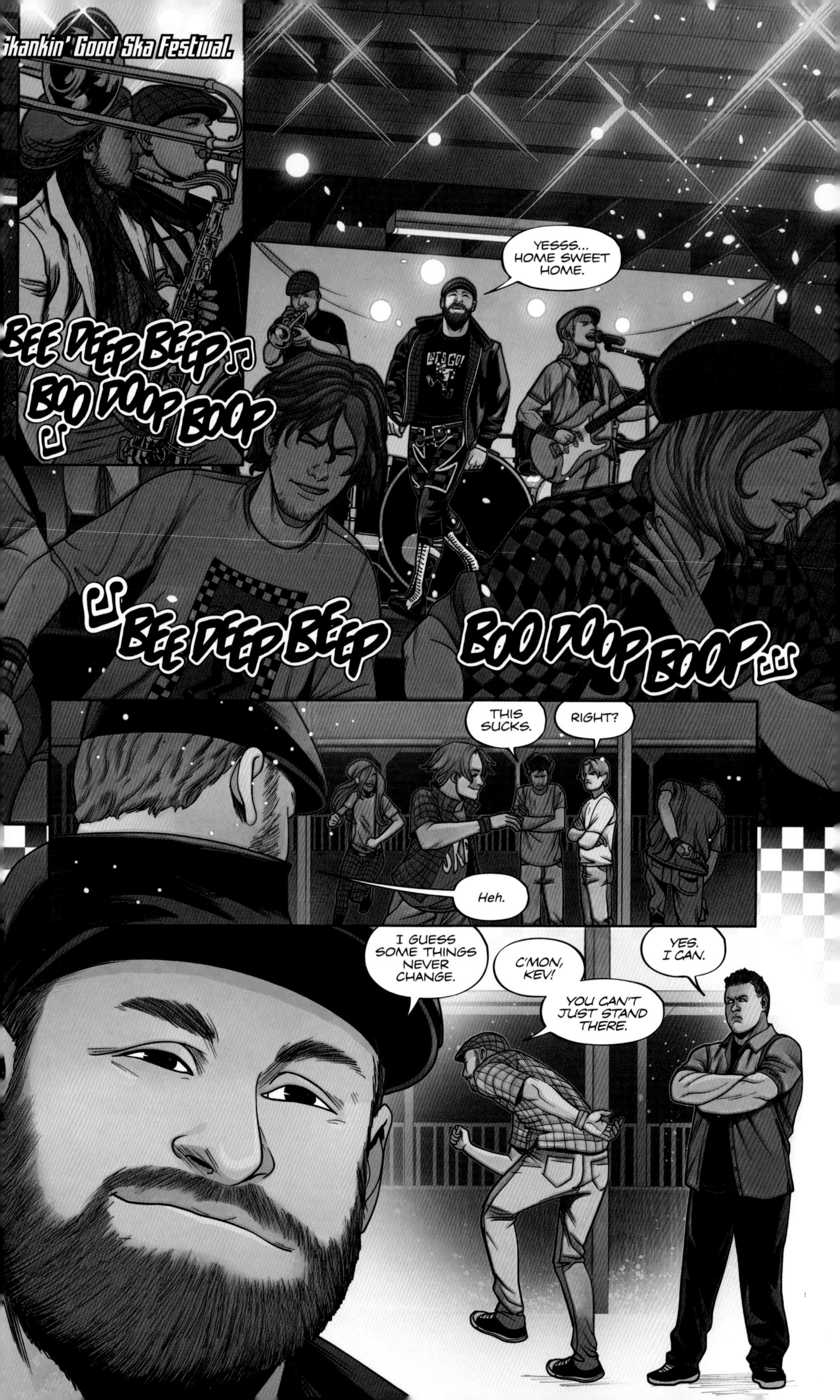
Skankin' Good Ska Festival.
BEE DEEP BEEP
BOO DOOP BOOP
YESSS... HOME SWEET HOME.
BEE DEEP BEEP
BOO DOOP BOOP
THIS SUCKS.
RIGHT?
Heh.
I GUESS SOME THINGS NEVER CHANGE.
C'MON, KEV!
YOU CAN'T JUST STAND THERE.
YES. I CAN.

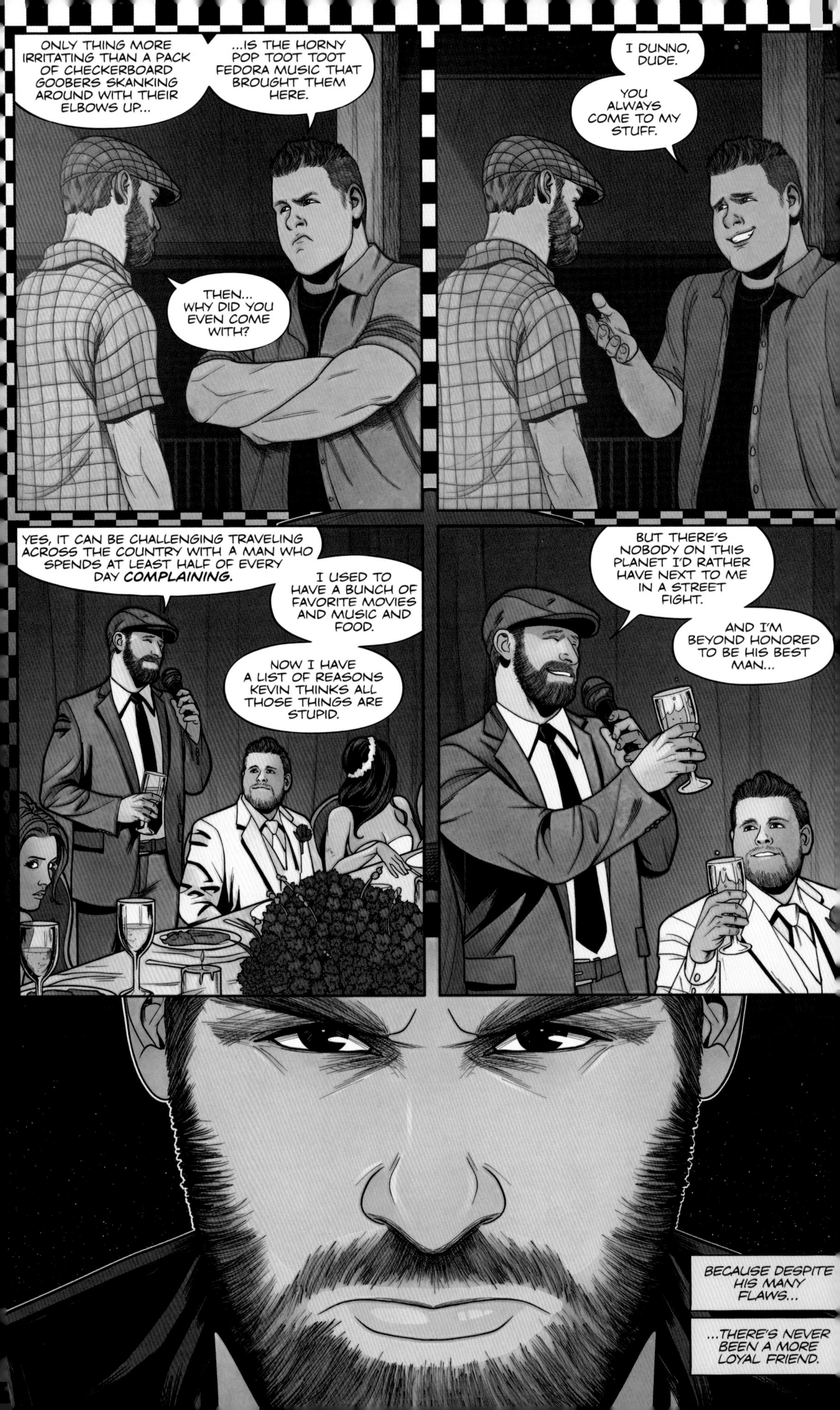
ONLY THING MORE IRRITATING THAN A PACK OF CHECKERBOARD GOOBERS SKANKING AROUND WITH THEIR ELBOWS UP...
...IS THE HORNY POP TOOT TOOT FEDORA MUSIC THAT BROUGHT THEM HERE.
THEN... WHY DID YOU EVEN COME WITH?
I DUNNO, DUDE.
YOU ALWAYS COME TO MY STUFF.
YES, IT CAN BE CHALLENGING TRAVELING ACROSS THE COUNTRY WITH A MAN WHO SPENDS AT LEAST HALF OF EVERY DAY **COMPLAINING.**
I USED TO HAVE A BUNCH OF FAVORITE MOVIES AND MUSIC AND FOOD.
NOW I HAVE A LIST OF REASONS KEVIN THINKS ALL THOSE THINGS ARE STUPID.
BUT THERE'S NOBODY ON THIS PLANET I'D RATHER HAVE NEXT TO ME IN A STREET FIGHT.
AND I'M BEYOND HONORED TO BE HIS BEST MAN...
BECAUSE DESPITE HIS MANY FLAWS...
...THERE'S NEVER BEEN A MORE LOYAL FRIEND.

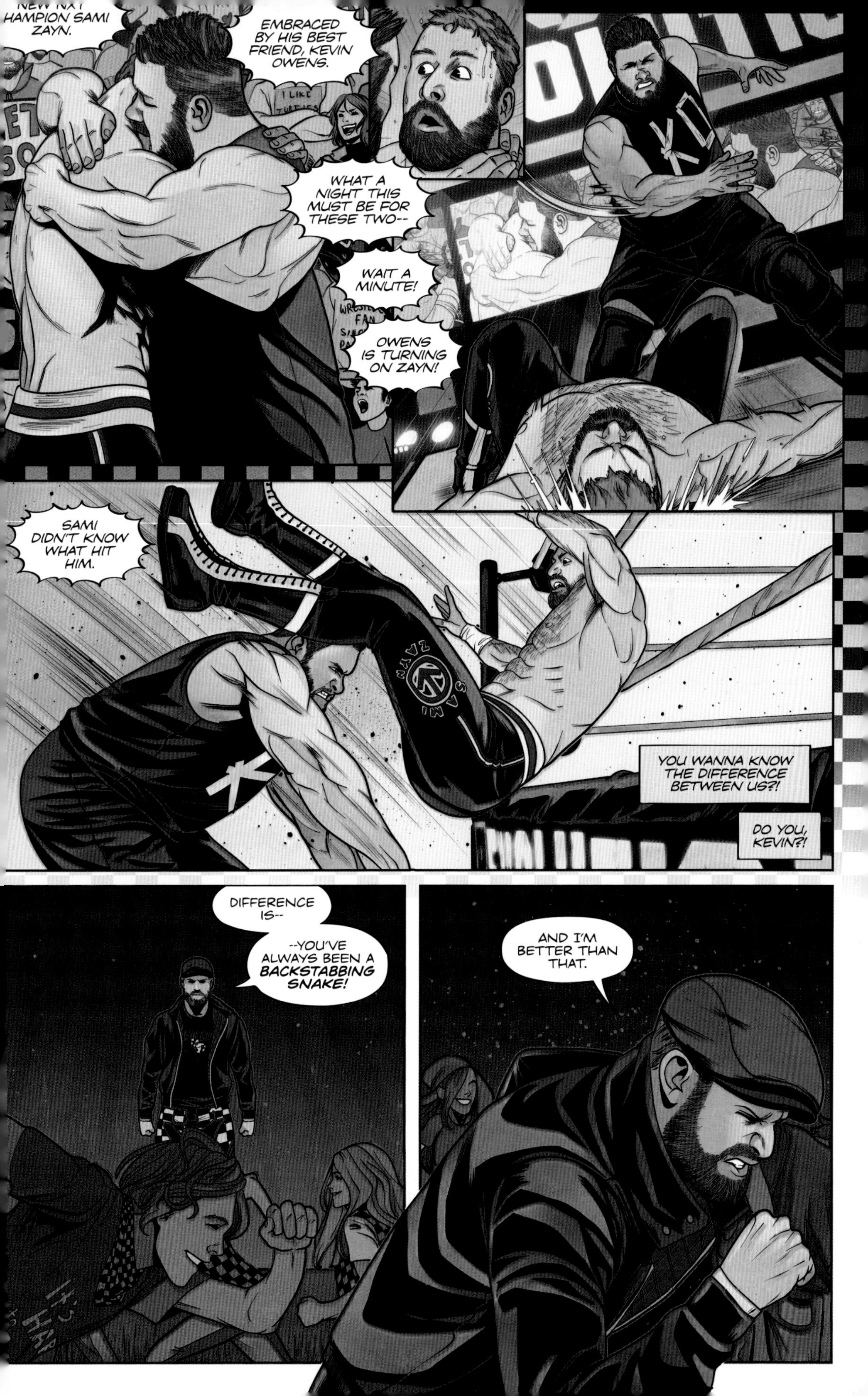
NEW NXT
HAMPION SAMI ZAYN.
EMBRACED BY HIS BEST FRIEND, KEVIN OWENS.
I LIKE TURTLES
WHAT A NIGHT THIS MUST BE FOR THESE TWO--
WAIT A MINUTE!
OWENS IS TURNING ON ZAYN!
SAMI DIDN'T KNOW WHAT HIT HIM.
SAMI ZAYN
YOU WANNA KNOW THE DIFFERENCE BETWEEN US?!
DO YOU, KEVIN?!
DIFFERENCE IS--
--YOU'VE ALWAYS BEEN A **BACKSTABBING SNAKE!**
AND I'M BETTER THAN THAT.

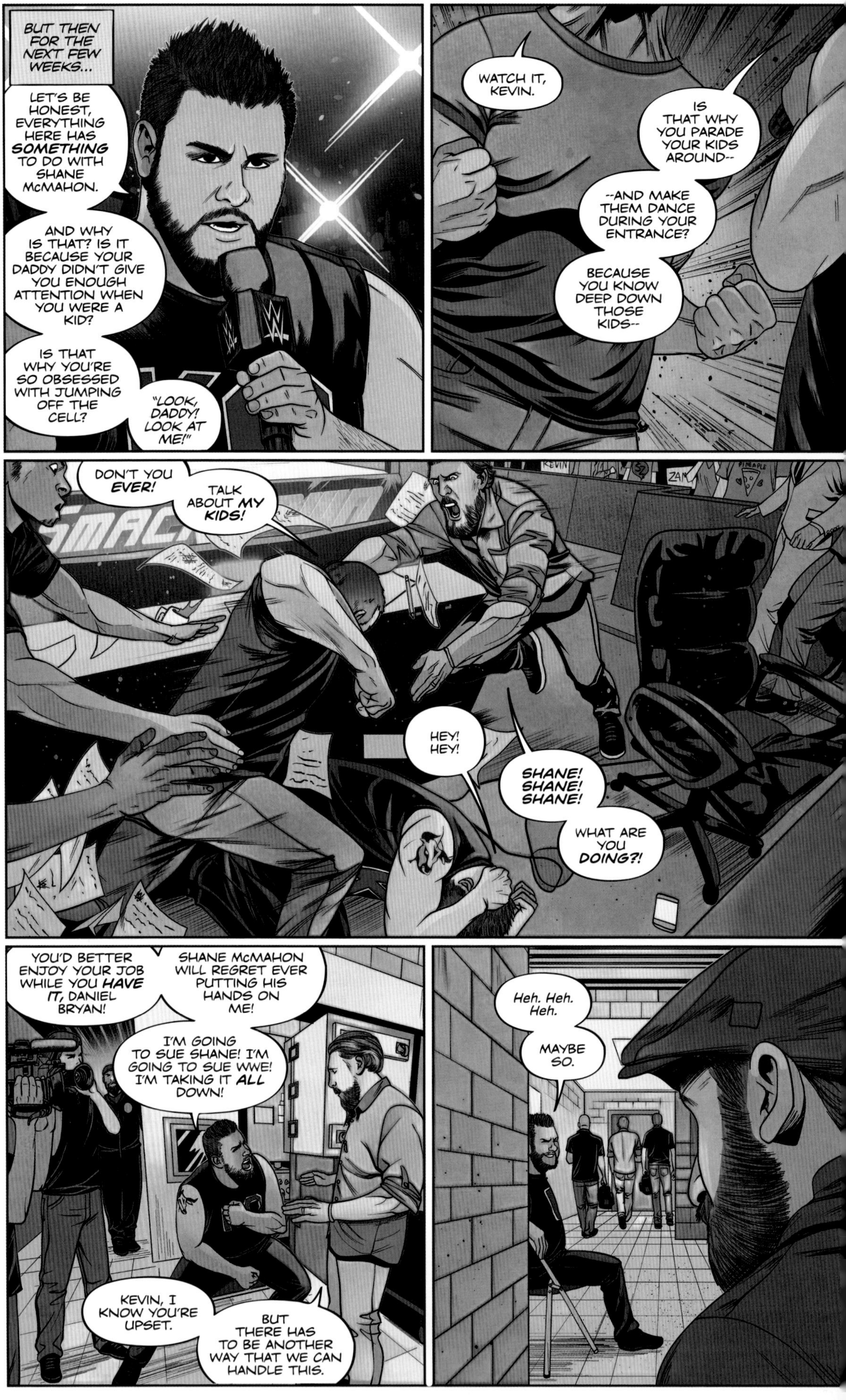

BUT THEN FOR THE NEXT FEW WEEKS...
LET'S BE HONEST, EVERYTHING HERE HAS **SOMETHING** TO DO WITH SHANE McMAHON.
AND WHY IS THAT? IS IT BECAUSE YOUR DADDY DIDN'T GIVE YOU ENOUGH ATTENTION WHEN YOU WERE A KID?
IS THAT WHY YOU'RE SO OBSESSED WITH JUMPING OFF THE CELL?
"LOOK, DADDY! LOOK AT ME!"
WATCH IT, KEVIN.
IS THAT WHY YOU PARADE YOUR KIDS AROUND--
--AND MAKE THEM DANCE DURING YOUR ENTRANCE?
BECAUSE YOU KNOW DEEP DOWN THOSE KIDS--
DON'T YOU ***EVER!***
TALK ABOUT ***MY KIDS!***
HEY! HEY!
SHANE! SHANE! SHANE!
WHAT ARE YOU ***DOING?!***
YOU'D BETTER ENJOY YOUR JOB WHILE YOU ***HAVE IT,*** DANIEL BRYAN!
SHANE McMAHON WILL REGRET EVER PUTTING HIS HANDS ON ME!
I'M GOING TO SUE SHANE! I'M GOING TO SUE WWE! I'M TAKING IT ***ALL*** DOWN!
KEVIN, I KNOW YOU'RE UPSET.
BUT THERE HAS TO BE ANOTHER WAY THAT WE CAN HANDLE THIS.
Heh. Heh. Heh.
MAYBE SO.

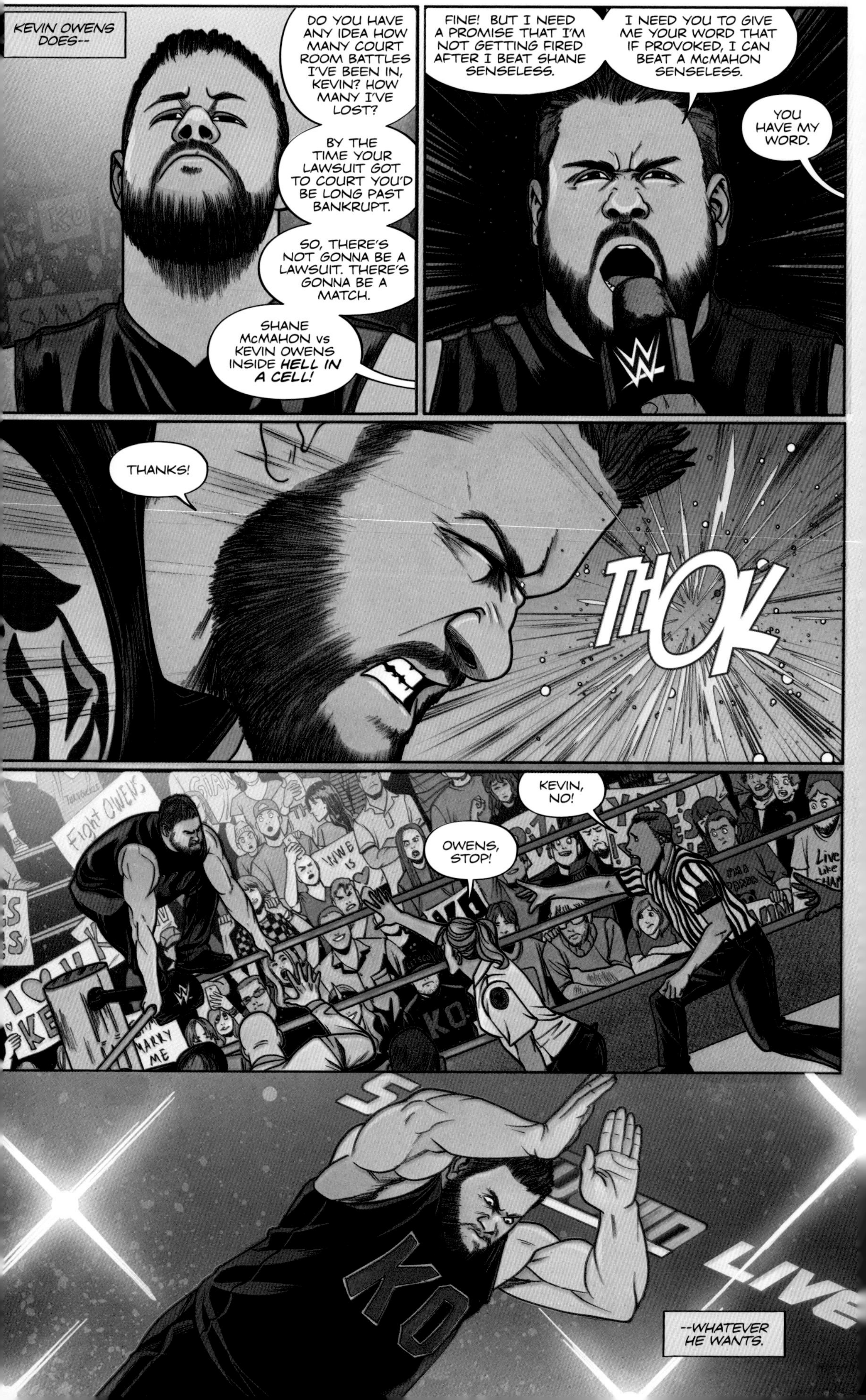

KEVIN OWENS DOES--
DO YOU HAVE ANY IDEA HOW MANY COURT ROOM BATTLES I'VE BEEN IN, KEVIN? HOW MANY I'VE LOST?
BY THE TIME YOUR LAWSUIT GOT TO COURT YOU'D BE LONG PAST BANKRUPT.
SO, THERE'S NOT GONNA BE A LAWSUIT. THERE'S GONNA BE A MATCH.
SHANE McMAHON vs KEVIN OWENS INSIDE HELL IN A CELL!
FINE! BUT I NEED A PROMISE THAT I'M NOT GETTING FIRED AFTER I BEAT SHANE SENSELESS.
I NEED YOU TO GIVE ME YOUR WORD THAT IF PROVOKED, I CAN BEAT A McMAHON SENSELESS.
YOU HAVE MY WORD.
THANKS!
THOK
KEVIN, NO!
OWENS, STOP!
Fight OWENS
WWE IS
MARRY ME
LIVE
--WHATEVER HE WANTS.

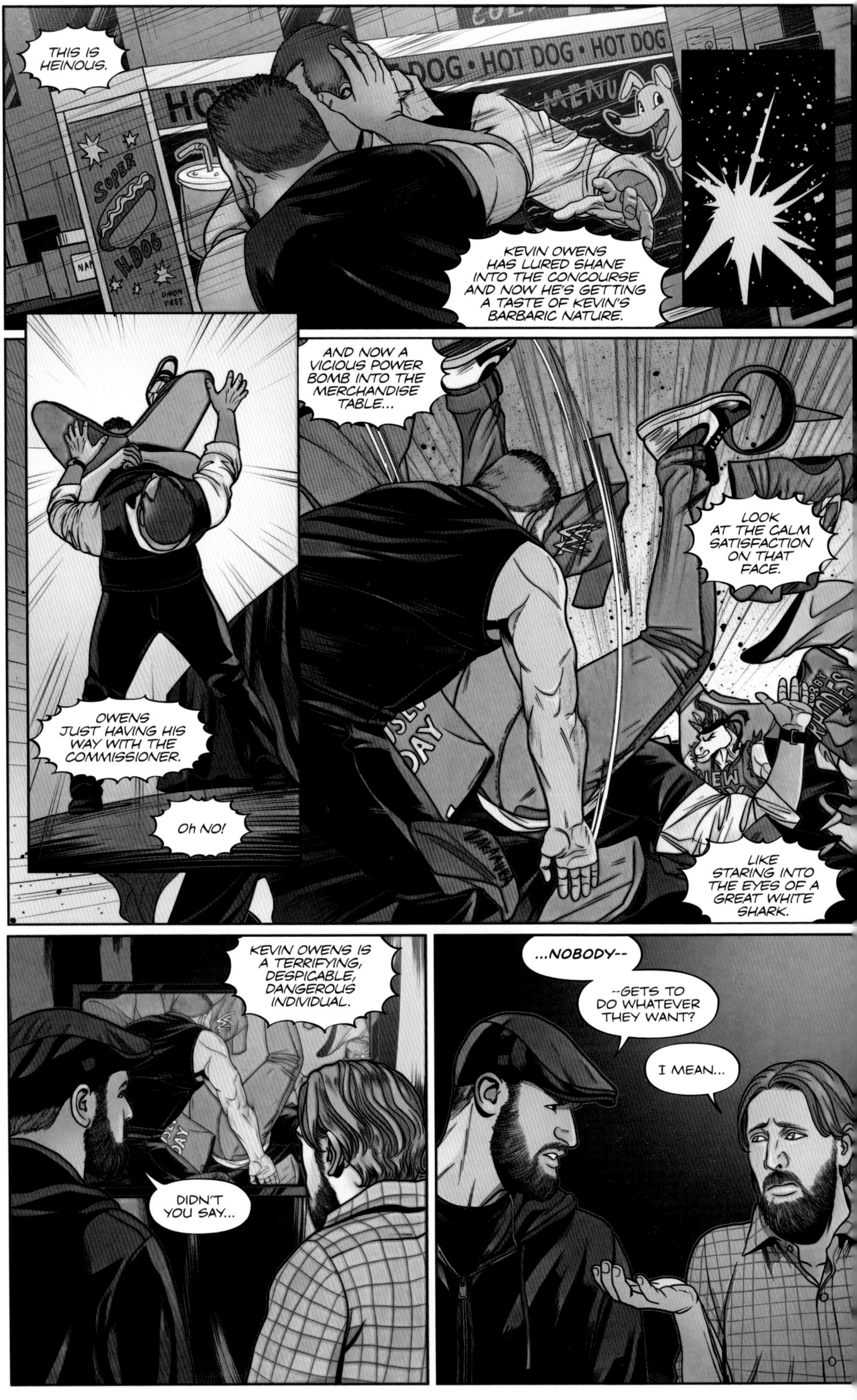
THIS IS HEINOUS.
HOT DOG • HOT DOG • HOT DOG
MENU
SUPER H.DOG
ONION FREE
KEVIN OWENS HAS LURED SHANE INTO THE CONCOURSE AND NOW HE'S GETTING A TASTE OF KEVIN'S BARBARIC NATURE.
OWENS JUST HAVING HIS WAY WITH THE COMMISSIONER.
Oh NO!
AND NOW A VICIOUS POWER BOMB INTO THE MERCHANDISE TABLE...
LOOK AT THE CALM SATISFACTION ON THAT FACE.
LIKE STARING INTO THE EYES OF A GREAT WHITE SHARK.
KEVIN OWENS IS A TERRIFYING, DESPICABLE, DANGEROUS INDIVIDUAL.
DIDN'T YOU SAY...
...NOBODY--
--GETS TO DO WHATEVER THEY WANT?
I MEAN...

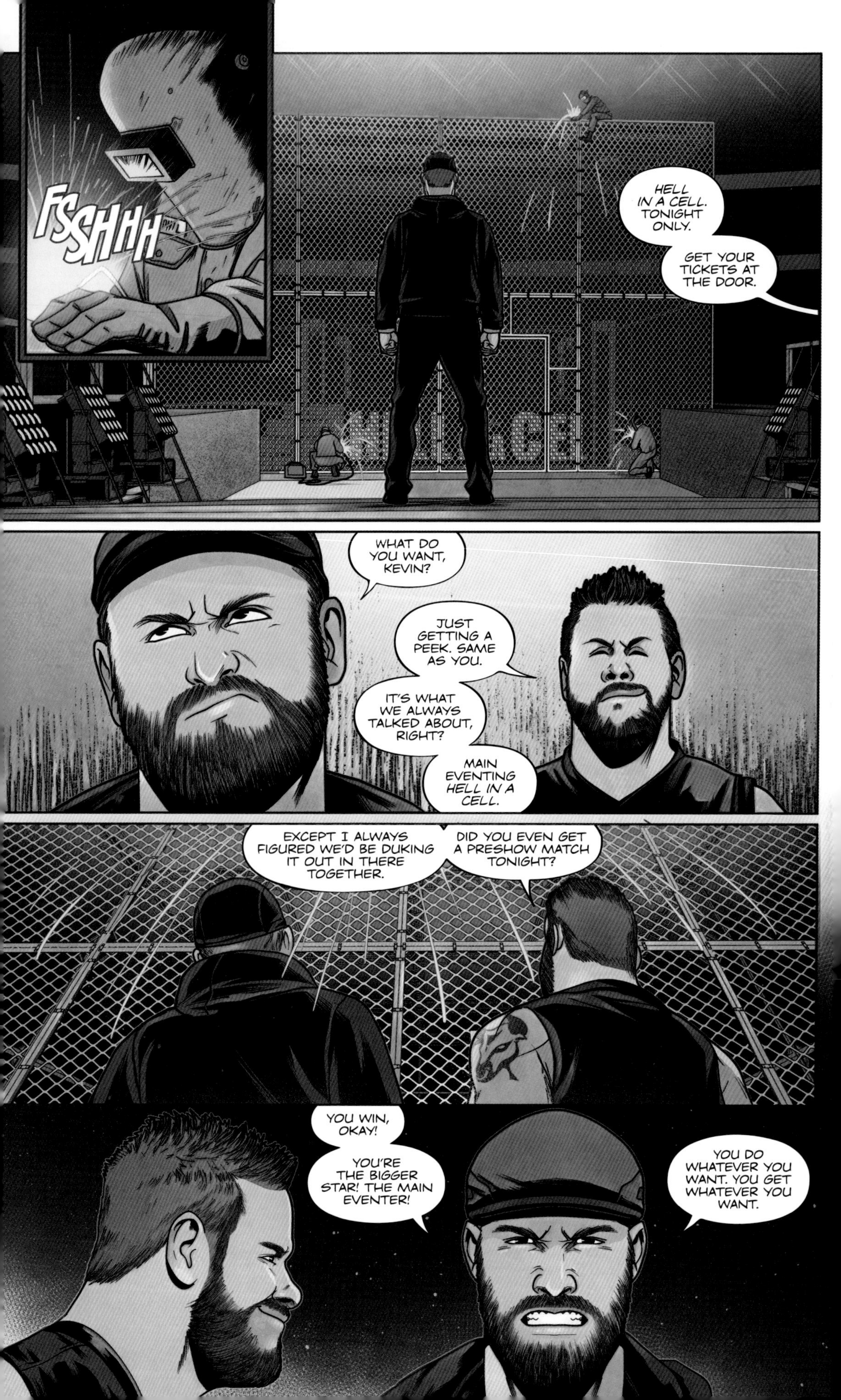
FSSHHH
PHIL
HELL IN A CELL. TONIGHT ONLY.
GET YOUR TICKETS AT THE DOOR.
WHAT DO YOU WANT, KEVIN?
JUST GETTING A PEEK. SAME AS YOU.
IT'S WHAT WE ALWAYS TALKED ABOUT, RIGHT?
MAIN EVENTING HELL IN A CELL.
EXCEPT I ALWAYS FIGURED WE'D BE DUKING IT OUT IN THERE TOGETHER.
DID YOU EVEN GET A PRESHOW MATCH TONIGHT?
YOU WIN, OKAY!
YOU'RE THE BIGGER STAR! THE MAIN EVENTER!
YOU DO WHATEVER YOU WANT. YOU GET WHATEVER YOU WANT.

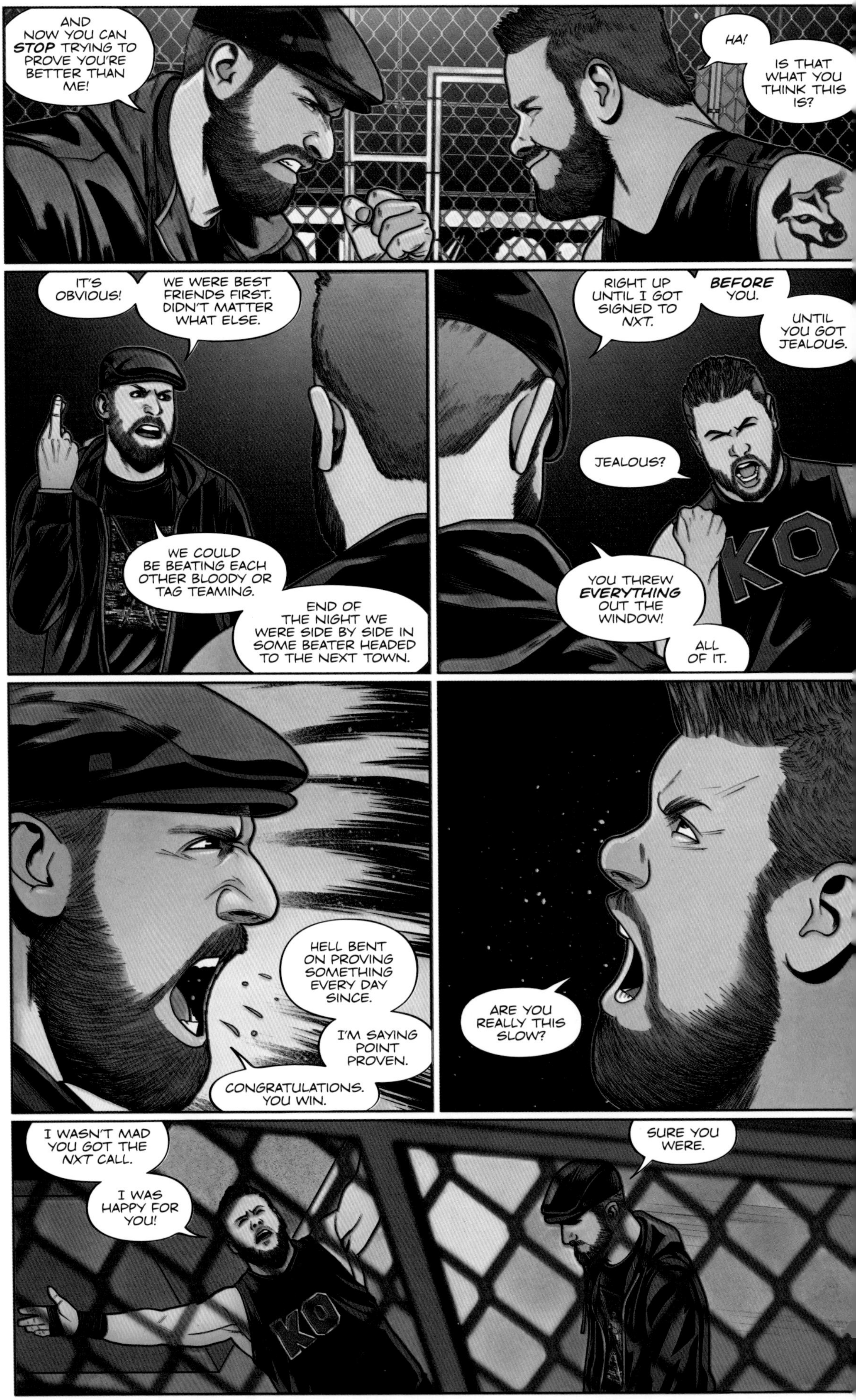
AND NOW YOU CAN STOP TRYING TO PROVE YOU'RE BETTER THAN ME!
HA!
IS THAT WHAT YOU THINK THIS IS?
IT'S OBVIOUS!
WE WERE BEST FRIENDS FIRST. DIDN'T MATTER WHAT ELSE.
WE COULD BE BEATING EACH OTHER BLOODY OR TAG TEAMING.
END OF THE NIGHT WE WERE SIDE BY SIDE IN SOME BEATER HEADED TO THE NEXT TOWN.
RIGHT UP UNTIL I GOT SIGNED TO NXT.
BEFORE YOU.
UNTIL YOU GOT JEALOUS.
JEALOUS?
YOU THREW EVERYTHING OUT THE WINDOW!
ALL OF IT.
HELL BENT ON PROVING SOMETHING EVERY DAY SINCE.
I'M SAYING POINT PROVEN.
CONGRATULATIONS. YOU WIN.
ARE YOU REALLY THIS SLOW?
I WASN'T MAD YOU GOT THE NXT CALL.
I WAS HAPPY FOR YOU!
SURE YOU WERE.
KO

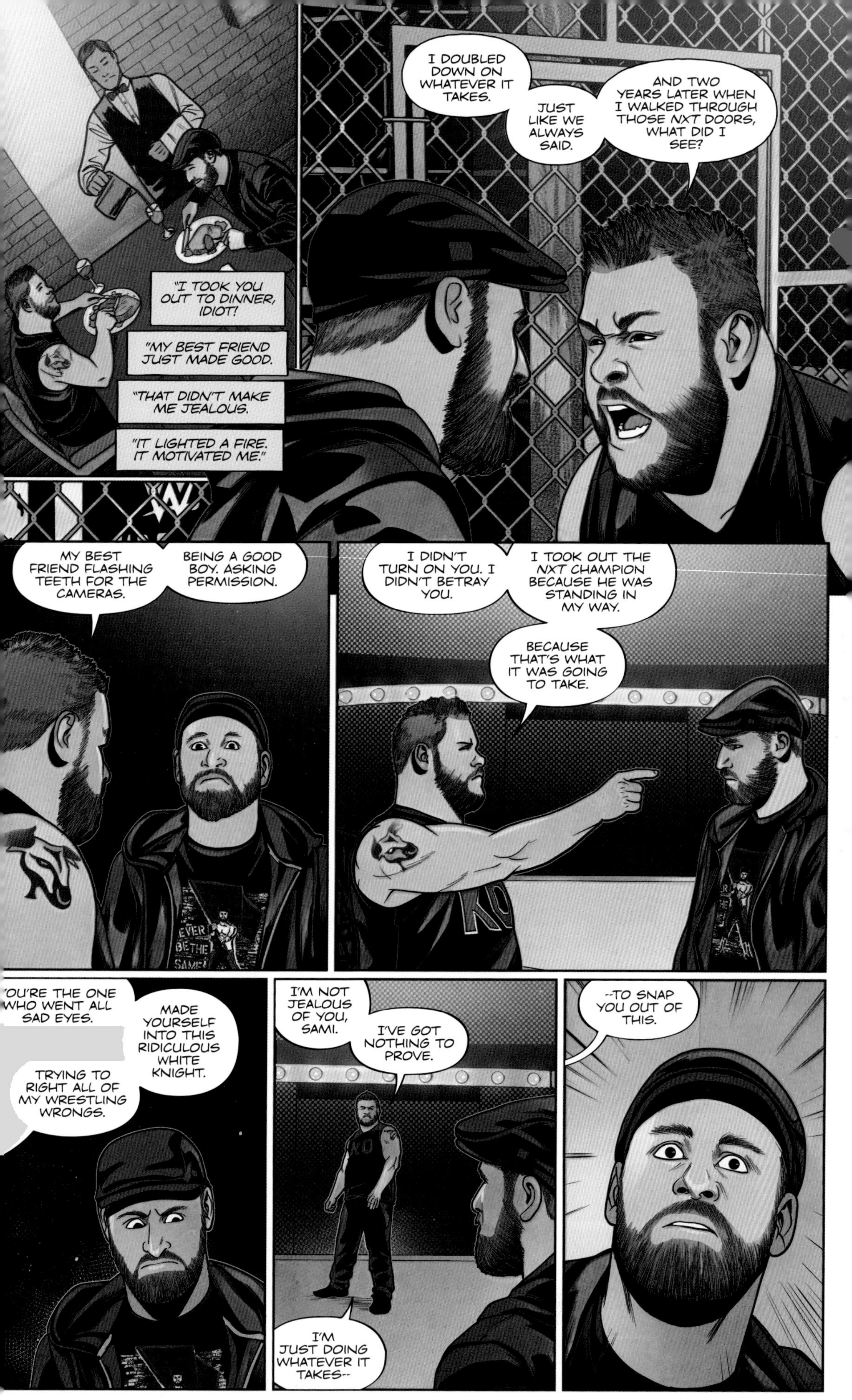

"I TOOK YOU OUT TO DINNER, IDIOT!
"MY BEST FRIEND JUST MADE GOOD.
"THAT DIDN'T MAKE ME JEALOUS.
"IT LIGHTED A FIRE. IT MOTIVATED ME."
I DOUBLED DOWN ON WHATEVER IT TAKES.
JUST LIKE WE ALWAYS SAID.
AND TWO YEARS LATER WHEN I WALKED THROUGH THOSE NXT DOORS, WHAT DID I SEE?
MY BEST FRIEND FLASHING TEETH FOR THE CAMERAS.
BEING A GOOD BOY. ASKING PERMISSION.
I DIDN'T TURN ON YOU. I DIDN'T BETRAY YOU.
I TOOK OUT THE NXT CHAMPION BECAUSE HE WAS STANDING IN MY WAY.
BECAUSE THAT'S WHAT IT WAS GOING TO TAKE.
YOU'RE THE ONE WHO WENT ALL SAD EYES.
MADE YOURSELF INTO THIS RIDICULOUS WHITE KNIGHT.
TRYING TO RIGHT ALL OF MY WRESTLING WRONGS.
I'M NOT JEALOUS OF YOU, SAMI.
I'VE GOT NOTHING TO PROVE.
I'M JUST DOING WHATEVER IT TAKES--
--TO SNAP YOU OUT OF THIS.

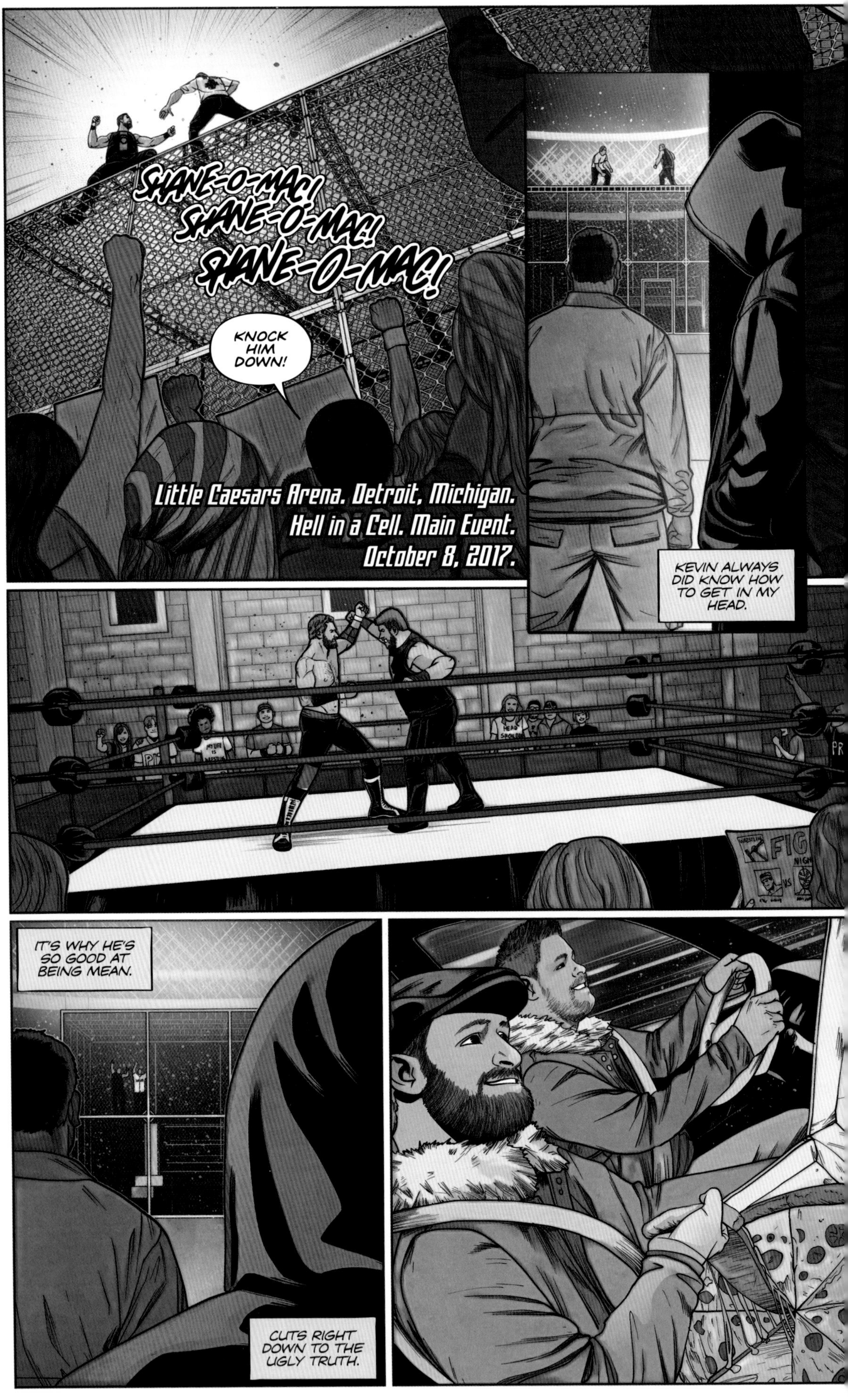
SHANE-O-MAC! SHANE-O-MAC! SHANE-O-MAC!
KNOCK HIM DOWN!
Little Caesars Arena. Detroit, Michigan. Hell in a Cell. Main Event. October 8, 2017.
KEVIN ALWAYS DID KNOW HOW TO GET IN MY HEAD.
IT'S WHY HE'S SO GOOD AT BEING MEAN.
CUTS RIGHT DOWN TO THE UGLY TRUTH.

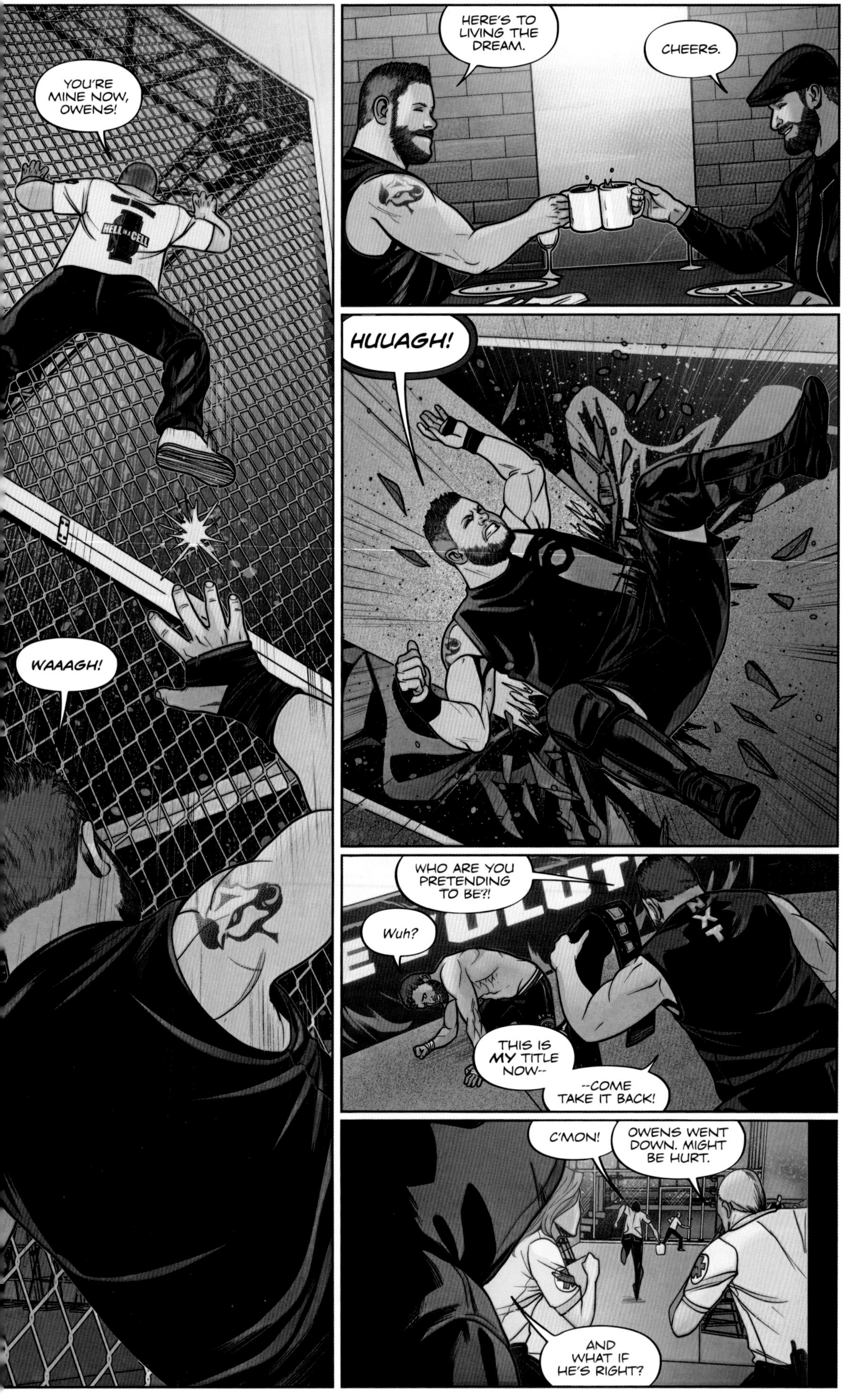

YOU'RE MINE NOW, OWENS!
WAAAGH!
HERE'S TO LIVING THE DREAM.
CHEERS.
HUUAGH!
WHO ARE YOU PRETENDING TO BE?!
Wuh?
THIS IS MY TITLE NOW--
--COME TAKE IT BACK!
C'MON!
OWENS WENT DOWN. MIGHT BE HURT.
AND WHAT IF HE'S RIGHT?

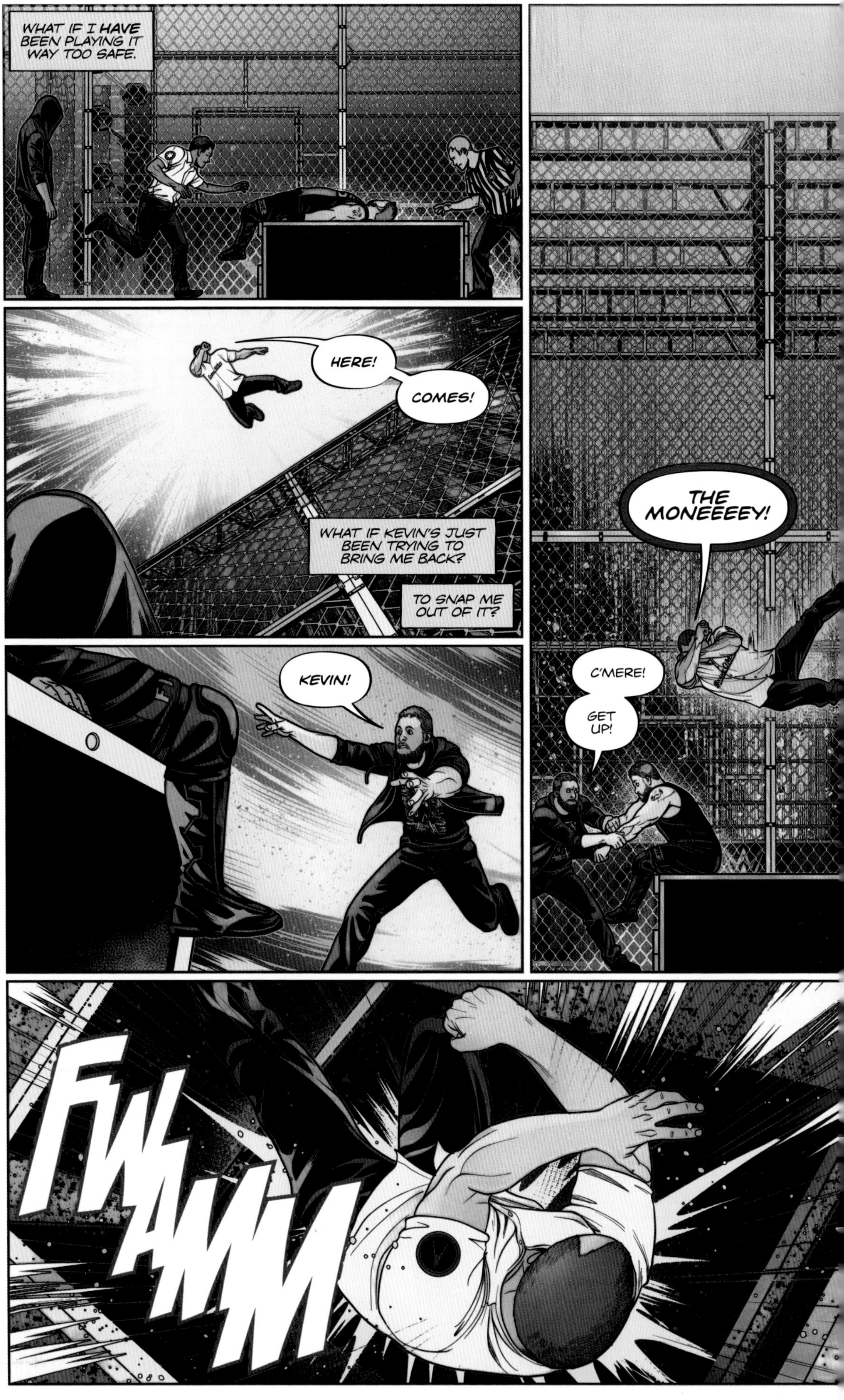
WHAT IF I HAVE BEEN PLAYING IT WAY TOO SAFE.
HERE!
COMES!
WHAT IF KEVIN'S JUST BEEN TRYING TO BRING ME BACK?
TO SNAP ME OUT OF IT?
KEVIN!
THE MONEEEEY!
C'MERE!
GET UP!
FWAMM

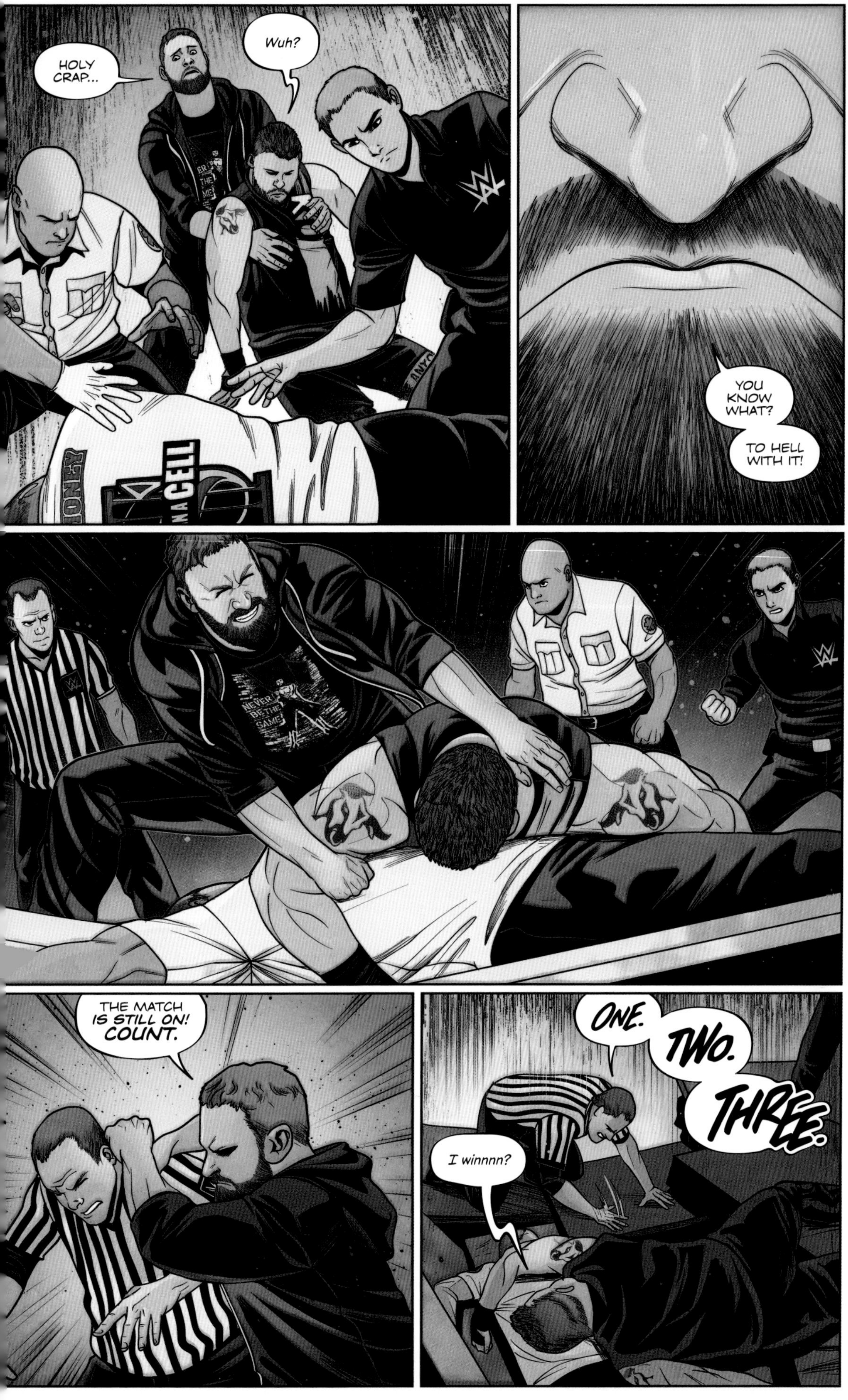
HOLY CRAP...
Wuh?
YOU KNOW WHAT?
TO HELL WITH IT!
THE MATCH IS STILL ON! COUNT.
ONE.
TWO.
THREE.
I winnnn?

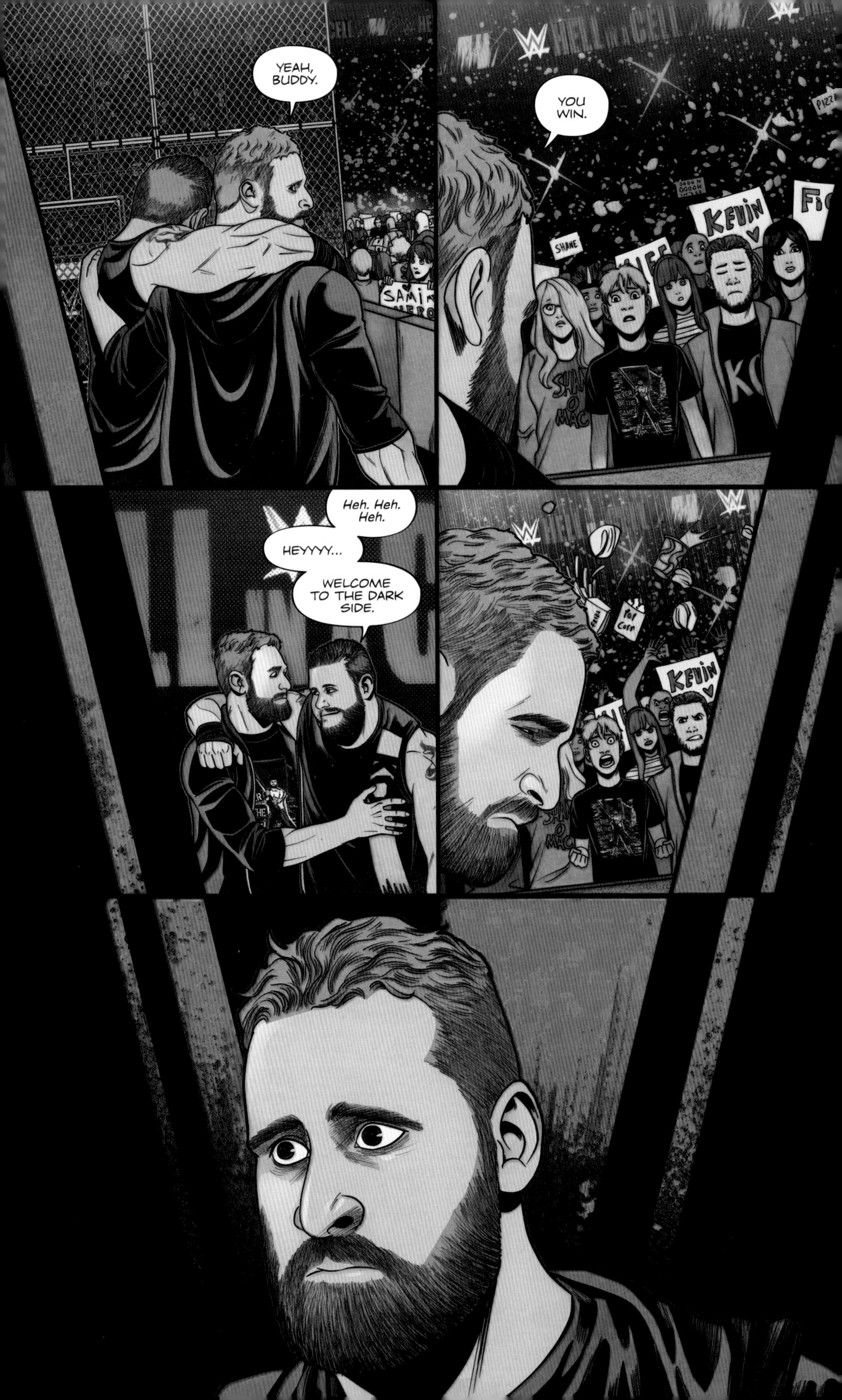
YEAH, BUDDY.
YOU WIN.
SHANE
KEVIN
Heh. Heh. Heh.
HEYYYY...
WELCOME TO THE DARK SIDE.
KEVIN

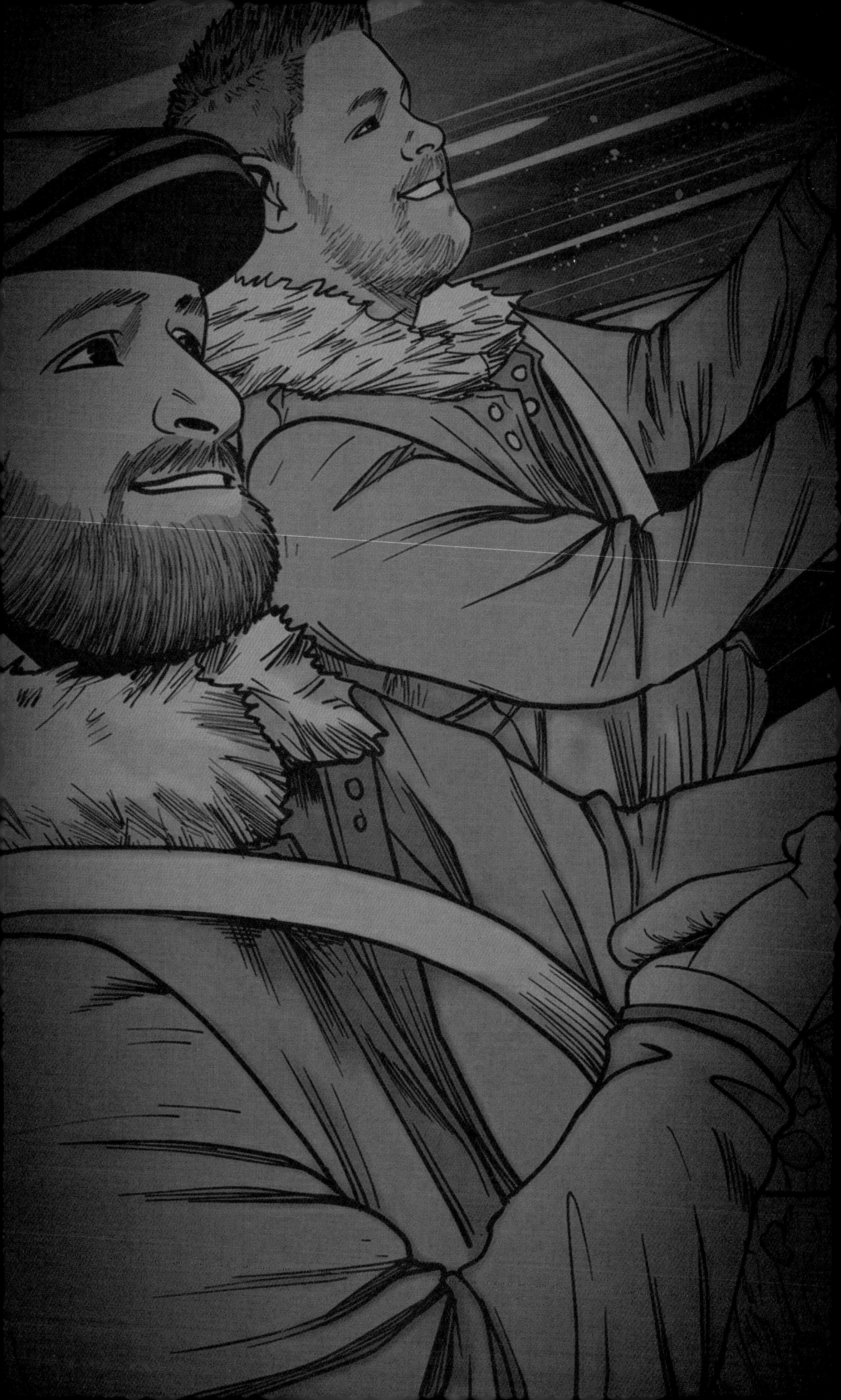

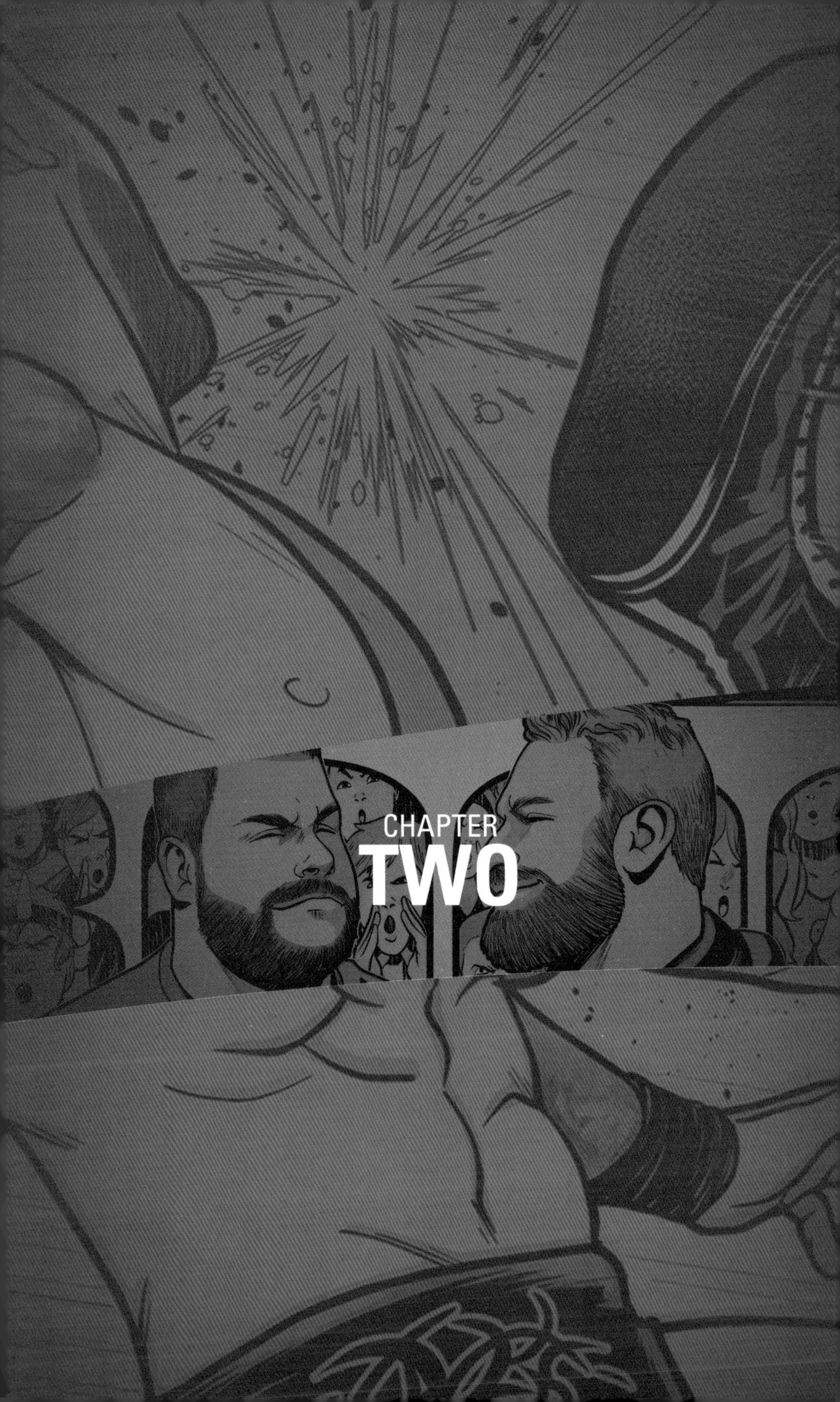
CHAPTER
TWO

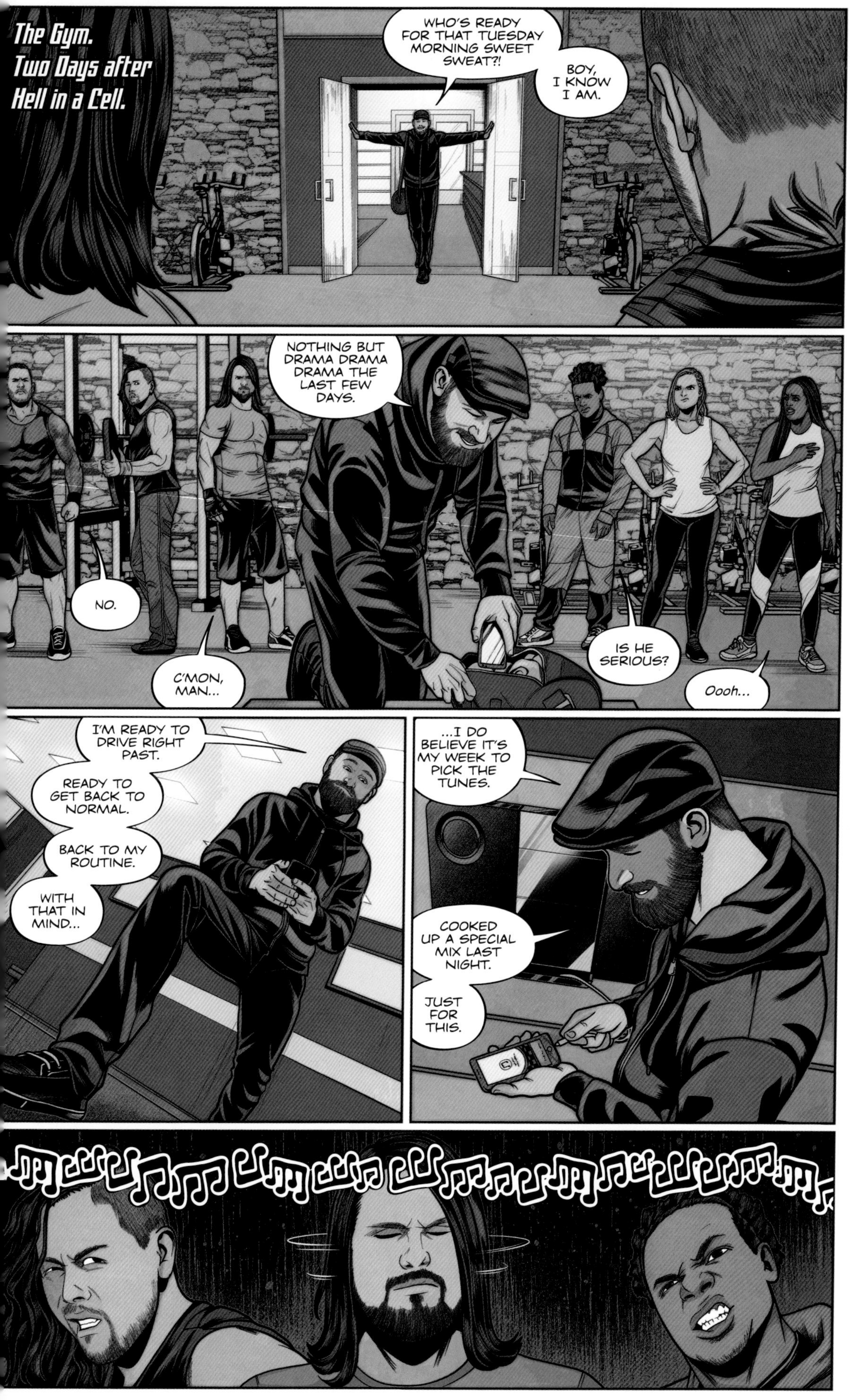
The Gym.
Two Days after
Hell in a Cell.
WHO'S READY FOR THAT TUESDAY MORNING SWEET SWEAT?!
BOY, I KNOW I AM.
NOTHING BUT DRAMA DRAMA DRAMA THE LAST FEW DAYS.
NO.
C'MON, MAN...
IS HE SERIOUS?
Oooh...
I'M READY TO DRIVE RIGHT PAST.
READY TO GET BACK TO NORMAL.
BACK TO MY ROUTINE.
WITH THAT IN MIND...
...I DO BELIEVE IT'S MY WEEK TO PICK THE TUNES.
COOKED UP A SPECIAL MIX LAST NIGHT.
JUST FOR THIS.

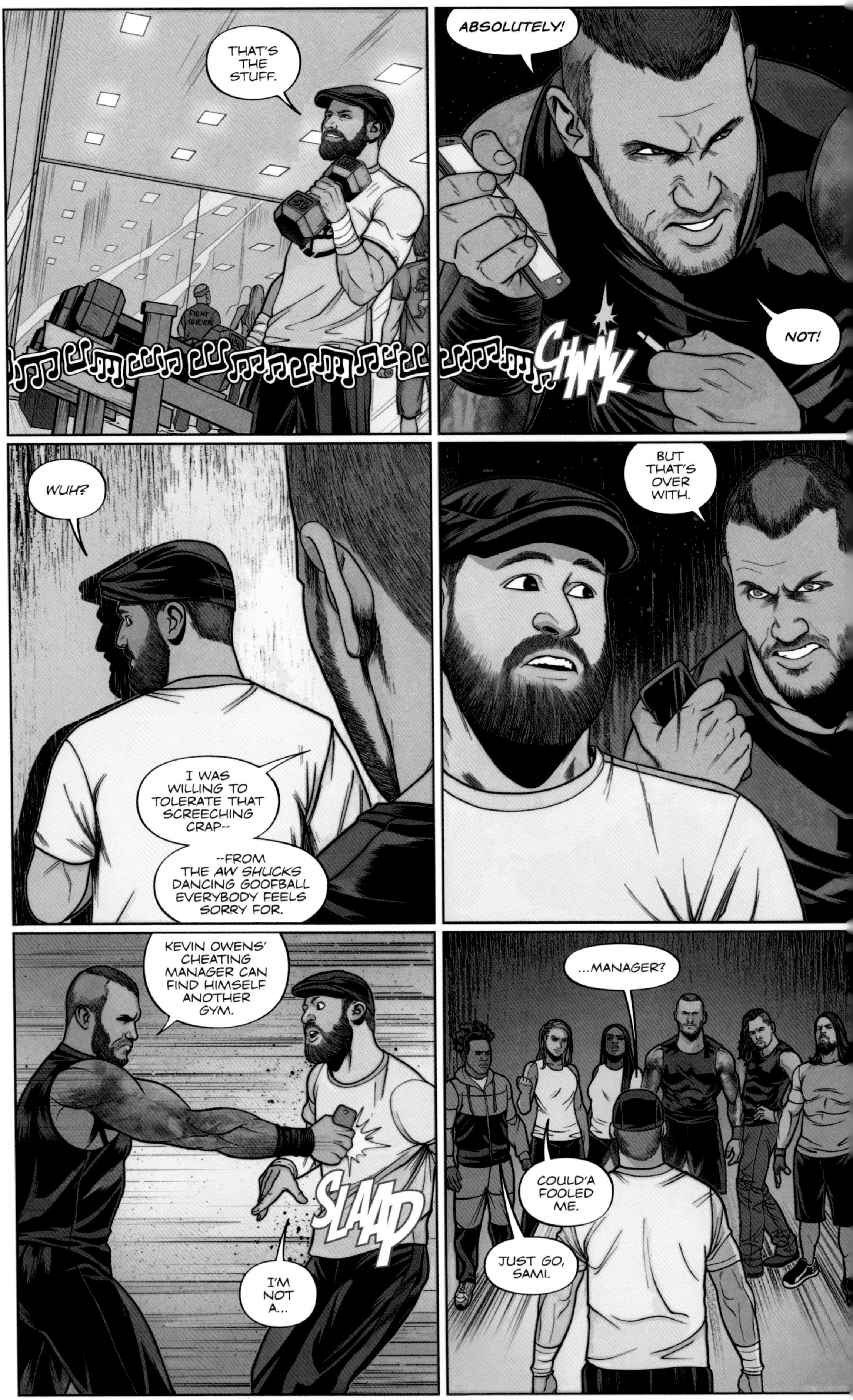
THAT'S THE STUFF.
FIGHT FOREVER
ABSOLUTELY!
CHNNK
NOT!
WUH?
I WAS WILLING TO TOLERATE THAT SCREECHING CRAP--
--FROM THE AW SHUCKS DANCING GOOFBALL EVERYBODY FEELS SORRY FOR.
BUT THAT'S OVER WITH.
KEVIN OWENS' CHEATING MANAGER CAN FIND HIMSELF ANOTHER GYM.
SLAAP
I'M NOT A...
...MANAGER?
COULD'A FOOLED ME.
JUST GO, SAMI.

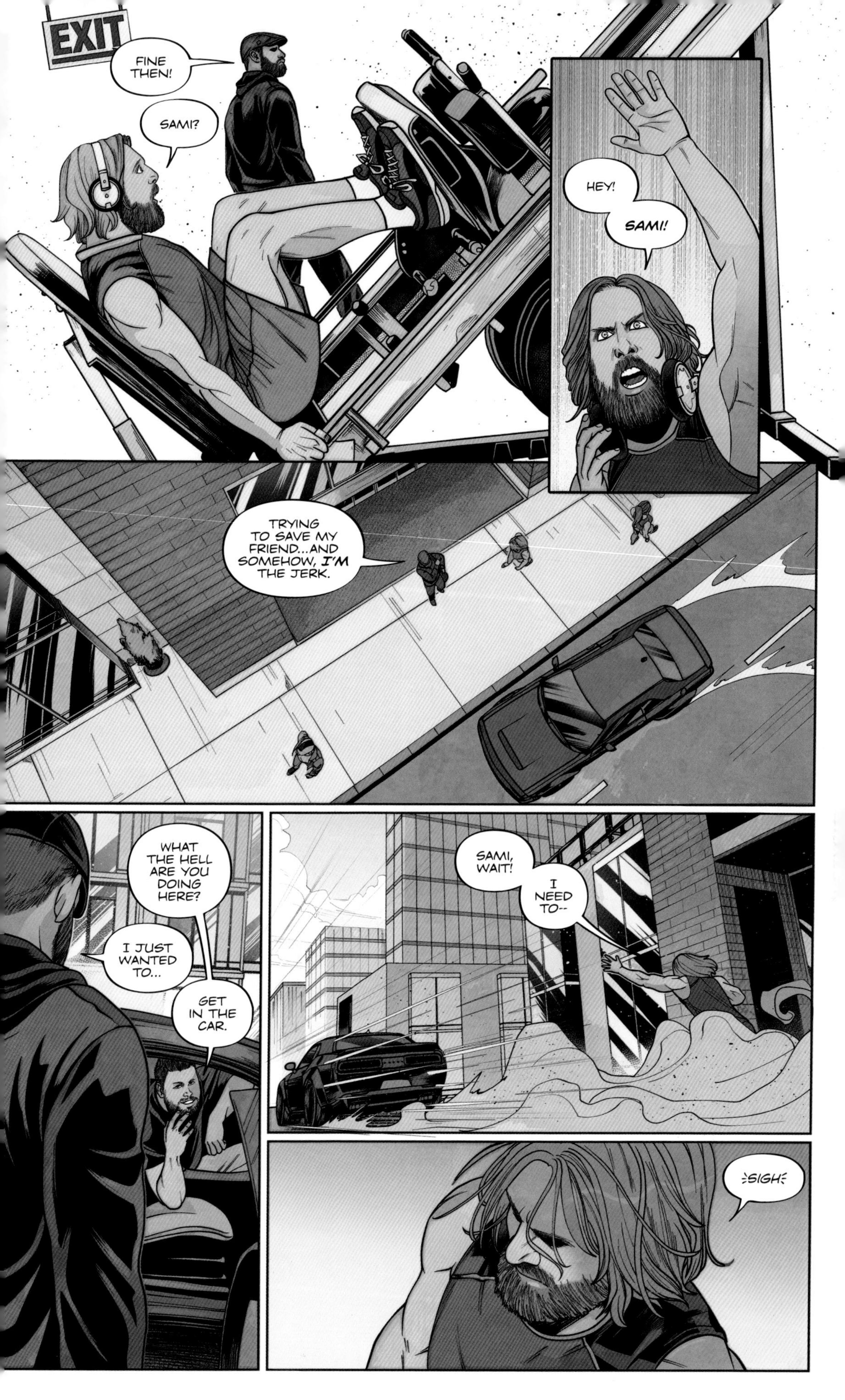
EXIT
FINE THEN!
SAMI?
HEY!
SAMI!
TRYING TO SAVE MY FRIEND...AND SOMEHOW, I'M THE JERK.
WHAT THE HELL ARE YOU DOING HERE?
I JUST WANTED TO...
GET IN THE CAR.
SAMI, WAIT!
I NEED TO--
SIGH

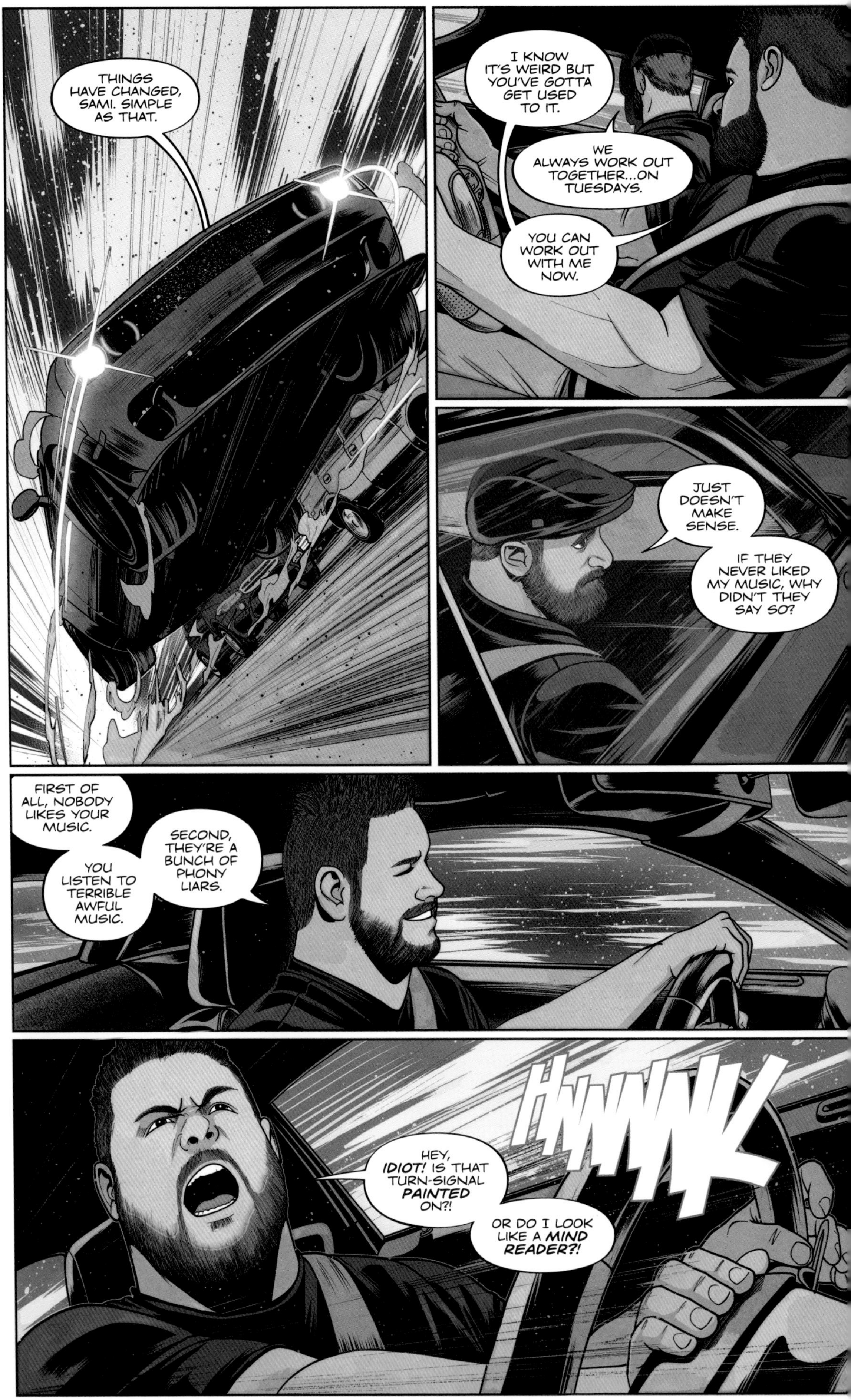
THINGS HAVE CHANGED, SAMI. SIMPLE AS THAT.
I KNOW IT'S WEIRD BUT YOU'VE GOTTA GET USED TO IT.
WE ALWAYS WORK OUT TOGETHER...ON TUESDAYS.
YOU CAN WORK OUT WITH ME NOW.
JUST DOESN'T MAKE SENSE.
IF THEY NEVER LIKED MY MUSIC, WHY DIDN'T THEY SAY SO?
FIRST OF ALL, NOBODY LIKES YOUR MUSIC.
YOU LISTEN TO TERRIBLE AWFUL MUSIC.
SECOND, THEY'RE A BUNCH OF PHONY LIARS.
HNNNNK
HEY, IDIOT! IS THAT TURN-SIGNAL PAINTED ON?!
OR DO I LOOK LIKE A MIND READER?!

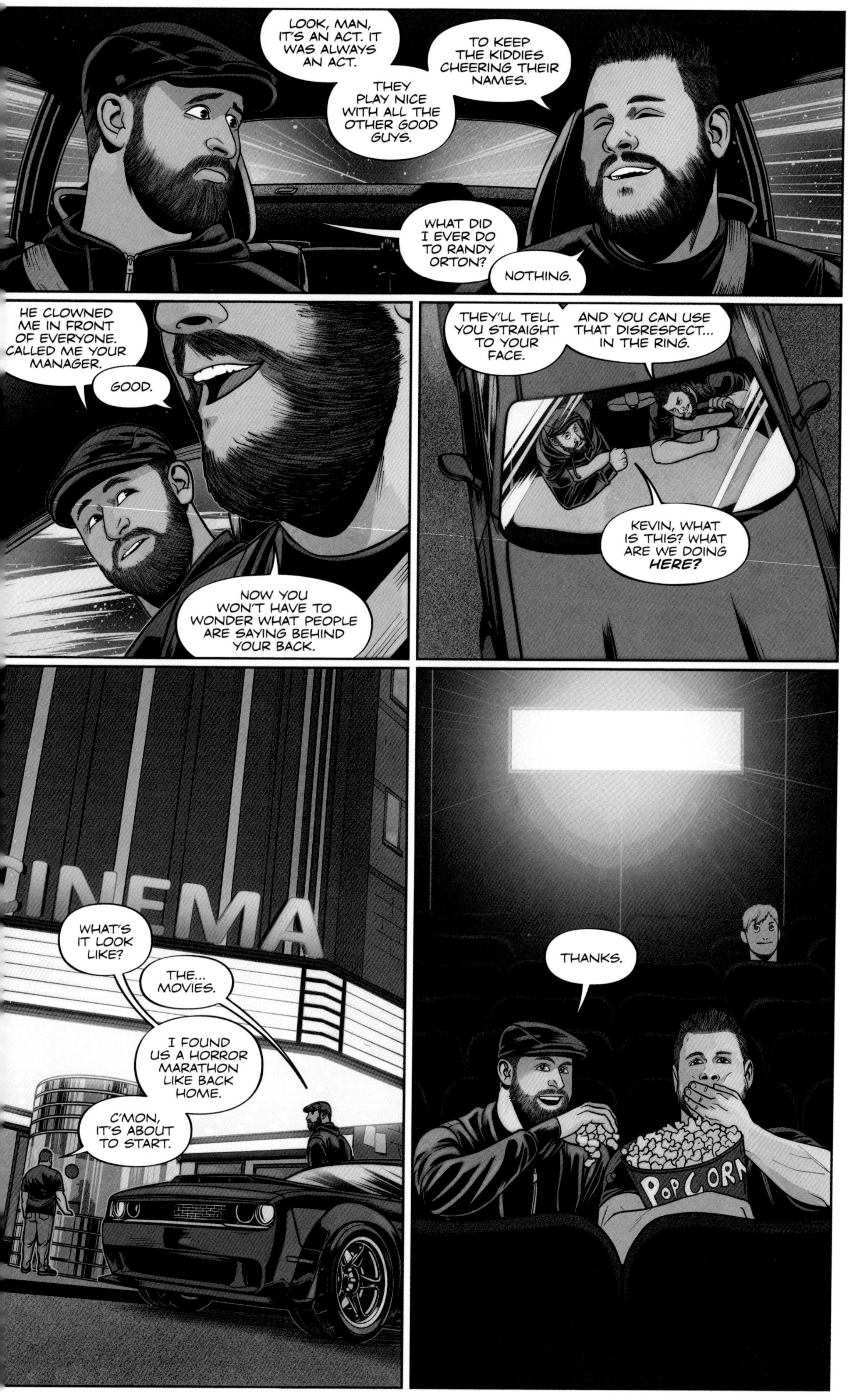
LOOK, MAN, IT'S AN ACT. IT WAS ALWAYS AN ACT.
THEY PLAY NICE WITH ALL THE OTHER GOOD GUYS.
TO KEEP THE KIDDIES CHEERING THEIR NAMES.
WHAT DID I EVER DO TO RANDY ORTON?
NOTHING.
HE CLOWNED ME IN FRONT OF EVERYONE. CALLED ME YOUR MANAGER.
GOOD.
NOW YOU WON'T HAVE TO WONDER WHAT PEOPLE ARE SAYING BEHIND YOUR BACK.
THEY'LL TELL YOU STRAIGHT TO YOUR FACE.
AND YOU CAN USE THAT DISRESPECT... IN THE RING.
KEVIN, WHAT IS THIS? WHAT ARE WE DOING *HERE?*
INEMA
WHAT'S IT LOOK LIKE?
THE... MOVIES.
I FOUND US A HORROR MARATHON LIKE BACK HOME.
C'MON, IT'S ABOUT TO START.
THANKS.
POPCORN

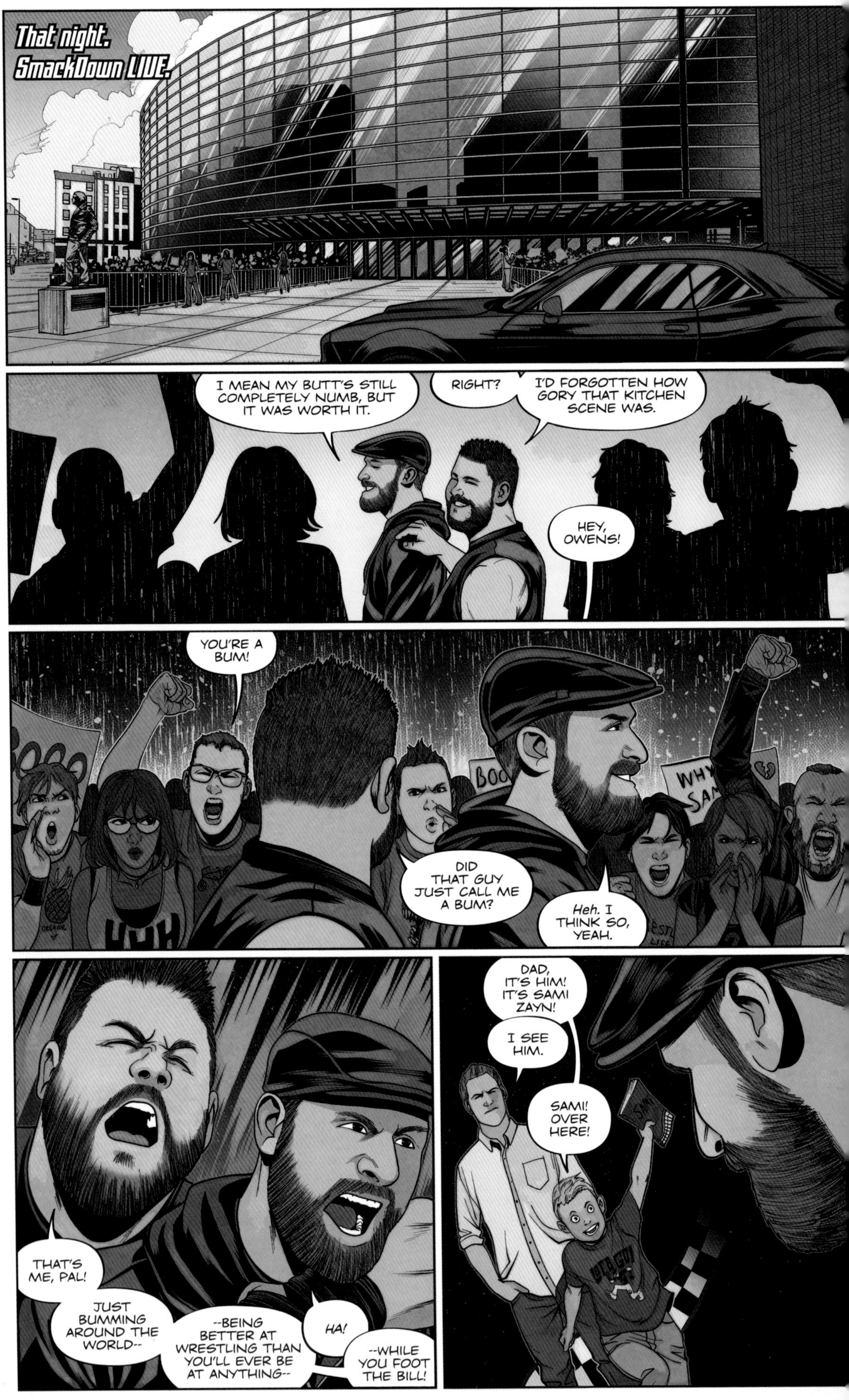
That night.
SmackDown LIVE.
I MEAN MY BUTT'S STILL COMPLETELY NUMB, BUT IT WAS WORTH IT.
RIGHT?
I'D FORGOTTEN HOW GORY THAT KITCHEN SCENE WAS.
HEY, OWENS!
YOU'RE A BUM!
BOOO
BOO
WHY SAM
DID THAT GUY JUST CALL ME A BUM?
Heh. I THINK SO, YEAH.
THAT'S ME, PAL!
JUST BUMMING AROUND THE WORLD--
--BEING BETTER AT WRESTLING THAN YOU'LL EVER BE AT ANYTHING--
HA!
--WHILE YOU FOOT THE BILL!
DAD, IT'S HIM! IT'S SAMI ZAYN!
I SEE HIM.
SAMI! OVER HERE!

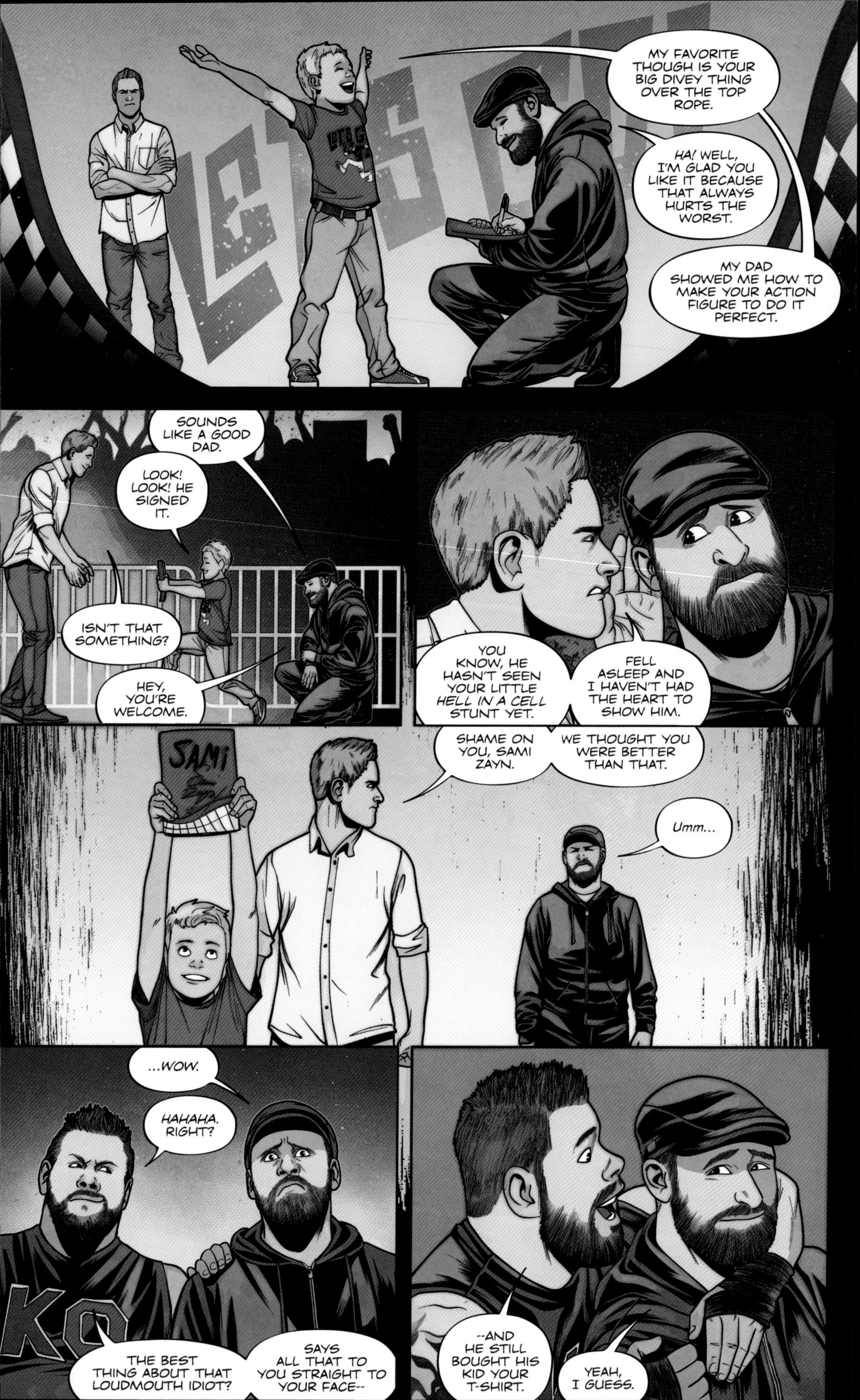
MY FAVORITE THOUGH IS YOUR BIG DIVEY THING OVER THE TOP ROPE.
HA! WELL, I'M GLAD YOU LIKE IT BECAUSE THAT ALWAYS HURTS THE WORST.
MY DAD SHOWED ME HOW TO MAKE YOUR ACTION FIGURE TO DO IT PERFECT.
SOUNDS LIKE A GOOD DAD.
LOOK! LOOK! HE SIGNED IT.
ISN'T THAT SOMETHING?
HEY, YOU'RE WELCOME.
YOU KNOW, HE HASN'T SEEN YOUR LITTLE HELL IN A CELL STUNT YET.
FELL ASLEEP AND I HAVEN'T HAD THE HEART TO SHOW HIM.
SAMI
SHAME ON YOU, SAMI ZAYN.
WE THOUGHT YOU WERE BETTER THAN THAT.
Umm...
...WOW.
HAHAHA. RIGHT?
THE BEST THING ABOUT THAT LOUDMOUTH IDIOT?
SAYS ALL THAT TO YOU STRAIGHT TO YOUR FACE--
--AND HE STILL BOUGHT HIS KID YOUR T-SHIRT.
YEAH, I GUESS.

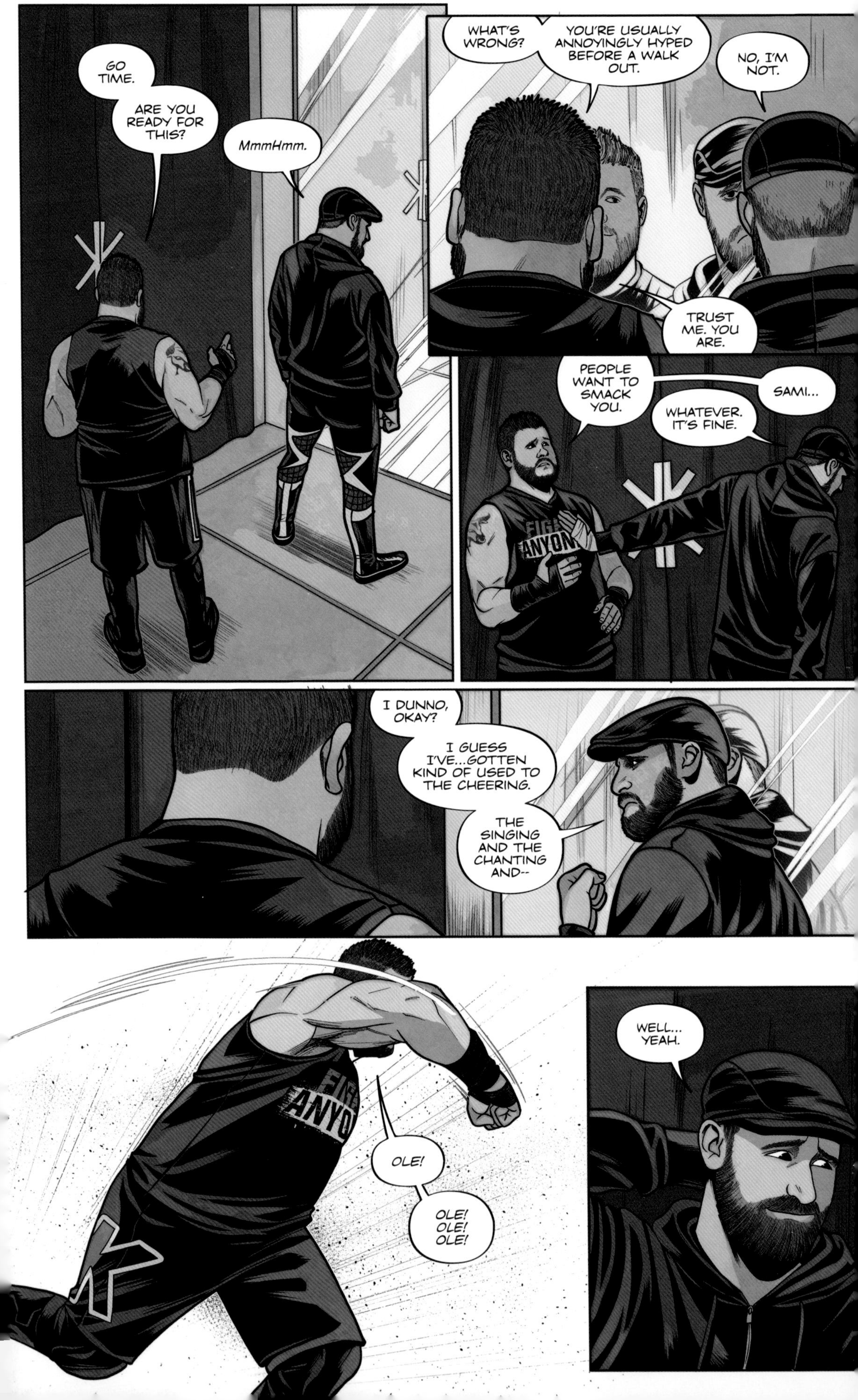
GO TIME.
ARE YOU READY FOR THIS?
MmmHmm.
WHAT'S WRONG?
YOU'RE USUALLY ANNOYINGLY HYPED BEFORE A WALK OUT.
NO, I'M NOT.
TRUST ME. YOU ARE.
PEOPLE WANT TO SMACK YOU.
SAMI...
WHATEVER. IT'S FINE.
I DUNNO, OKAY?
I GUESS I'VE...GOTTEN KIND OF USED TO THE CHEERING.
THE SINGING AND THE CHANTING AND--
OLE!
OLE! OLE! OLE!
WELL... YEAH.

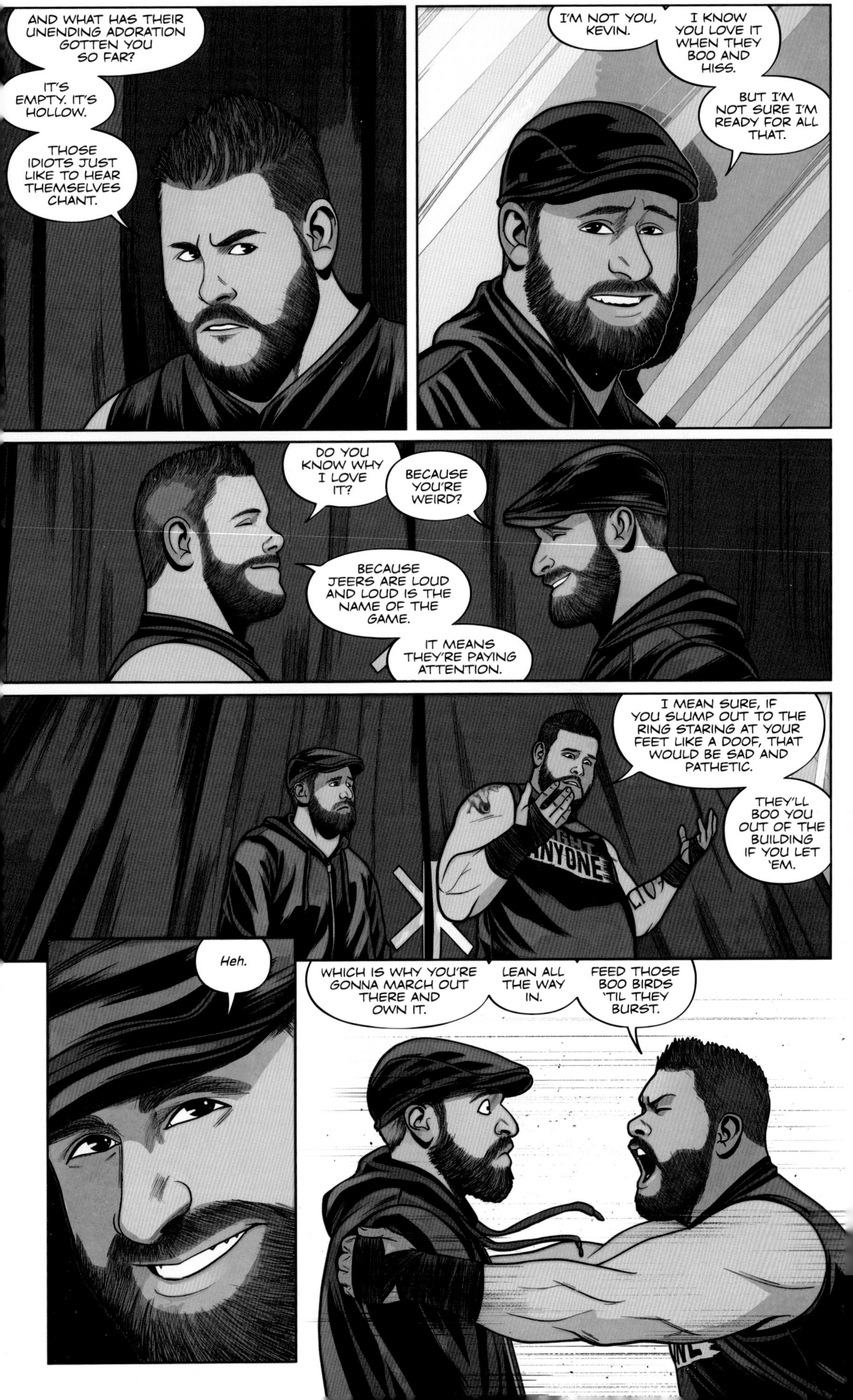

AND WHAT HAS THEIR UNENDING ADORATION GOTTEN YOU SO FAR?
IT'S EMPTY. IT'S HOLLOW.
THOSE IDIOTS JUST LIKE TO HEAR THEMSELVES CHANT.
I'M NOT YOU, KEVIN.
I KNOW YOU LOVE IT WHEN THEY BOO AND HISS.
BUT I'M NOT SURE I'M READY FOR ALL THAT.
DO YOU KNOW WHY I LOVE IT?
BECAUSE YOU'RE WEIRD?
BECAUSE JEERS ARE LOUD AND LOUD IS THE NAME OF THE GAME.
IT MEANS THEY'RE PAYING ATTENTION.
I MEAN SURE, IF YOU SLUMP OUT TO THE RING STARING AT YOUR FEET LIKE A DOOF, THAT WOULD BE SAD AND PATHETIC.
THEY'LL BOO YOU OUT OF THE BUILDING IF YOU LET 'EM.
Heh.
WHICH IS WHY YOU'RE GONNA MARCH OUT THERE AND OWN IT.
LEAN ALL THE WAY IN.
FEED THOSE BOO BIRDS 'TIL THEY BURST.

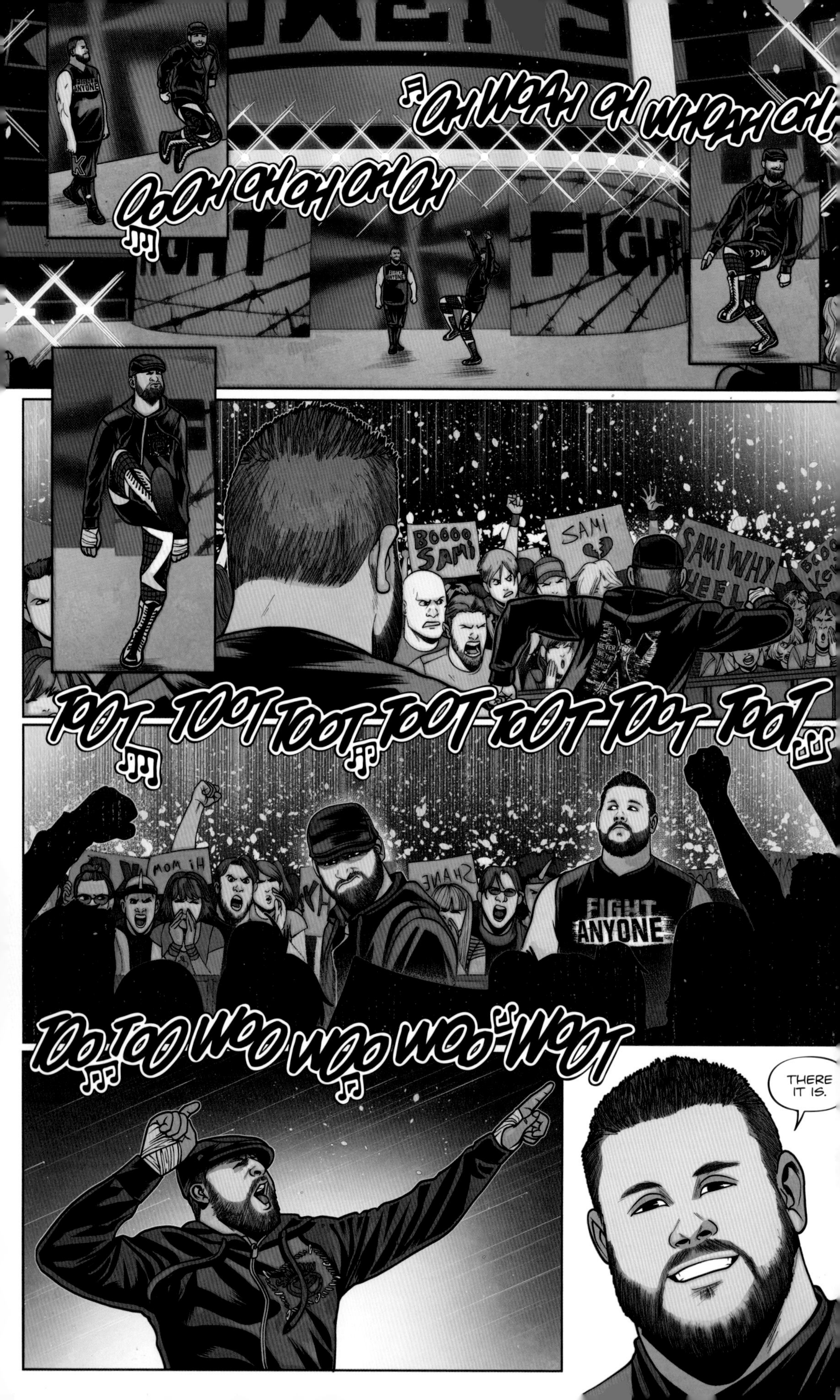
OH WOAH OH WHOAH OH!
OOOH OH OH OH OH
FIGHT ANYONE
FIGHT
BOOOO SAMI
SAMI
SAMI WHY HEEL
TOOT TOOT TOOT TOOT TOOT TOOT TOOT
FIGHT ANYONE
TOO TOO WOO WOO WOO WOOT
THERE IT IS.

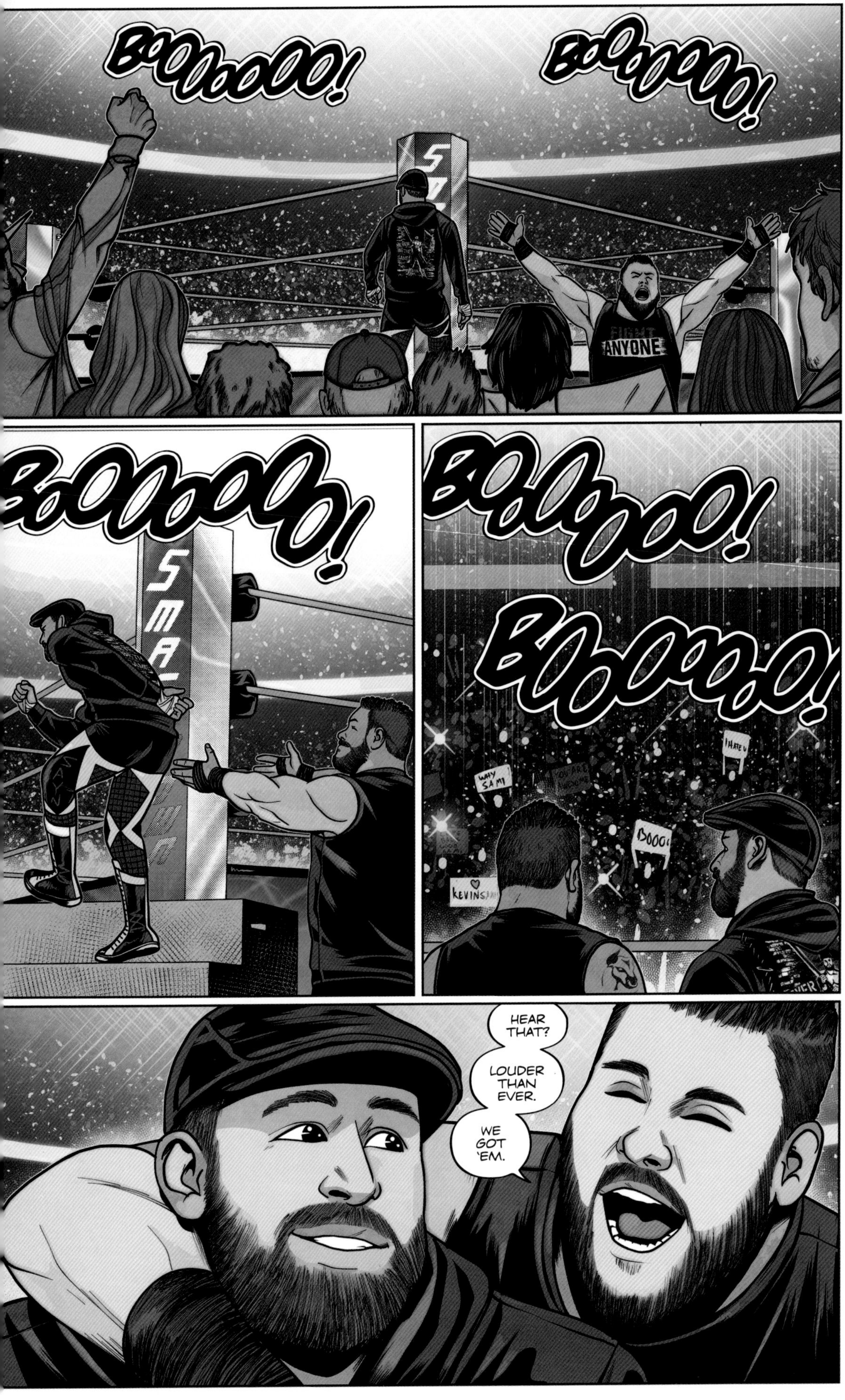

BOOOOOOOO!
BOOOOOOOO!
ANYONE
BOOOOOOOO!
BOOOOOOO!
BOOOOOOO!
HEAR THAT?
LOUDER THAN EVER.
WE GOT 'EM.

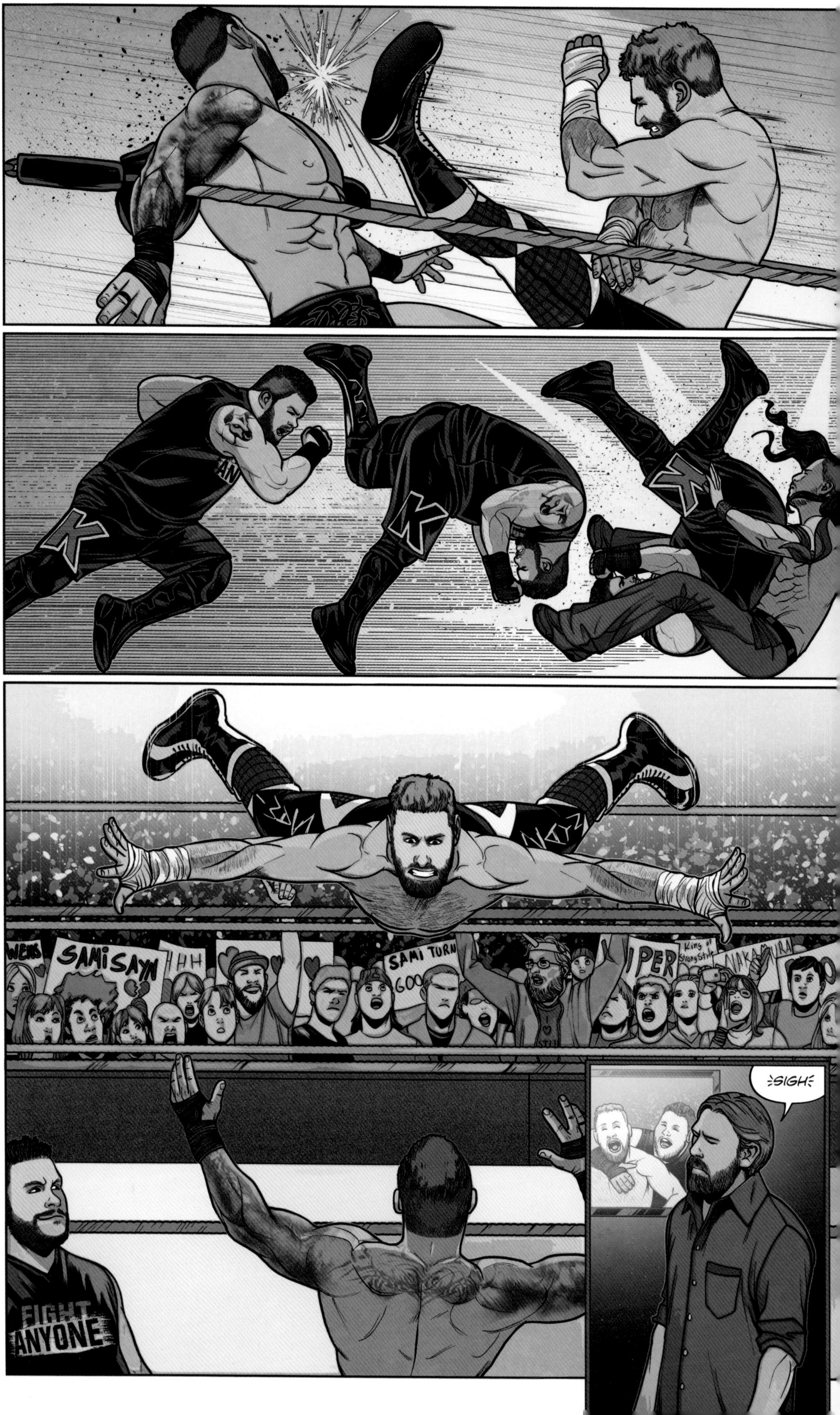
SAMI SAYN
SAMI TURN
King of Strong Style
NAKAMURA
SIGH
FIGHT ANYONE

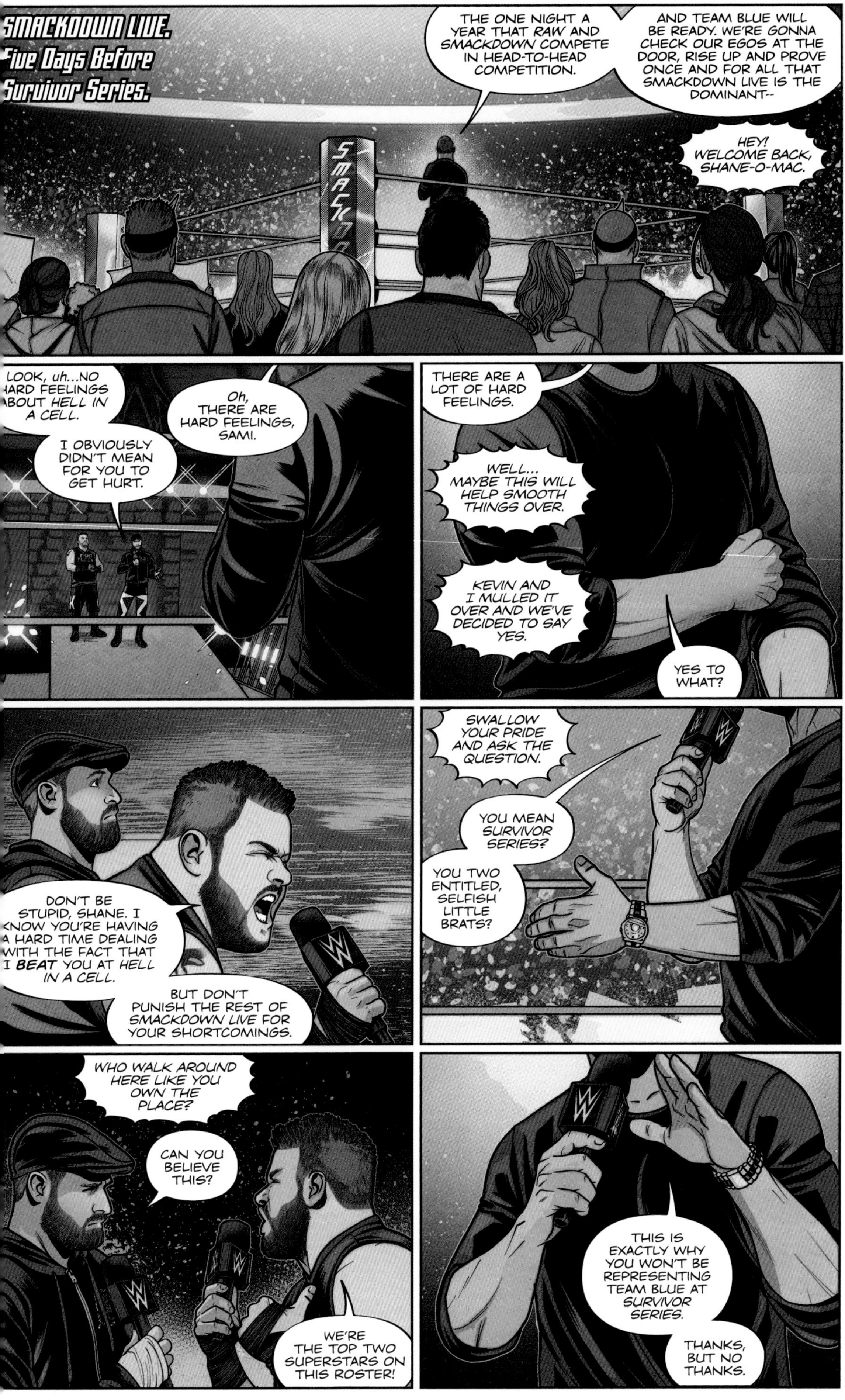

SMACKDOWN LIVE. Five Days Before Survivor Series.
THE ONE NIGHT A YEAR THAT RAW AND SMACKDOWN COMPETE IN HEAD-TO-HEAD COMPETITION.
AND TEAM BLUE WILL BE READY. WE'RE GONNA CHECK OUR EGOS AT THE DOOR, RISE UP AND PROVE ONCE AND FOR ALL THAT SMACKDOWN LIVE IS THE DOMINANT--
HEY! WELCOME BACK, SHANE-O-MAC.
LOOK, uh...NO HARD FEELINGS ABOUT HELL IN A CELL.
I OBVIOUSLY DIDN'T MEAN FOR YOU TO GET HURT.
Oh, THERE ARE HARD FEELINGS, SAMI.
THERE ARE A LOT OF HARD FEELINGS.
WELL... MAYBE THIS WILL HELP SMOOTH THINGS OVER.
KEVIN AND I MULLED IT OVER AND WE'VE DECIDED TO SAY YES.
YES TO WHAT?
SWALLOW YOUR PRIDE AND ASK THE QUESTION.
YOU MEAN SURVIVOR SERIES?
YOU TWO ENTITLED, SELFISH LITTLE BRATS?
DON'T BE STUPID, SHANE. I KNOW YOU'RE HAVING A HARD TIME DEALING WITH THE FACT THAT I BEAT YOU AT HELL IN A CELL.
BUT DON'T PUNISH THE REST OF SMACKDOWN LIVE FOR YOUR SHORTCOMINGS.
WHO WALK AROUND HERE LIKE YOU OWN THE PLACE?
CAN YOU BELIEVE THIS?
WE'RE THE TOP TWO SUPERSTARS ON THIS ROSTER!
THIS IS EXACTLY WHY YOU WON'T BE REPRESENTING TEAM BLUE AT SURVIVOR SERIES.
THANKS, BUT NO THANKS.

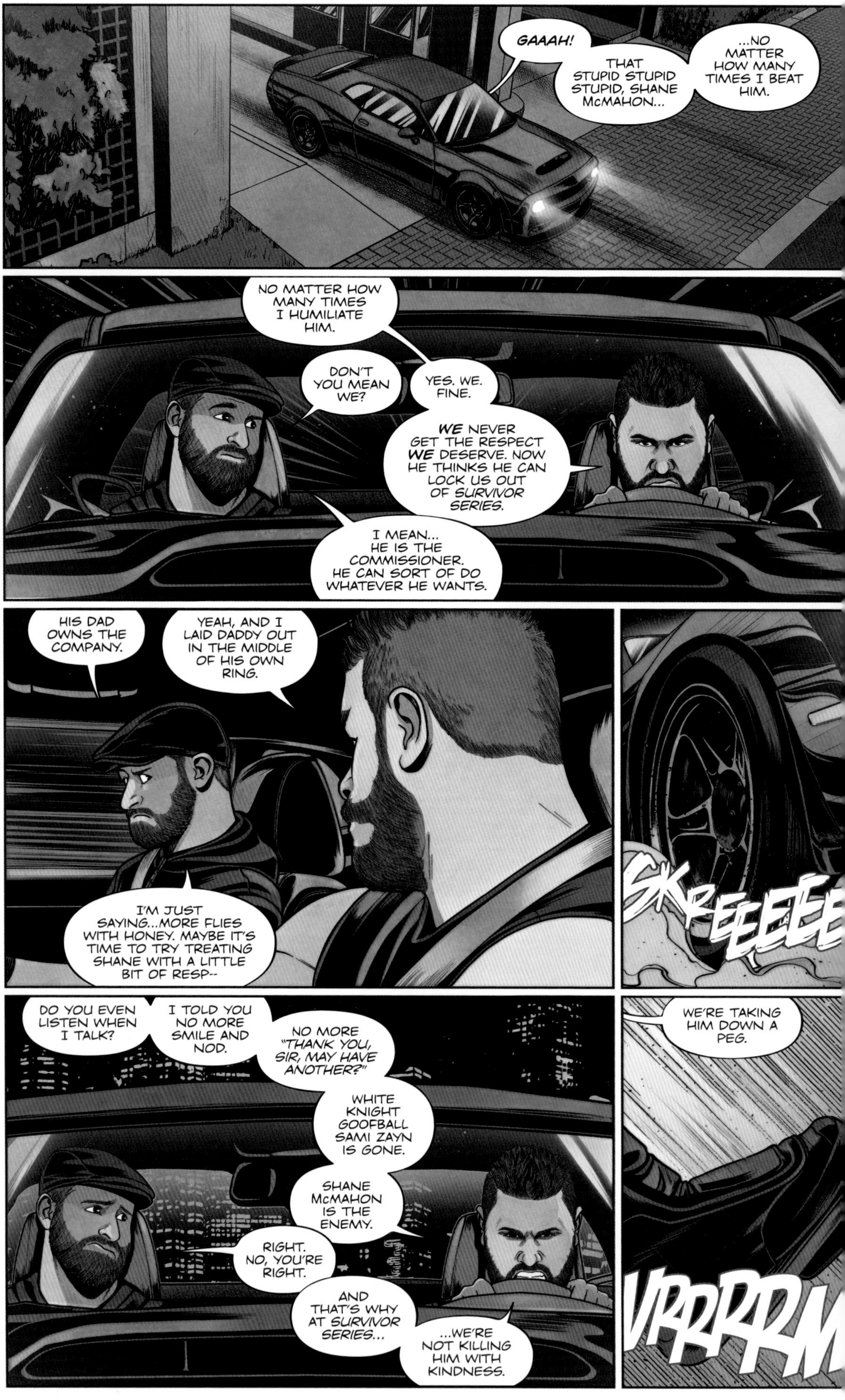
GAAAH!
THAT STUPID STUPID STUPID, SHANE McMAHON...
...NO MATTER HOW MANY TIMES I BEAT HIM.
NO MATTER HOW MANY TIMES I HUMILIATE HIM.
DON'T YOU MEAN WE?
YES. WE. FINE.
WE NEVER GET THE RESPECT WE DESERVE. NOW HE THINKS HE CAN LOCK US OUT OF SURVIVOR SERIES.
I MEAN... HE IS THE COMMISSIONER. HE CAN SORT OF DO WHATEVER HE WANTS.
HIS DAD OWNS THE COMPANY.
YEAH, AND I LAID DADDY OUT IN THE MIDDLE OF HIS OWN RING.
I'M JUST SAYING...MORE FLIES WITH HONEY. MAYBE IT'S TIME TO TRY TREATING SHANE WITH A LITTLE BIT OF RESP--
SKREEEEEE
DO YOU EVEN LISTEN WHEN I TALK?
I TOLD YOU NO MORE SMILE AND NOD.
NO MORE "THANK YOU, SIR, MAY HAVE ANOTHER?"
WHITE KNIGHT GOOFBALL SAMI ZAYN IS GONE.
SHANE McMAHON IS THE ENEMY.
RIGHT. NO, YOU'RE RIGHT.
AND THAT'S WHY AT SURVIVOR SERIES...
...WE'RE NOT KILLING HIM WITH KINDNESS.
WE'RE TAKING HIM DOWN A PEG.
VRRRRM

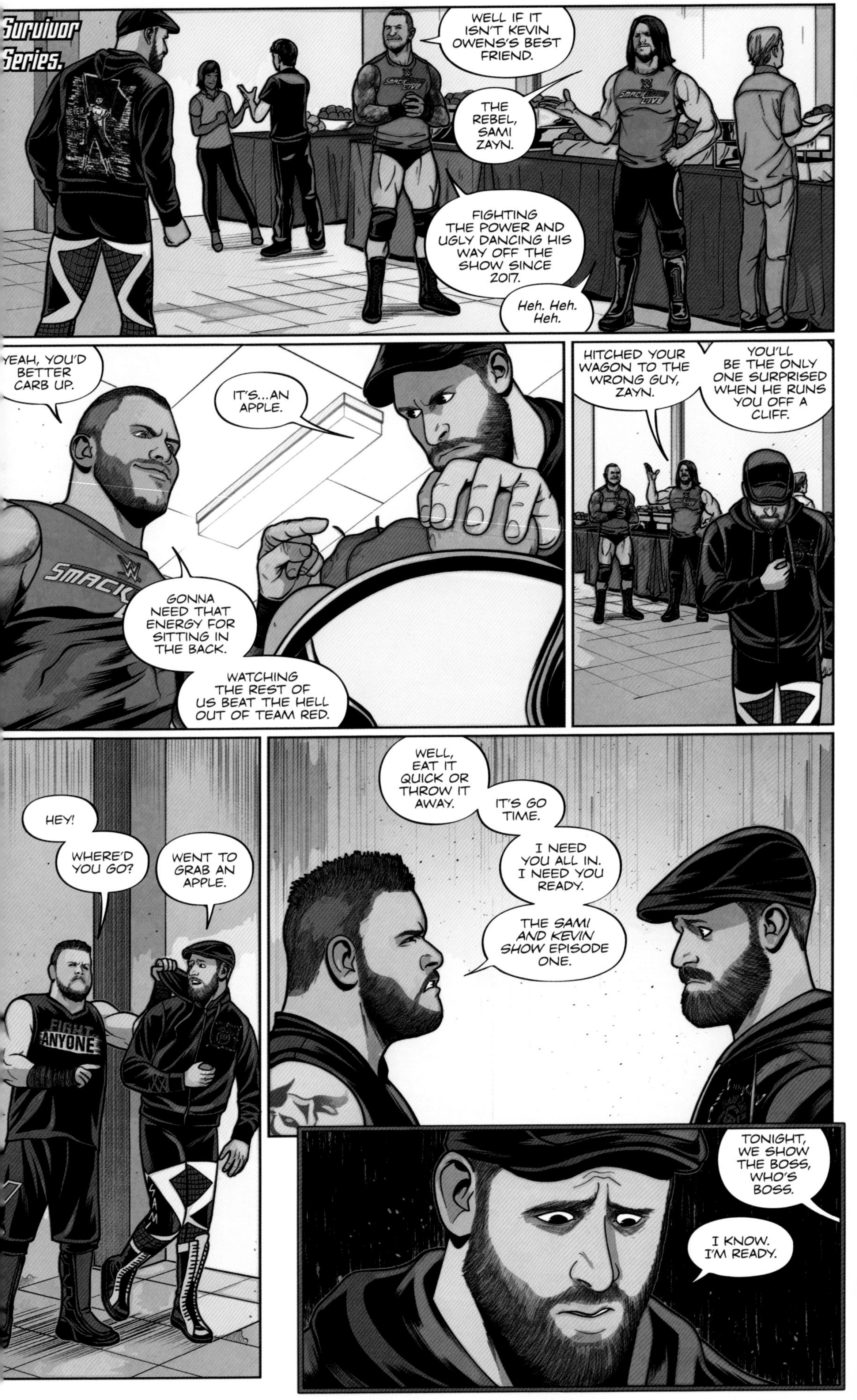
Survivor Series.
WELL IF IT ISN'T KEVIN OWENS'S BEST FRIEND.
THE REBEL, SAMI ZAYN.
FIGHTING THE POWER AND UGLY DANCING HIS WAY OFF THE SHOW SINCE 2017.
Heh. Heh. Heh.
YEAH, YOU'D BETTER CARB UP.
IT'S...AN APPLE.
GONNA NEED THAT ENERGY FOR SITTING IN THE BACK.
WATCHING THE REST OF US BEAT THE HELL OUT OF TEAM RED.
HITCHED YOUR WAGON TO THE WRONG GUY, ZAYN.
YOU'LL BE THE ONLY ONE SURPRISED WHEN HE RUNS YOU OFF A CLIFF.
HEY!
WHERE'D YOU GO?
WENT TO GRAB AN APPLE.
WELL, EAT IT QUICK OR THROW IT AWAY.
IT'S GO TIME.
I NEED YOU ALL IN. I NEED YOU READY.
THE SAMI AND KEVIN SHOW EPISODE ONE.
TONIGHT, WE SHOW THE BOSS, WHO'S BOSS.
I KNOW. I'M READY.

November 19th, 2017.
Survivor Series.

SURVIVOR SERIES

"THE PLAN IS SIMPLE.

"SHANE'S GONNA HAVE HIS HANDS FULL TRYING TO CAPTAIN TEAM BLUE.

OUTTA NOWHERE!

LET'S GO, RANDY!

"AS ALWAYS, THE WEAKEST LINK PUT HIMSELF IN CHARGE.

"HE'LL BE ON THE RING APRON CHEERLEADING IN HIS BASEBALL SHIRT.

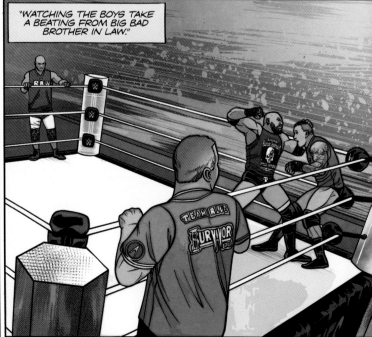

"WATCHING THE BOYS TAKE A BEATING FROM BIG BAD BROTHER IN LAW."

"DISTRACTED.

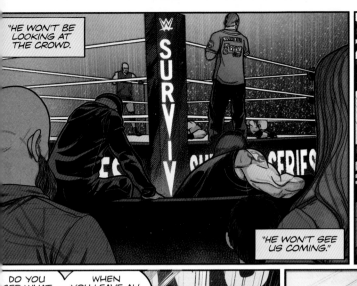

"HE WON'T BE LOOKING AT THE CROWD.

"HE WON'T SEE US COMING."

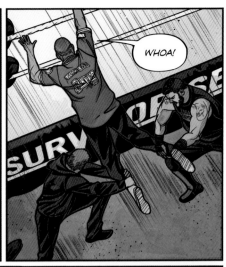

WHOA!

DO YOU SEE WHAT HAPPENS, SHANE?!

WHEN YOU LEAVE ALL THE TALENT ON THE BENCH?!

YOU GET BEATEN!

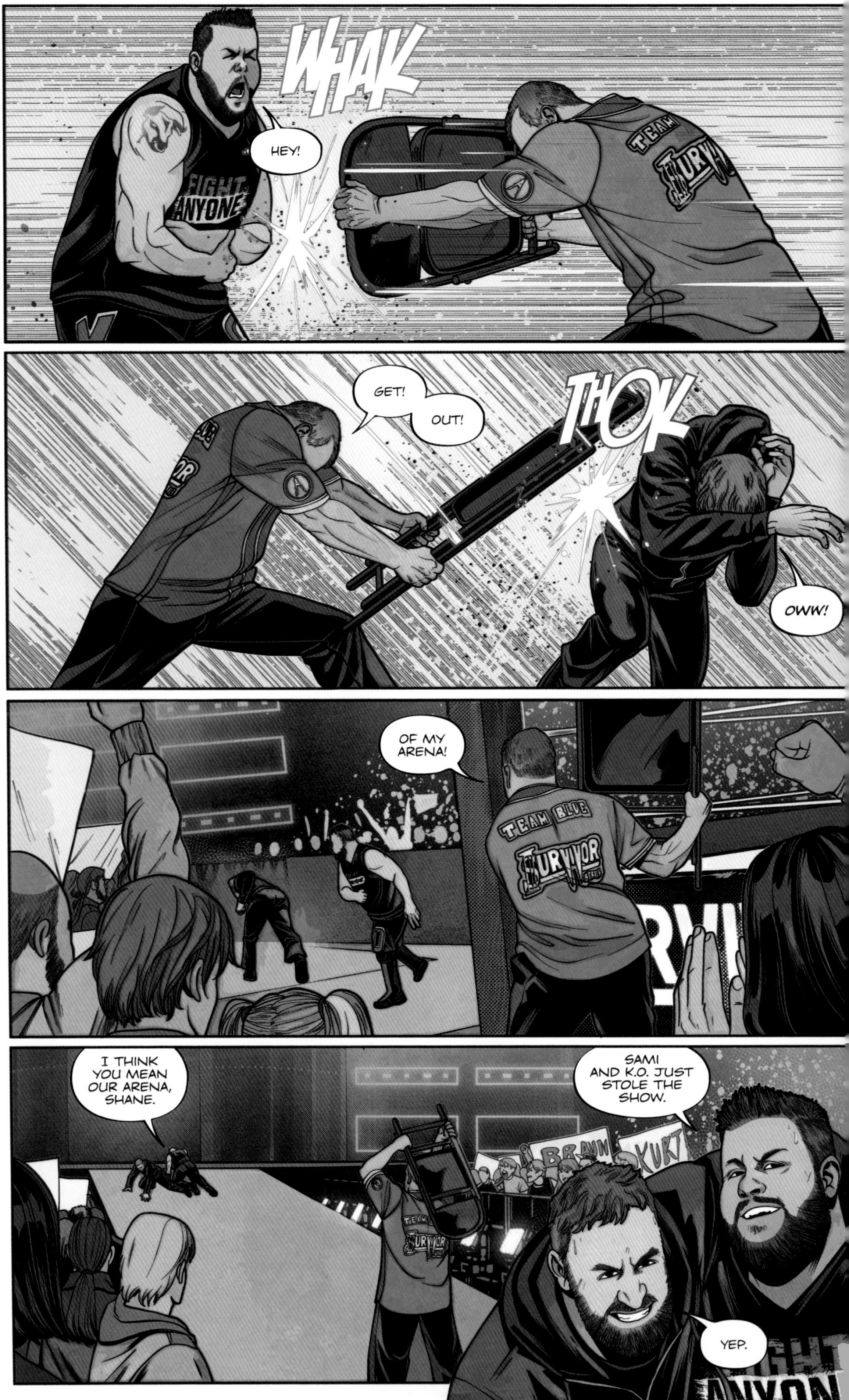
WHAK
HEY!
FIGHT ANYONE
TEAM SURVIVOR
GET!
OUT!
THOK
OWW!
OF MY ARENA!
TEAM BLUE SURVIVOR
I THINK YOU MEAN OUR ARENA, SHANE.
SAMI AND K.O. JUST STOLE THE SHOW.
BRAUN
KURT
YEP.

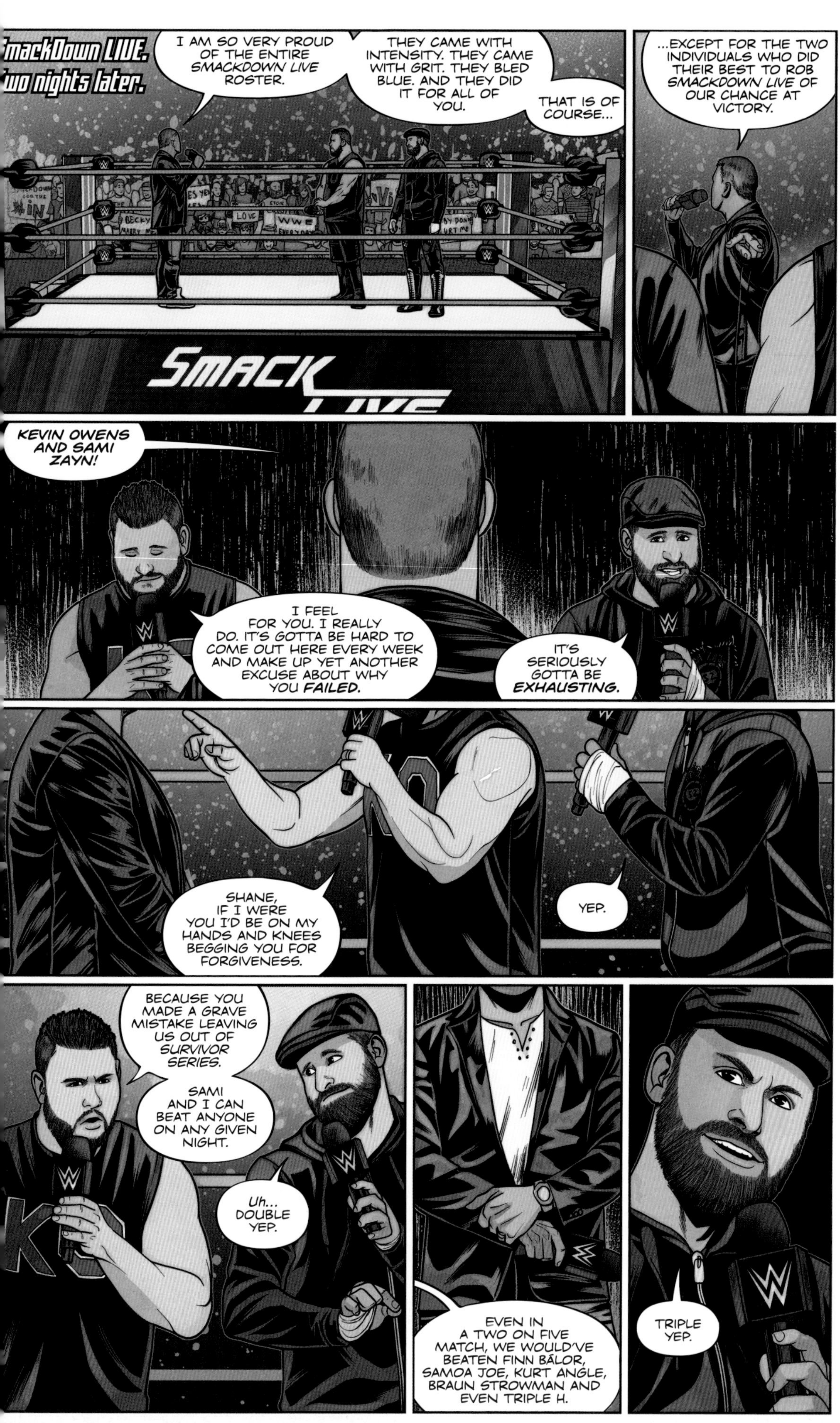
SmackDown LIVE. Two nights later.
I AM SO VERY PROUD OF THE ENTIRE SMACKDOWN LIVE ROSTER.
THEY CAME WITH INTENSITY. THEY CAME WITH GRIT. THEY BLED BLUE. AND THEY DID IT FOR ALL OF YOU.
THAT IS OF COURSE...
...EXCEPT FOR THE TWO INDIVIDUALS WHO DID THEIR BEST TO ROB SMACKDOWN LIVE OF OUR CHANCE AT VICTORY.
KEVIN OWENS AND SAMI ZAYN!
I FEEL FOR YOU. I REALLY DO. IT'S GOTTA BE HARD TO COME OUT HERE EVERY WEEK AND MAKE UP YET ANOTHER EXCUSE ABOUT WHY YOU FAILED.
IT'S SERIOUSLY GOTTA BE EXHAUSTING.
SHANE, IF I WERE YOU I'D BE ON MY HANDS AND KNEES BEGGING YOU FOR FORGIVENESS.
YEP.
BECAUSE YOU MADE A GRAVE MISTAKE LEAVING US OUT OF SURVIVOR SERIES.
SAMI AND I CAN BEAT ANYONE ON ANY GIVEN NIGHT.
Uh... DOUBLE YEP.
EVEN IN A TWO ON FIVE MATCH, WE WOULD'VE BEATEN FINN BÁLOR, SAMOA JOE, KURT ANGLE, BRAUN STROWMAN AND EVEN TRIPLE H.
TRIPLE YEP.

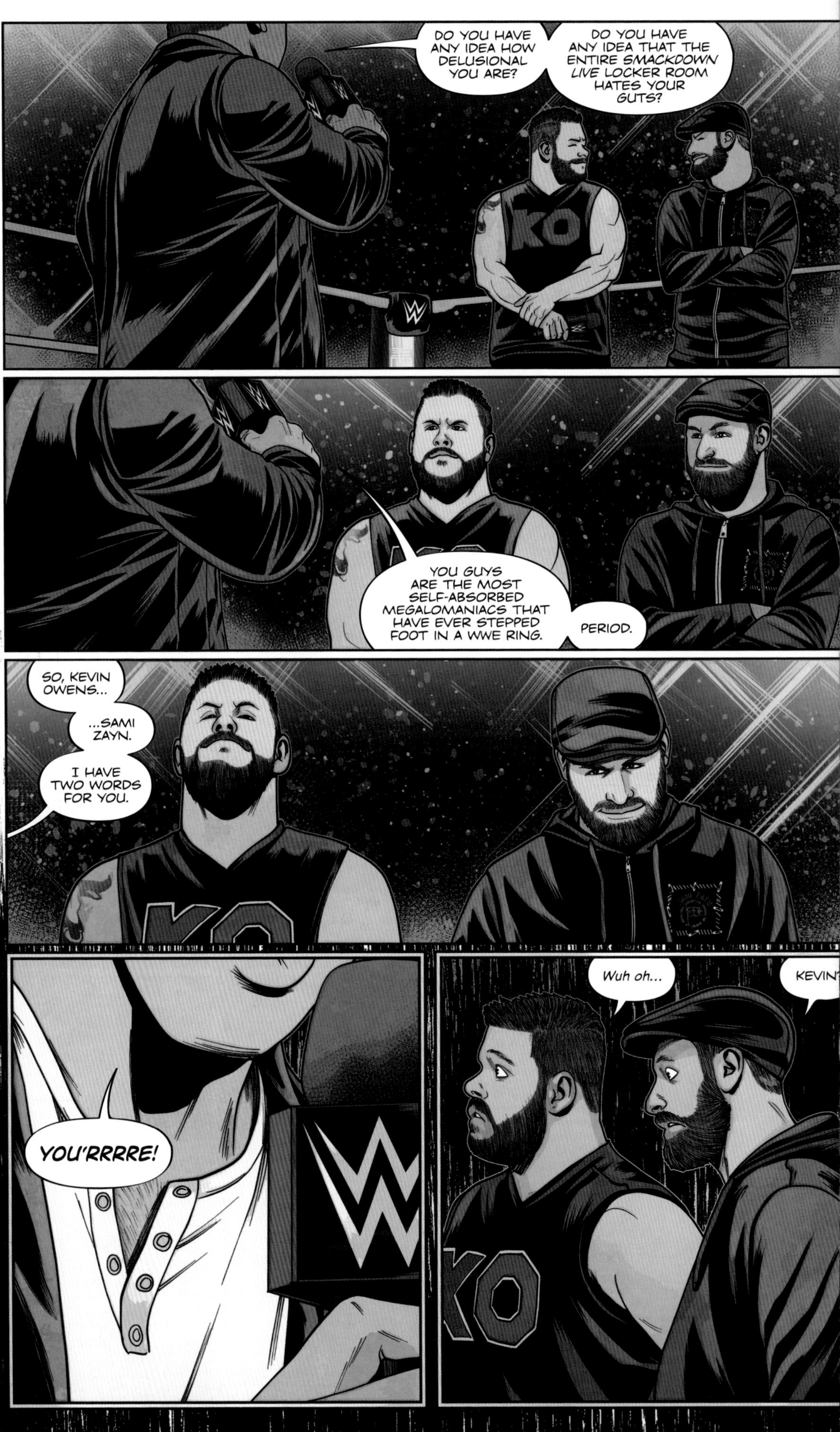
DO YOU HAVE ANY IDEA HOW DELUSIONAL YOU ARE?
DO YOU HAVE ANY IDEA THAT THE ENTIRE *SMACKDOWN LIVE* LOCKER ROOM HATES YOUR GUTS?
YOU GUYS ARE THE MOST SELF-ABSORBED MEGALOMANIACS THAT HAVE EVER STEPPED FOOT IN A WWE RING.
PERIOD.
SO, KEVIN OWENS...
...SAMI ZAYN.
I HAVE TWO WORDS FOR YOU.
YOU'RRRRE!
Wuh oh...

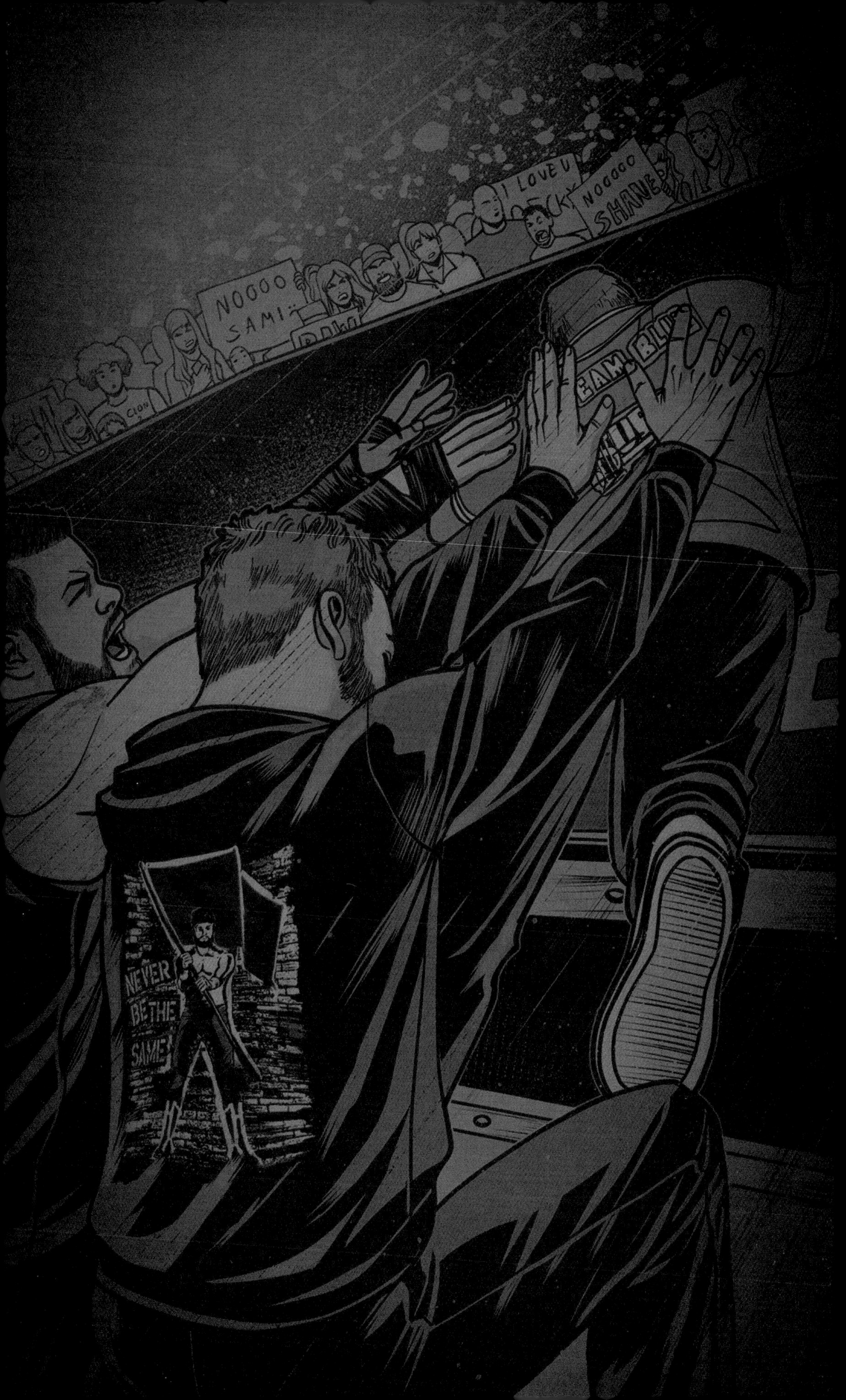
NOOOO SAMI
I LOVE U
NOOOOO SHANE
NEVER BE THE SAME!

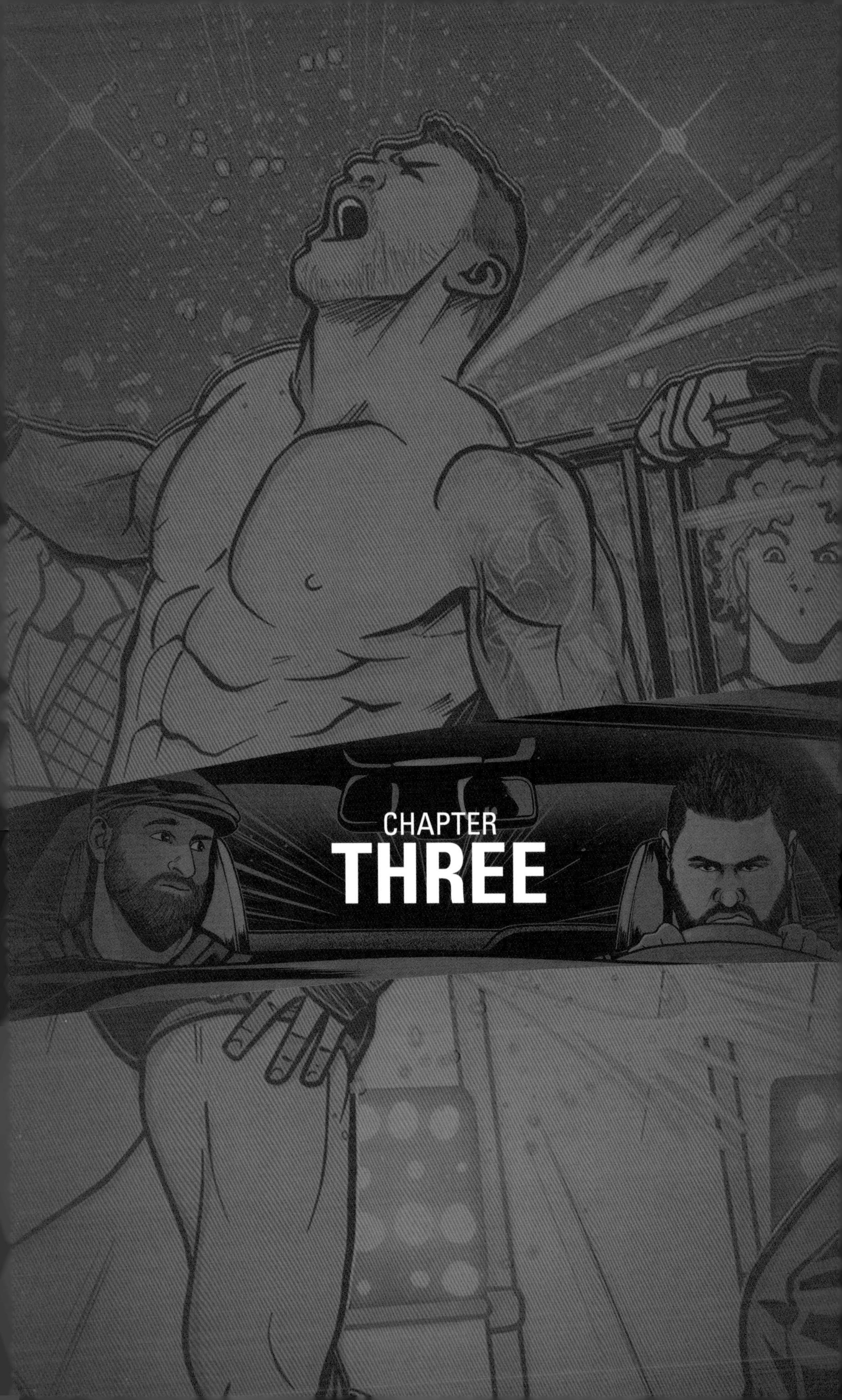
CHAPTER
THREE

YOU'RRRRE!

BUM BUM BUM♫

...DANIEL?

HOLD ON.

HOLD ON, SHANE.

HOLD ON.

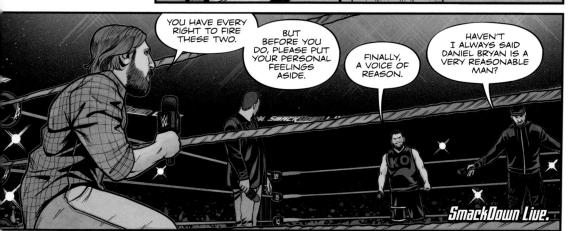

YOU HAVE EVERY RIGHT TO FIRE THESE TWO.

BUT BEFORE YOU DO, PLEASE PUT YOUR PERSONAL FEELINGS ASIDE.

FINALLY, A VOICE OF REASON.

HAVEN'T I ALWAYS SAID DANIEL BRYAN IS A VERY REASONABLE MAN?

SmackDown Live.

YEP.

AND FINALLY, HE'S STEPPING IN AND STOPPING SHANE McMAHON'S PERSONAL VEND--

SAMI.

SHUT UP.

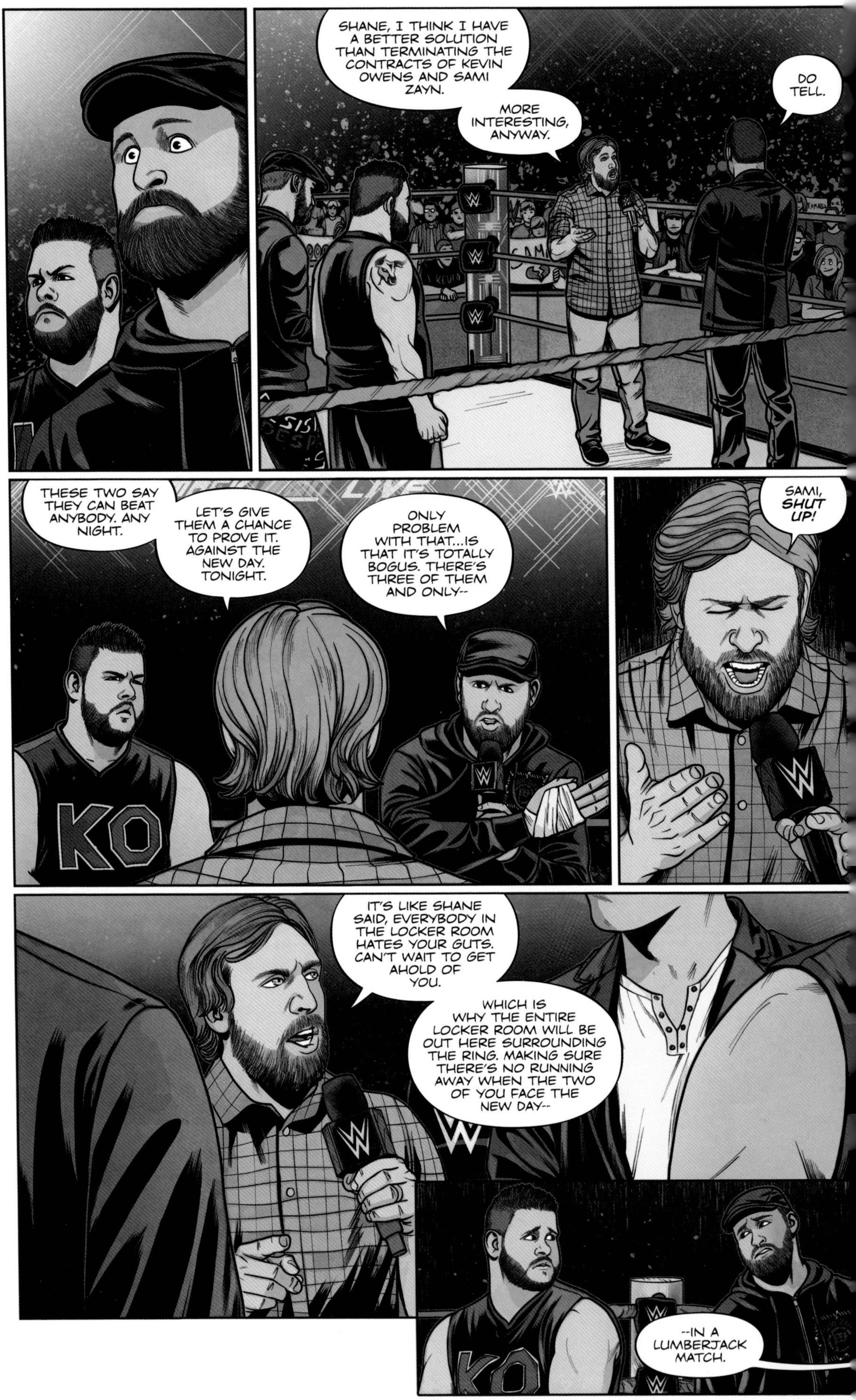
SHANE, I THINK I HAVE A BETTER SOLUTION THAN TERMINATING THE CONTRACTS OF KEVIN OWENS AND SAMI ZAYN.
MORE INTERESTING, ANYWAY.
DO TELL.
THESE TWO SAY THEY CAN BEAT ANYBODY. ANY NIGHT.
LET'S GIVE THEM A CHANCE TO PROVE IT. AGAINST THE NEW DAY. TONIGHT.
ONLY PROBLEM WITH THAT...IS THAT IT'S TOTALLY BOGUS. THERE'S THREE OF THEM AND ONLY--
SAMI, SHUT UP!
IT'S LIKE SHANE SAID, EVERYBODY IN THE LOCKER ROOM HATES YOUR GUTS. CAN'T WAIT TO GET AHOLD OF YOU.
WHICH IS WHY THE ENTIRE LOCKER ROOM WILL BE OUT HERE SURROUNDING THE RING. MAKING SURE THERE'S NO RUNNING AWAY WHEN THE TWO OF YOU FACE THE NEW DAY--
--IN A LUMBERJACK MATCH.

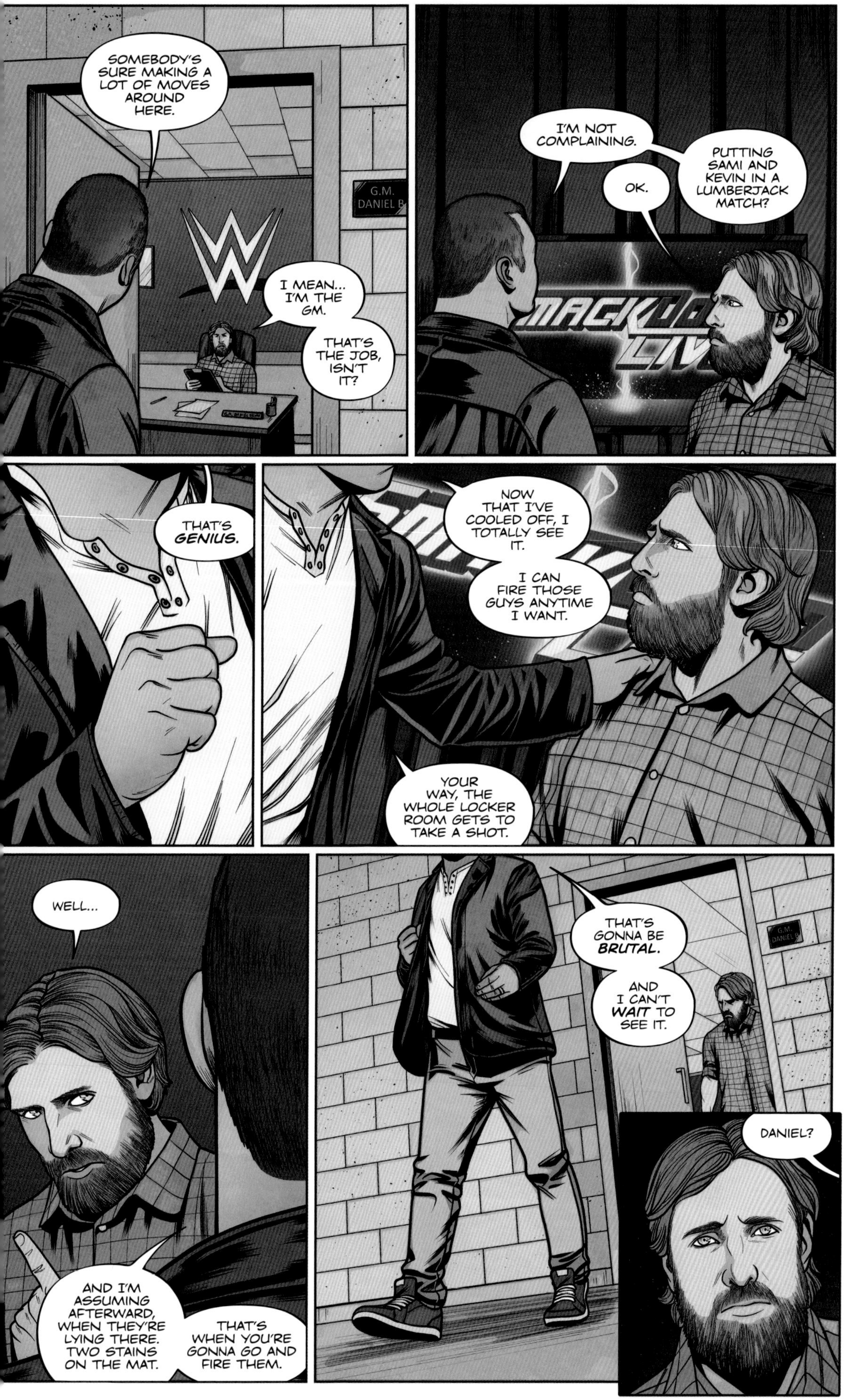

SOMEBODY'S SURE MAKING A LOT OF MOVES AROUND HERE.
G.M. DANIEL B
I MEAN... I'M THE GM.
THAT'S THE JOB, ISN'T IT?
I'M NOT COMPLAINING.
PUTTING SAMI AND KEVIN IN A LUMBERJACK MATCH?
OK.
THAT'S GENIUS.
NOW THAT I'VE COOLED OFF, I TOTALLY SEE IT.
I CAN FIRE THOSE GUYS ANYTIME I WANT.
YOUR WAY, THE WHOLE LOCKER ROOM GETS TO TAKE A SHOT.
WELL...
AND I'M ASSUMING AFTERWARD, WHEN THEY'RE LYING THERE. TWO STAINS ON THE MAT.
THAT'S WHEN YOU'RE GONNA GO AND FIRE THEM.
THAT'S GONNA BE BRUTAL.
AND I CAN'T WAIT TO SEE IT.
DANIEL?

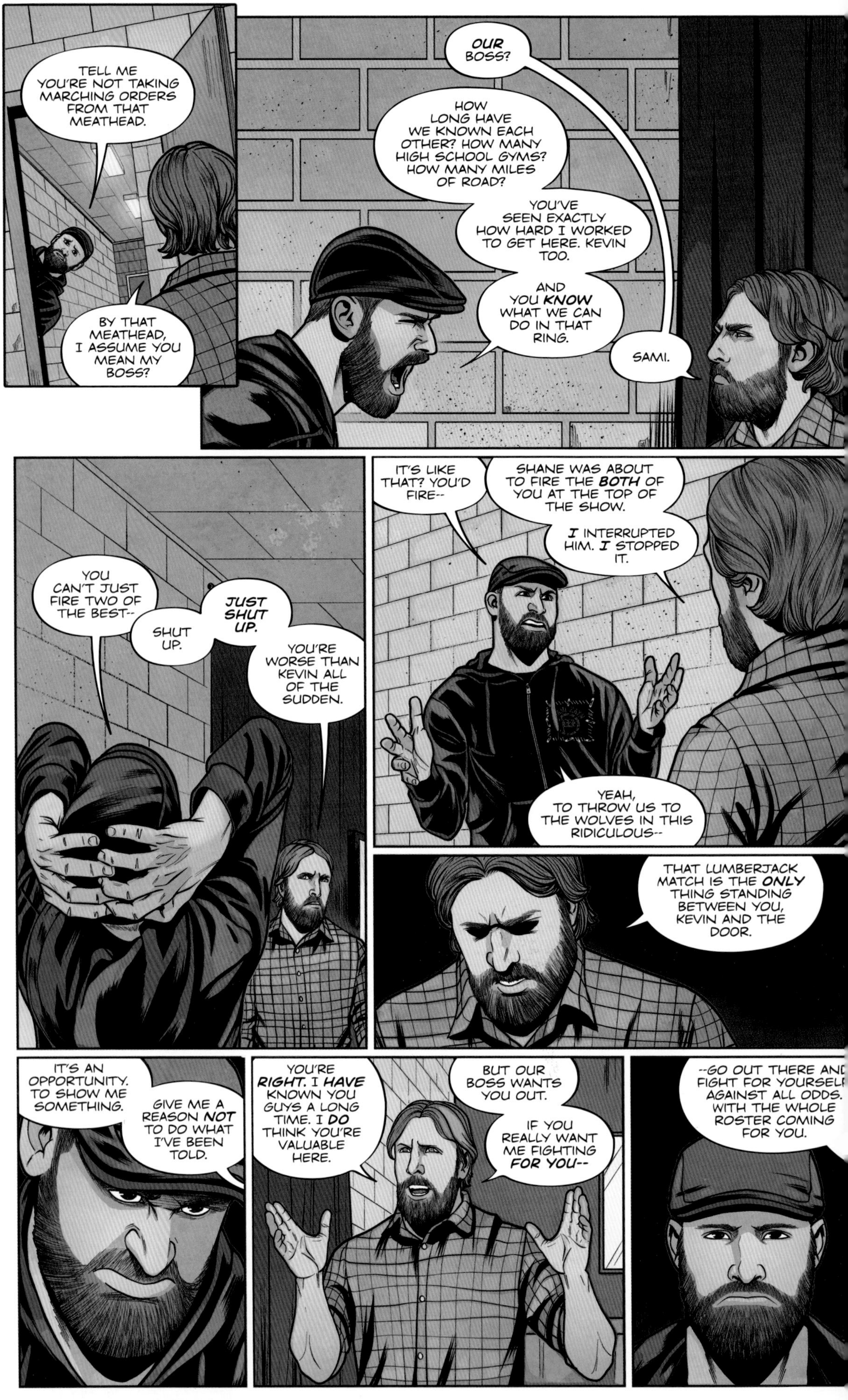
TELL ME YOU'RE NOT TAKING MARCHING ORDERS FROM THAT MEATHEAD.
BY THAT MEATHEAD, I ASSUME YOU MEAN MY BOSS?
OUR BOSS?
HOW LONG HAVE WE KNOWN EACH OTHER? HOW MANY HIGH SCHOOL GYMS? HOW MANY MILES OF ROAD?
YOU'VE SEEN EXACTLY HOW HARD I WORKED TO GET HERE. KEVIN TOO.
AND YOU KNOW WHAT WE CAN DO IN THAT RING.
SAMI.
YOU CAN'T JUST FIRE TWO OF THE BEST--
SHUT UP.
JUST SHUT UP.
YOU'RE WORSE THAN KEVIN ALL OF THE SUDDEN.
IT'S LIKE THAT? YOU'D FIRE--
SHANE WAS ABOUT TO FIRE THE BOTH OF YOU AT THE TOP OF THE SHOW.
I INTERRUPTED HIM. I STOPPED IT.
YEAH, TO THROW US TO THE WOLVES IN THIS RIDICULOUS--
THAT LUMBERJACK MATCH IS THE ONLY THING STANDING BETWEEN YOU, KEVIN AND THE DOOR.
IT'S AN OPPORTUNITY. TO SHOW ME SOMETHING.
GIVE ME A REASON NOT TO DO WHAT I'VE BEEN TOLD.
YOU'RE RIGHT. I HAVE KNOWN YOU GUYS A LONG TIME. I DO THINK YOU'RE VALUABLE HERE.
BUT OUR BOSS WANTS YOU OUT.
IF YOU REALLY WANT ME FIGHTING FOR YOU--
--GO OUT THERE AND FIGHT FOR YOURSELF AGAINST ALL ODDS. WITH THE WHOLE ROSTER COMING FOR YOU.

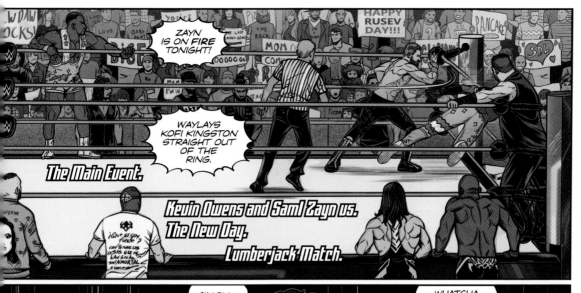

ZAYN IS ON **FIRE** TONIGHT!

WAYLAYS KOFI KINGSTON STRAIGHT OUT OF THE RING.

The Main Event.

Kevin Owens and Sami Zayn vs. The New Day. Lumberjack Match.

C'MON...

WHATCHA WAITING FOR, SAMI?

I'M JUST PUTTING KOFI BACK IN THE RING.

TRY IT, GINGER.

GOT NO BEEF WITH THE REST OF--

STOMP STOMP STOMP

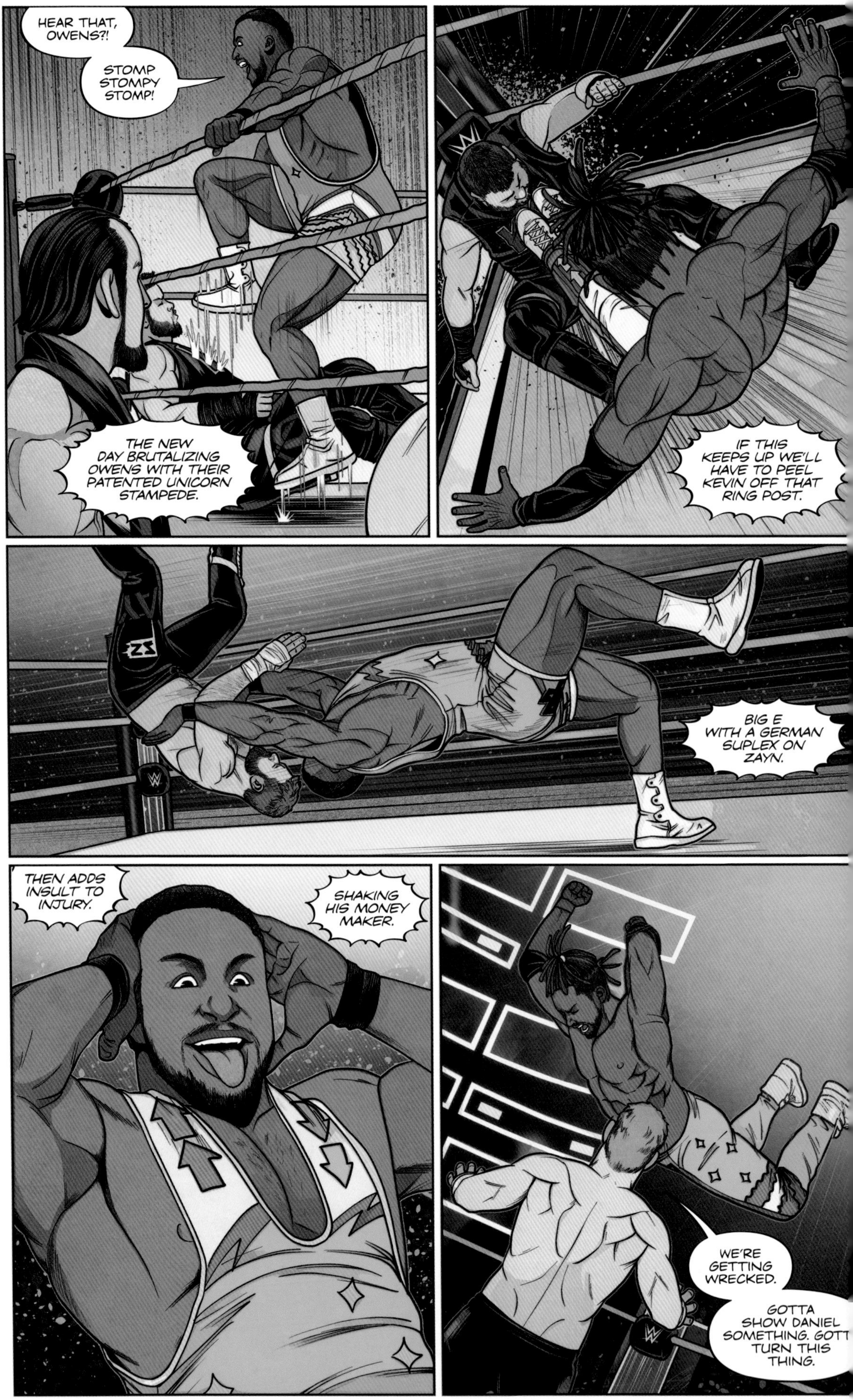
HEAR THAT, OWENS?!
STOMP STOMPY STOMP!
THE NEW DAY BRUTALIZING OWENS WITH THEIR PATENTED UNICORN STAMPEDE.
IF THIS KEEPS UP WE'LL HAVE TO PEEL KEVIN OFF THAT RING POST.
BIG E WITH A GERMAN SUPLEX ON ZAYN.
THEN ADDS INSULT TO INJURY.
SHAKING HIS MONEY MAKER.
WE'RE GETTING WRECKED.
GOTTA SHOW DANIEL SOMETHING. GOTT TURN THIS THING.

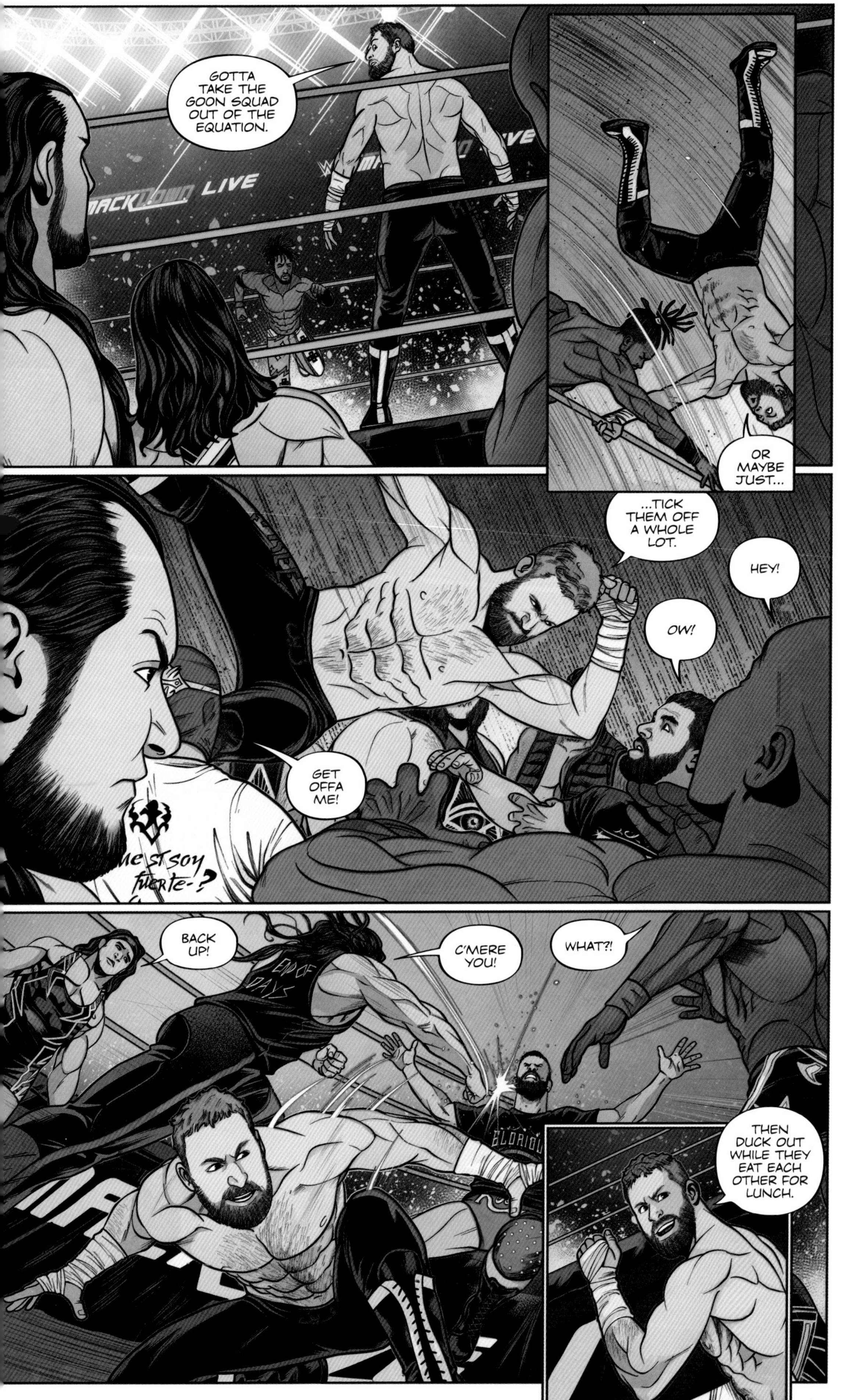
GOTTA TAKE THE GOON SQUAD OUT OF THE EQUATION.
LIVE
OR MAYBE JUST...
...TICK THEM OFF A WHOLE LOT.
HEY!
OW!
GET OFFA ME!
BACK UP!
END OF DAYS
C'MERE YOU!
WHAT?!
THEN DUCK OUT WHILE THEY EAT EACH OTHER FOR LUNCH.

NOW NOBODY'S LOOKING.

I'M THE LEGAL MAN.

AND KOFI DOESN'T KNOW KEVIN NEVER TAGGED IN.

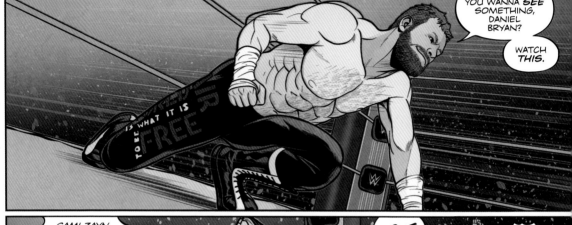

YOU WANNA *SEE* SOMETHING, DANIEL BRYAN?

WATCH *THIS.*

SAMI ZAYN ROLLS UP KINGSTON AND...

ONE TWO THREE

...STEALS THE PRIZE!

HEY!

KEVIN?

LOOK AT OWENS RUNNING OFF INTO THE CROWD.

HARD TO BLAME HIM.

THE NEW DAY DOES NOT LOOK PLEASED ABOUT THAT ENDING.

I WOULDN'T WANT TO BE SAMI ZAYN RIGHT NOW.

Kevin...

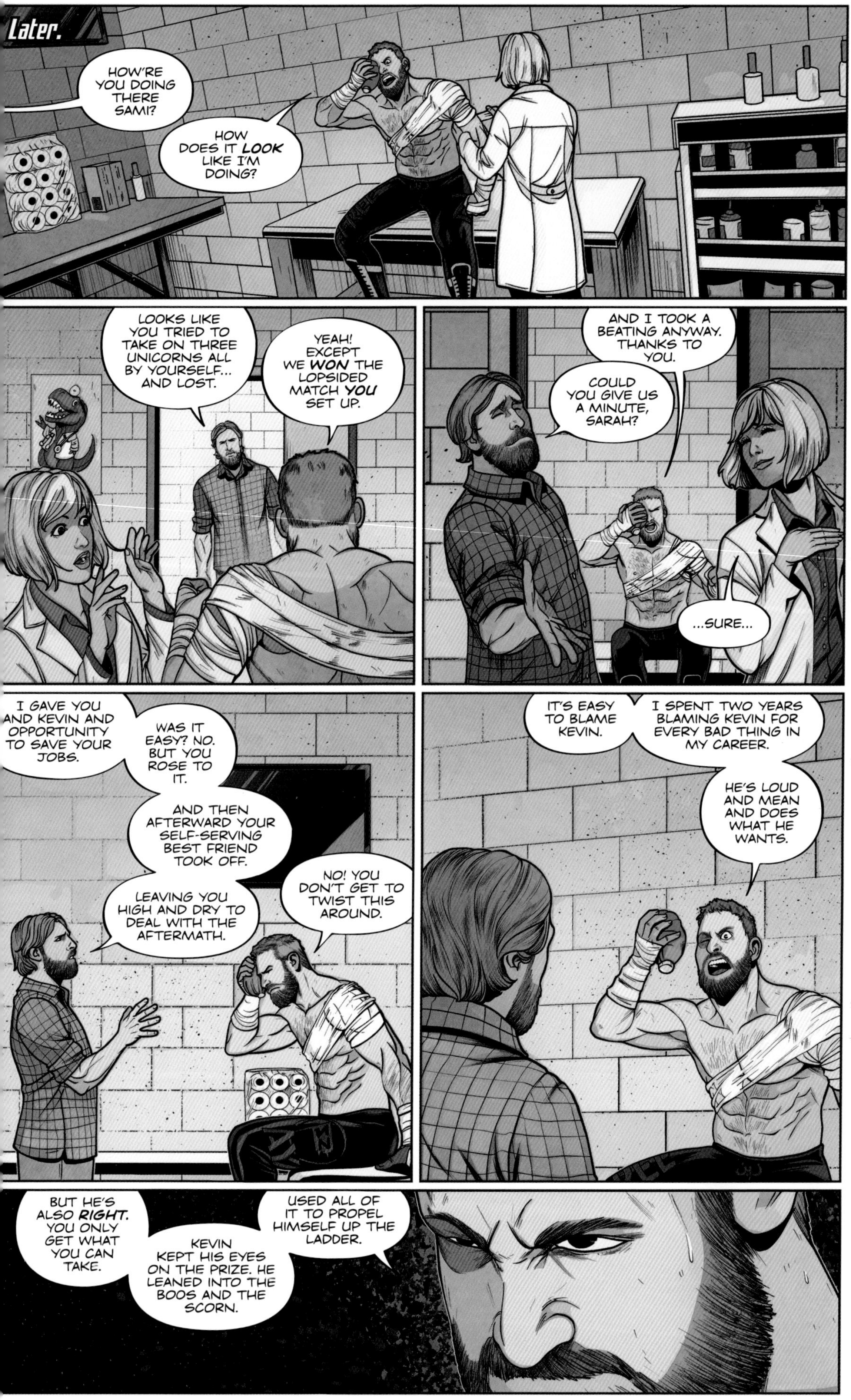
Later.
HOW'RE YOU DOING THERE SAMI?
HOW DOES IT LOOK LIKE I'M DOING?
LOOKS LIKE YOU TRIED TO TAKE ON THREE UNICORNS ALL BY YOURSELF... AND LOST.
YEAH! EXCEPT WE WON THE LOPSIDED MATCH YOU SET UP.
AND I TOOK A BEATING ANYWAY. THANKS TO YOU.
COULD YOU GIVE US A MINUTE, SARAH?
...SURE...
I GAVE YOU AND KEVIN AND OPPORTUNITY TO SAVE YOUR JOBS.
WAS IT EASY? NO. BUT YOU ROSE TO IT.
AND THEN AFTERWARD YOUR SELF-SERVING BEST FRIEND TOOK OFF.
LEAVING YOU HIGH AND DRY TO DEAL WITH THE AFTERMATH.
NO! YOU DON'T GET TO TWIST THIS AROUND.
IT'S EASY TO BLAME KEVIN.
I SPENT TWO YEARS BLAMING KEVIN FOR EVERY BAD THING IN MY CAREER.
HE'S LOUD AND MEAN AND DOES WHAT HE WANTS.
BUT HE'S ALSO RIGHT. YOU ONLY GET WHAT YOU CAN TAKE.
KEVIN KEPT HIS EYES ON THE PRIZE. HE LEANED INTO THE BOOS AND THE SCORN.
USED ALL OF IT TO PROPEL HIMSELF UP THE LADDER.

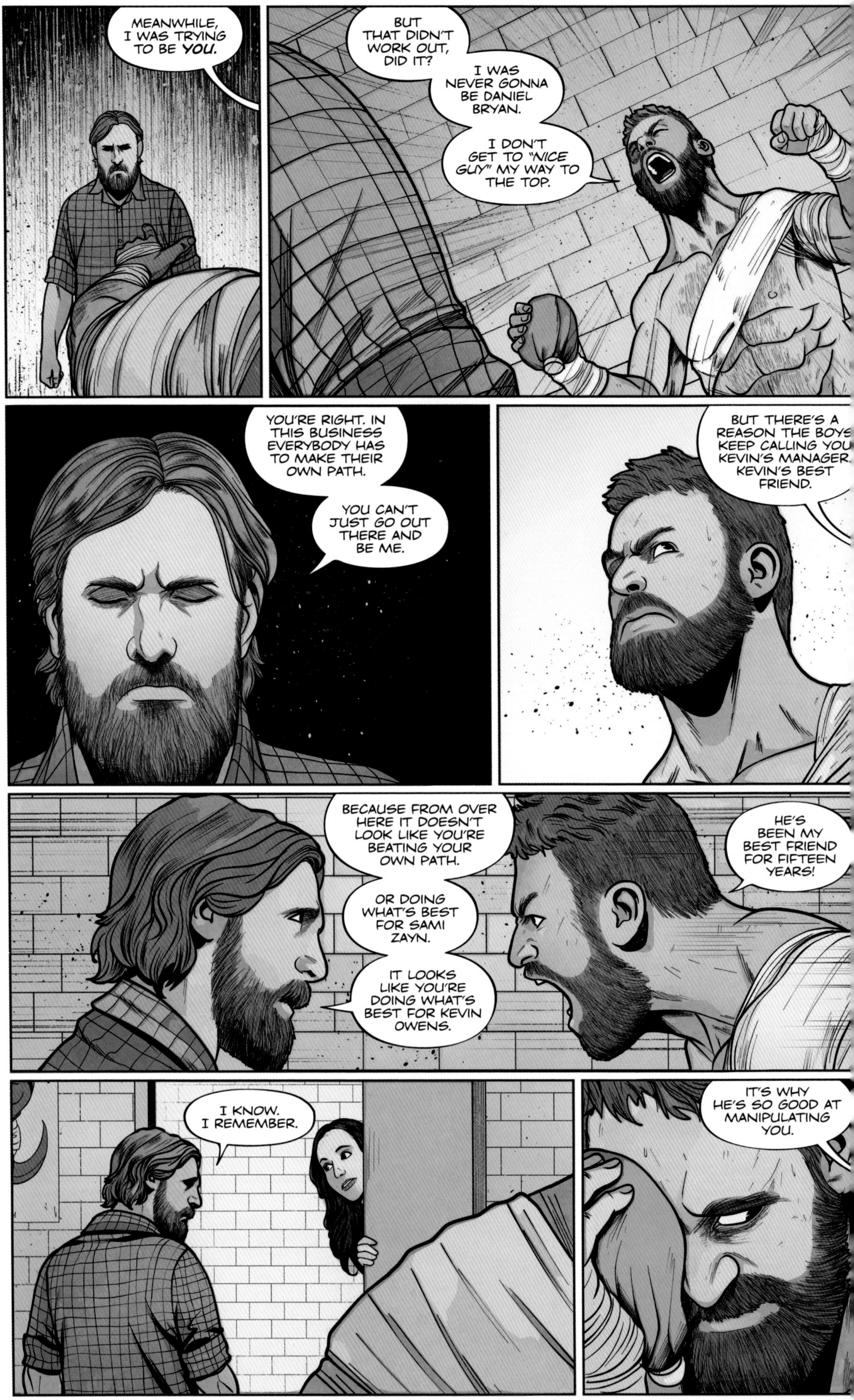
MEANWHILE, I WAS TRYING TO BE YOU.
BUT THAT DIDN'T WORK OUT, DID IT?
I WAS NEVER GONNA BE DANIEL BRYAN.
I DON'T GET TO "NICE GUY" MY WAY TO THE TOP.
YOU'RE RIGHT. IN THIS BUSINESS EVERYBODY HAS TO MAKE THEIR OWN PATH.
YOU CAN'T JUST GO OUT THERE AND BE ME.
BUT THERE'S A REASON THE BOYS KEEP CALLING YOU KEVIN'S MANAGER. KEVIN'S BEST FRIEND.
BECAUSE FROM OVER HERE IT DOESN'T LOOK LIKE YOU'RE BEATING YOUR OWN PATH.
OR DOING WHAT'S BEST FOR SAMI ZAYN.
IT LOOKS LIKE YOU'RE DOING WHAT'S BEST FOR KEVIN OWENS.
HE'S BEEN MY BEST FRIEND FOR FIFTEEN YEARS!
I KNOW. I REMEMBER.
IT'S WHY HE'S SO GOOD AT MANIPULATING YOU.

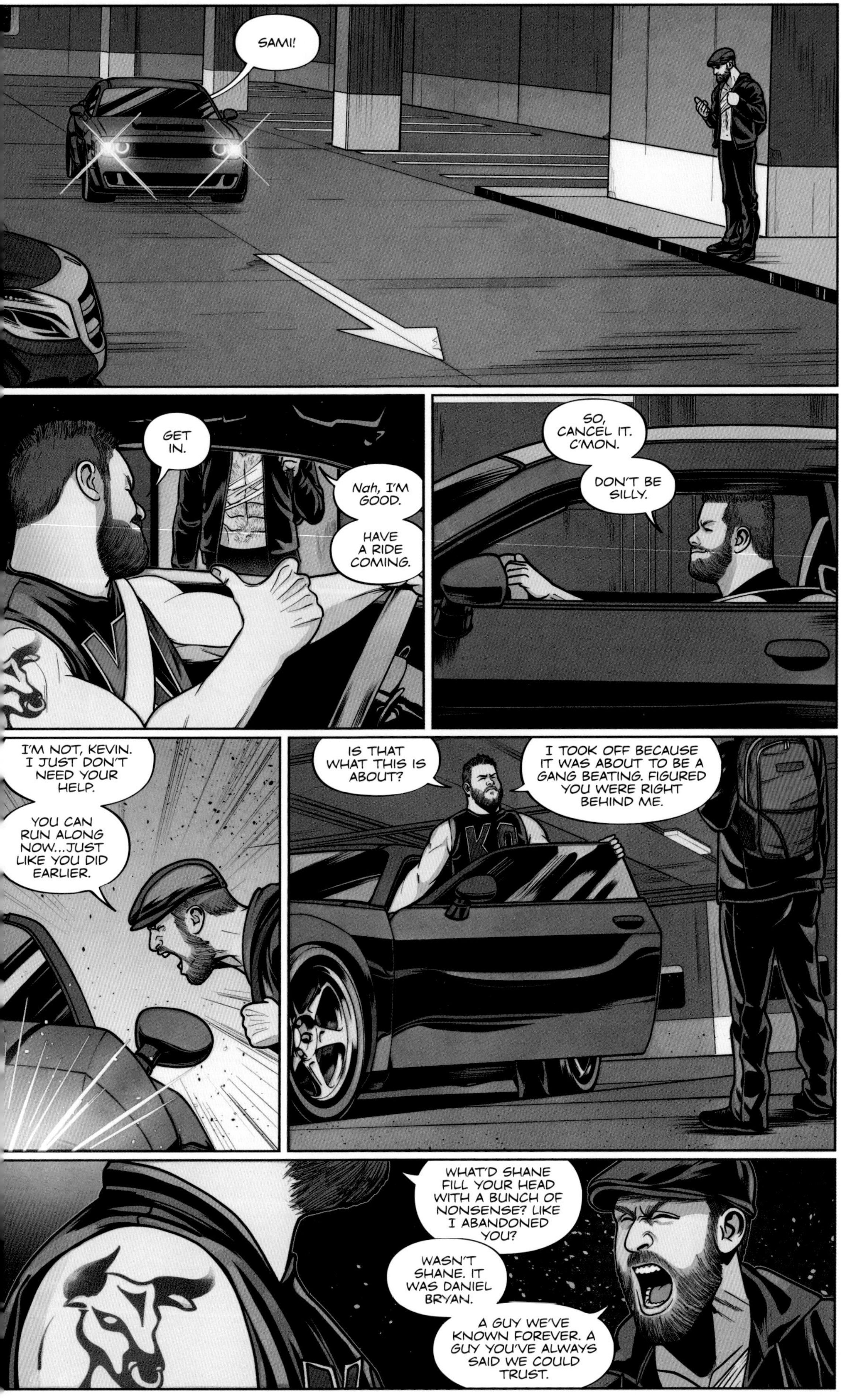
SAMI!
GET IN.
Nah, I'M GOOD.
HAVE A RIDE COMING.
SO, CANCEL IT. C'MON.
DON'T BE SILLY.
I'M NOT, KEVIN. I JUST DON'T NEED YOUR HELP.
YOU CAN RUN ALONG NOW...JUST LIKE YOU DID EARLIER.
IS THAT WHAT THIS IS ABOUT?
I TOOK OFF BECAUSE IT WAS ABOUT TO BE A GANG BEATING. FIGURED YOU WERE RIGHT BEHIND ME.
WHAT'D SHANE FILL YOUR HEAD WITH A BUNCH OF NONSENSE? LIKE I ABANDONED YOU?
WASN'T SHANE. IT WAS DANIEL BRYAN.
A GUY WE'VE KNOWN FOREVER. A GUY YOU'VE ALWAYS SAID WE COULD TRUST.

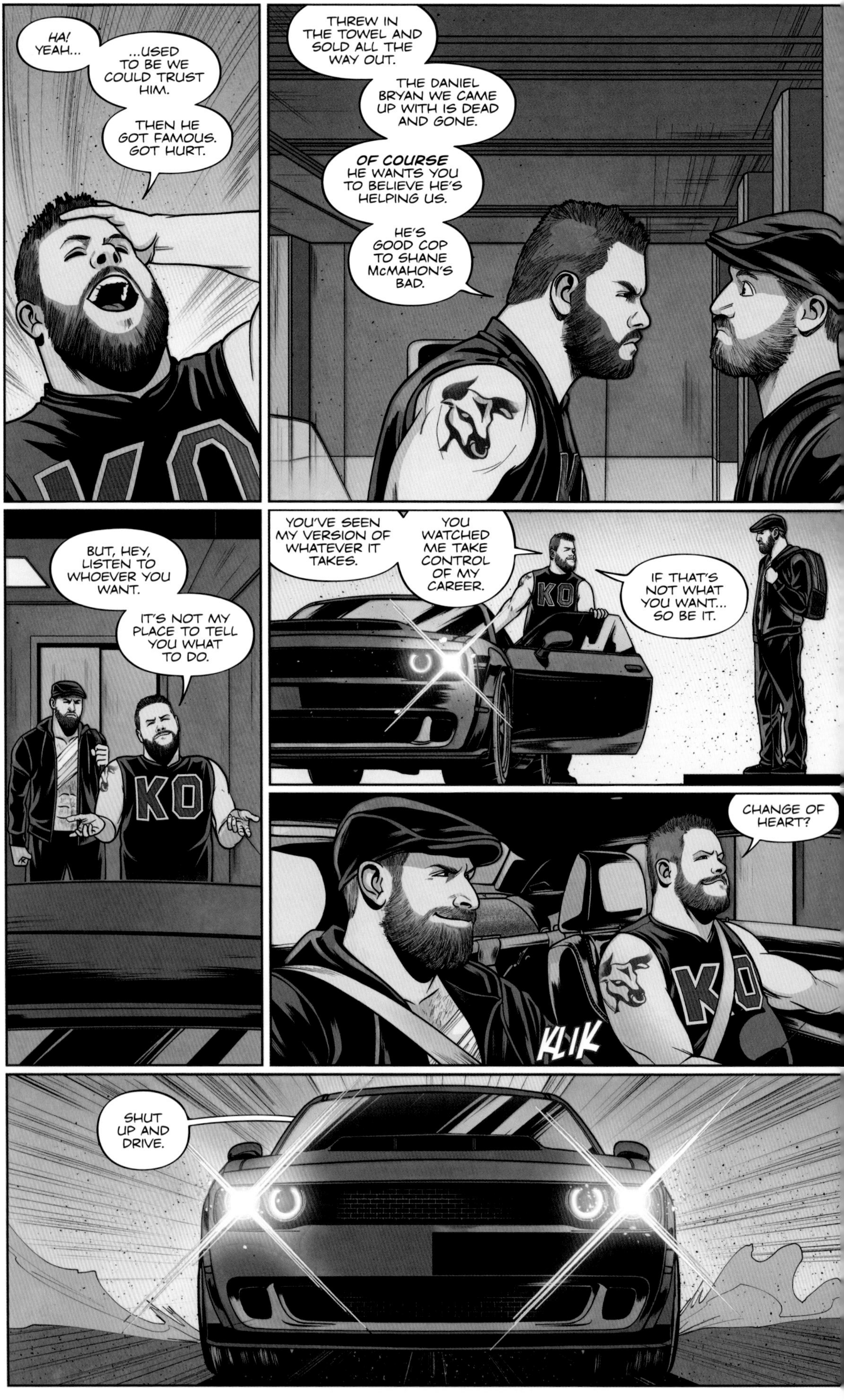
HA! YEAH...
...USED TO BE WE COULD TRUST HIM.
THEN HE GOT FAMOUS. GOT HURT.
THREW IN THE TOWEL AND SOLD ALL THE WAY OUT.
THE DANIEL BRYAN WE CAME UP WITH IS DEAD AND GONE.
OF COURSE HE WANTS YOU TO BELIEVE HE'S HELPING US.
HE'S GOOD COP TO SHANE McMAHON'S BAD.
BUT, HEY, LISTEN TO WHOEVER YOU WANT.
IT'S NOT MY PLACE TO TELL YOU WHAT TO DO.
YOU'VE SEEN MY VERSION OF WHATEVER IT TAKES.
YOU WATCHED ME TAKE CONTROL OF MY CAREER.
IF THAT'S NOT WHAT YOU WANT... SO BE IT.
CHANGE OF HEART?
KLIK
SHUT UP AND DRIVE.

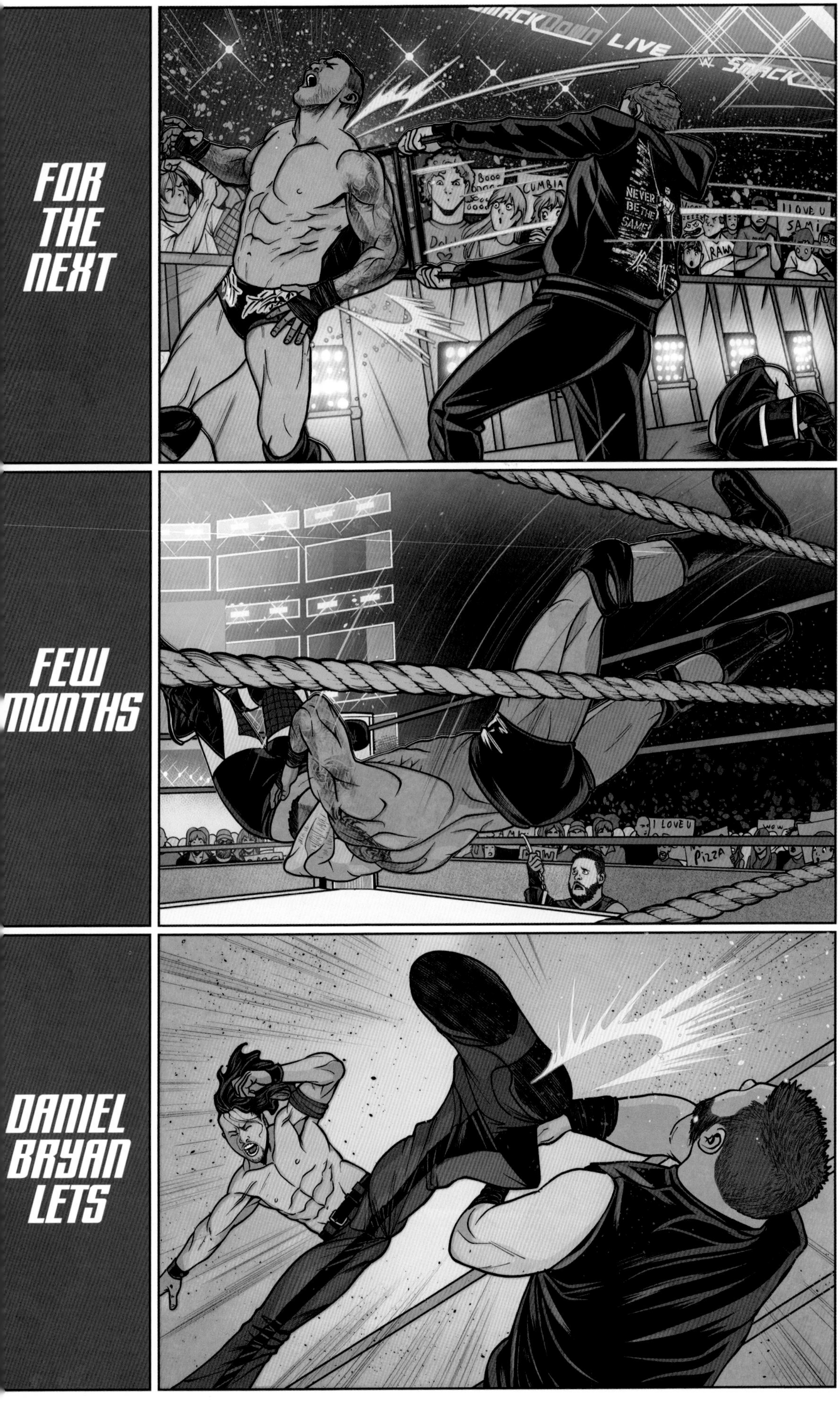
FOR THE NEXT
FEW MONTHS
DANIEL BRYAN LETS
LIVE
NEVER BE THE SAME
CUMBIA
I LOVE U SAMI
RAW
I LOVE U
PIZZA
WOW

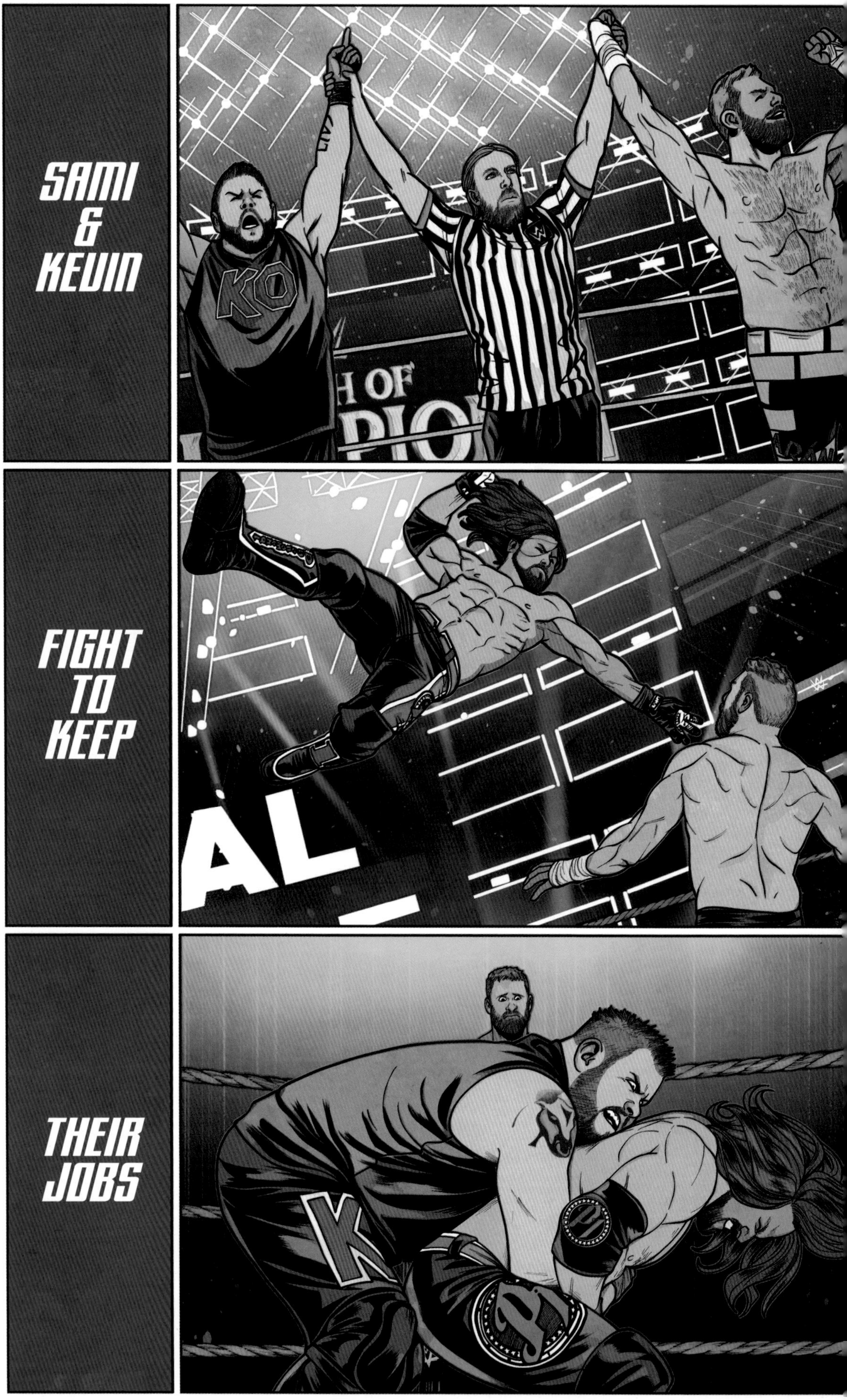
SAMI & KEVIN
FIGHT TO KEEP
THEIR JOBS

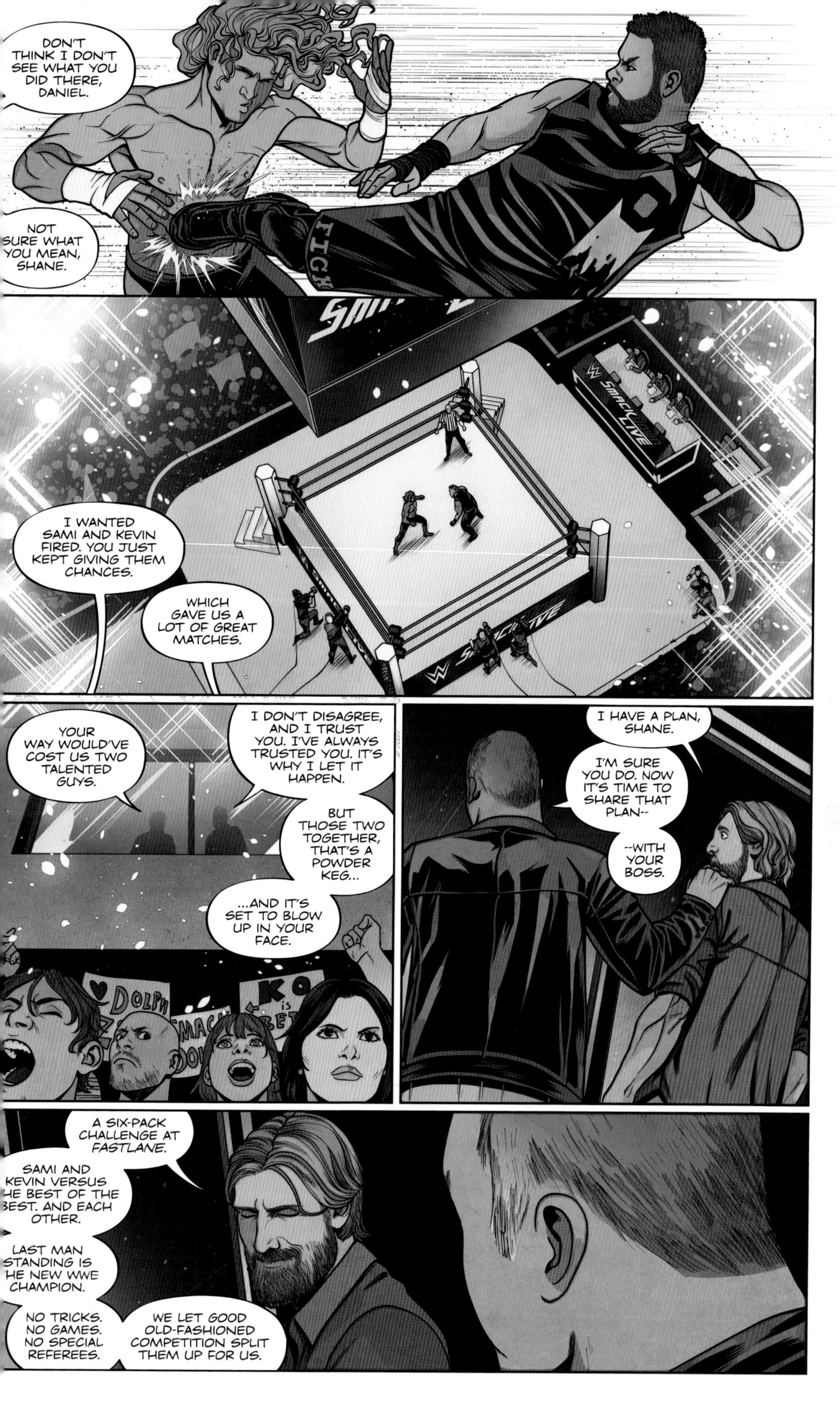

DON'T THINK I DON'T SEE WHAT YOU DID THERE, DANIEL.
NOT SURE WHAT YOU MEAN, SHANE.
I WANTED SAMI AND KEVIN FIRED. YOU JUST KEPT GIVING THEM CHANCES.
WHICH GAVE US A LOT OF GREAT MATCHES.
YOUR WAY WOULD'VE COST US TWO TALENTED GUYS.
I DON'T DISAGREE, AND I TRUST YOU. I'VE ALWAYS TRUSTED YOU. IT'S WHY I LET IT HAPPEN.
BUT THOSE TWO TOGETHER, THAT'S A POWDER KEG...
...AND IT'S SET TO BLOW UP IN YOUR FACE.
I HAVE A PLAN, SHANE.
I'M SURE YOU DO. NOW IT'S TIME TO SHARE THAT PLAN--
--WITH YOUR BOSS.
A SIX-PACK CHALLENGE AT FASTLANE.
SAMI AND KEVIN VERSUS THE BEST OF THE BEST. AND EACH OTHER.
LAST MAN STANDING IS THE NEW WWE CHAMPION.
NO TRICKS. NO GAMES. NO SPECIAL REFEREES.
WE LET GOOD OLD-FASHIONED COMPETITION SPLIT THEM UP FOR US.

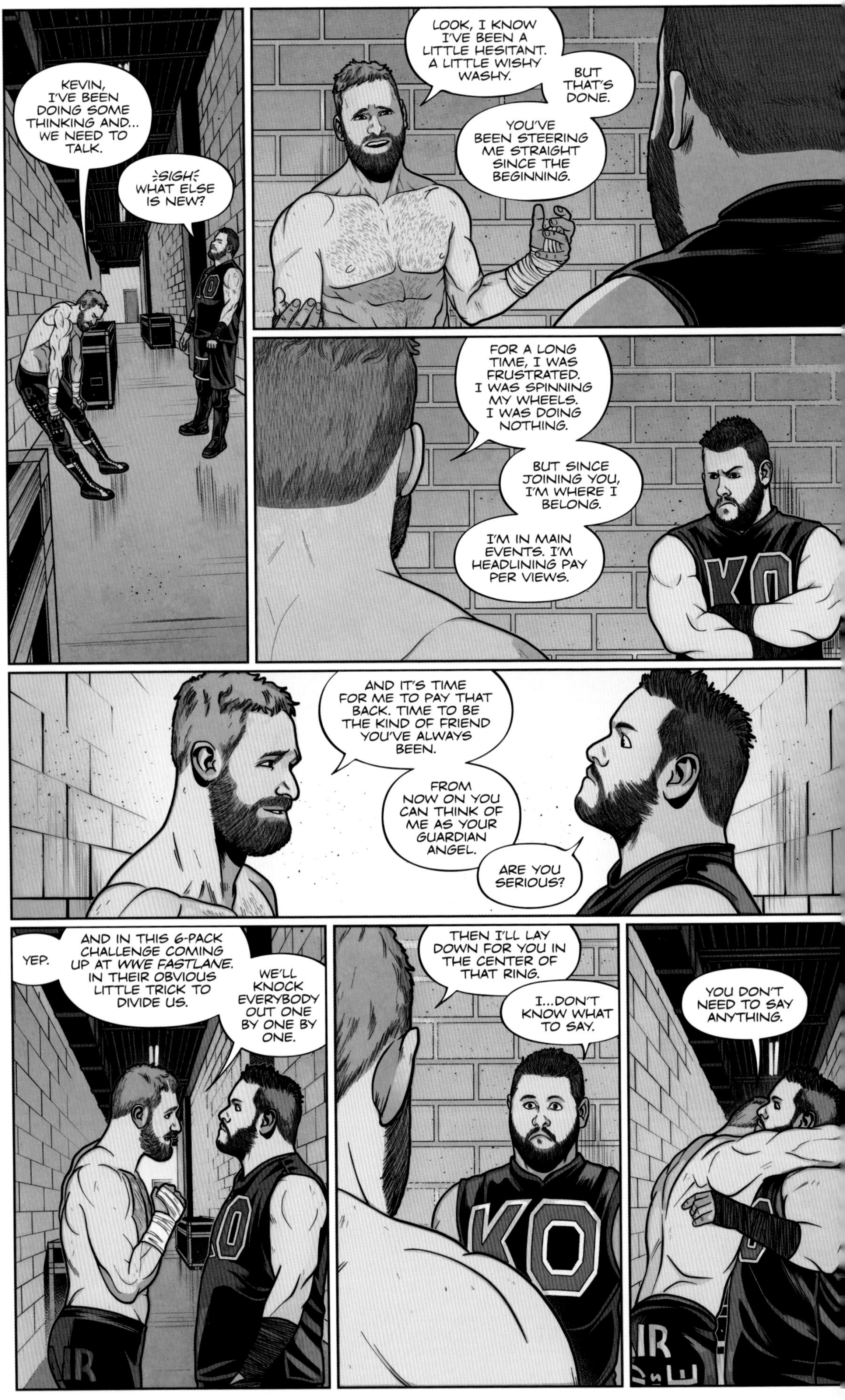

KEVIN, I'VE BEEN DOING SOME THINKING AND... WE NEED TO TALK.
SIGH WHAT ELSE IS NEW?
LOOK, I KNOW I'VE BEEN A LITTLE HESITANT. A LITTLE WISHY WASHY.
BUT THAT'S DONE.
YOU'VE BEEN STEERING ME STRAIGHT SINCE THE BEGINNING.
FOR A LONG TIME, I WAS FRUSTRATED. I WAS SPINNING MY WHEELS. I WAS DOING NOTHING.
BUT SINCE JOINING YOU, I'M WHERE I BELONG.
I'M IN MAIN EVENTS. I'M HEADLINING PAY PER VIEWS.
AND IT'S TIME FOR ME TO PAY THAT BACK. TIME TO BE THE KIND OF FRIEND YOU'VE ALWAYS BEEN.
FROM NOW ON YOU CAN THINK OF ME AS YOUR GUARDIAN ANGEL.
ARE YOU SERIOUS?
YEP.
AND IN THIS 6-PACK CHALLENGE COMING UP AT *WWE FASTLANE*. IN THEIR OBVIOUS LITTLE TRICK TO DIVIDE US.
WE'LL KNOCK EVERYBODY OUT ONE BY ONE BY ONE.
THEN I'LL LAY DOWN FOR YOU IN THE CENTER OF THAT RING.
I...DON'T KNOW WHAT TO SAY.
YOU DON'T NEED TO SAY ANYTHING.

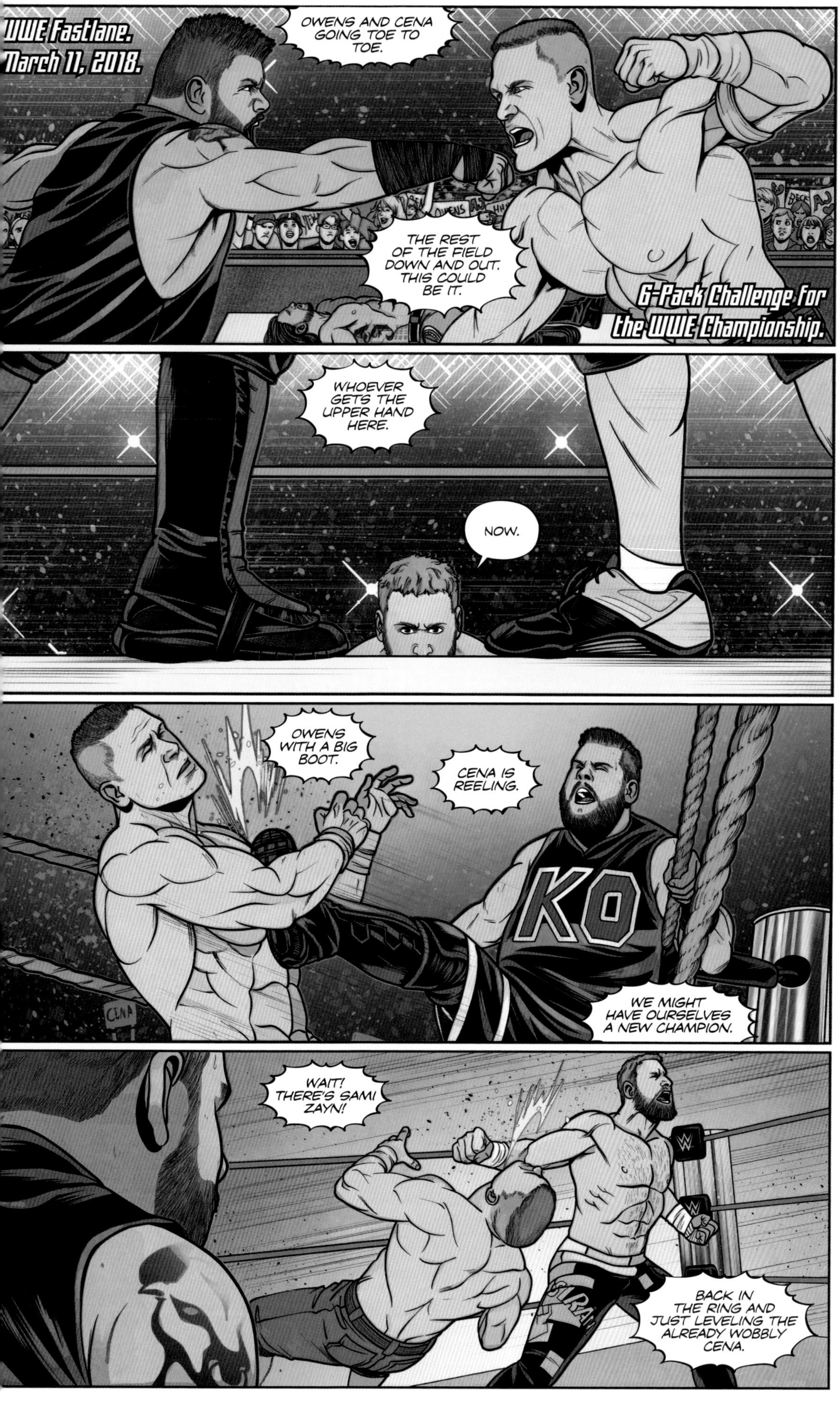
WWE Fastlane.
March 11, 2018.
OWENS AND CENA GOING TOE TO TOE.
THE REST OF THE FIELD DOWN AND OUT. THIS COULD BE IT.
6-Pack Challenge for the WWE Championship.
WHOEVER GETS THE UPPER HAND HERE.
NOW.
OWENS WITH A BIG BOOT.
CENA IS REELING.
KO
WE MIGHT HAVE OURSELVES A NEW CHAMPION.
WAIT! THERE'S SAMI ZAYN!
BACK IN THE RING AND JUST LEVELING THE ALREADY WOBBLY CENA.

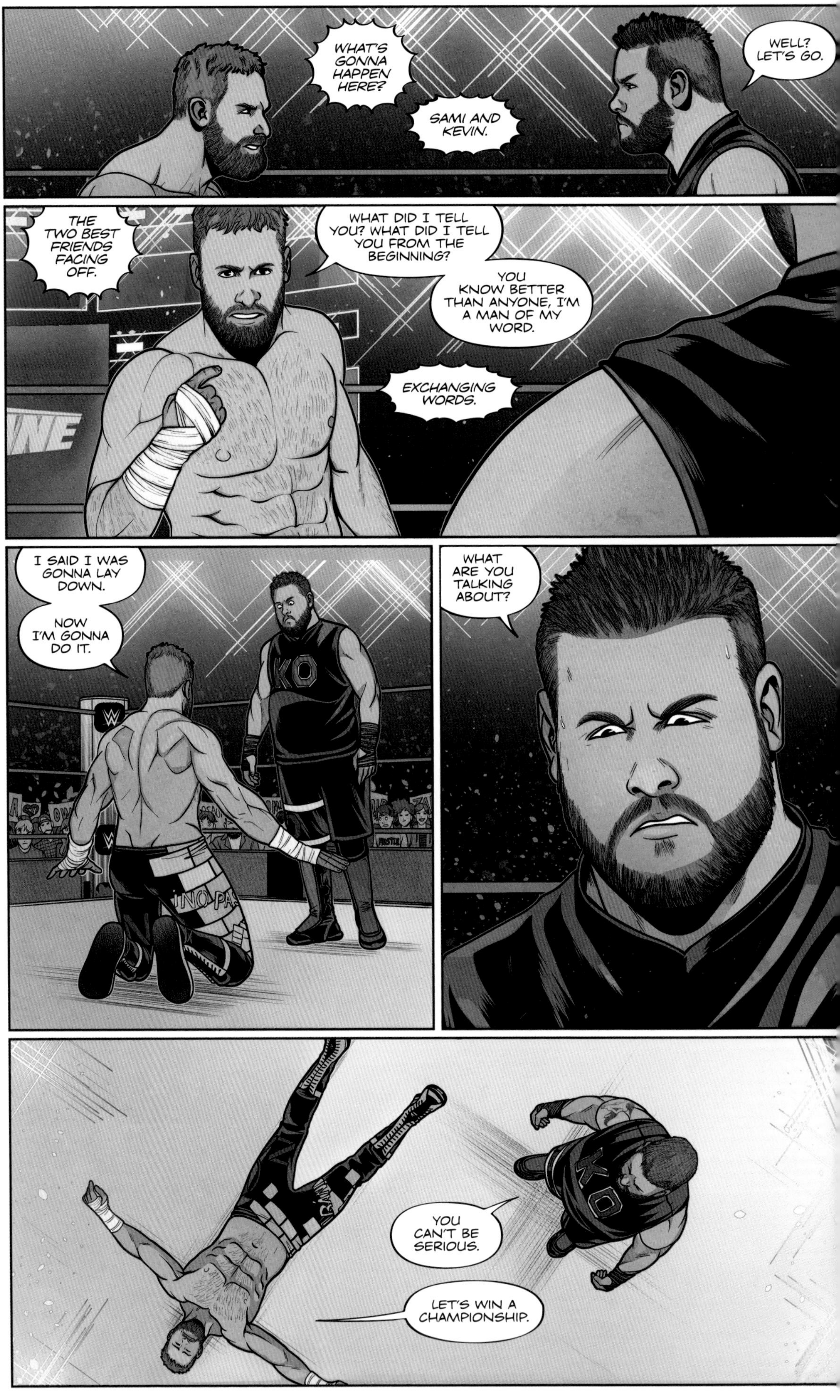

WHAT'S GONNA HAPPEN HERE?
SAMI AND KEVIN.
WELL? LET'S GO.
THE TWO BEST FRIENDS FACING OFF.
WHAT DID I TELL YOU? WHAT DID I TELL YOU FROM THE BEGINNING?
YOU KNOW BETTER THAN ANYONE, I'M A MAN OF MY WORD.
EXCHANGING WORDS.
I SAID I WAS GONNA LAY DOWN.
NOW I'M GONNA DO IT.
KO
WHAT ARE YOU TALKING ABOUT?
YOU CAN'T BE SERIOUS.
LET'S WIN A CHAMPIONSHIP.

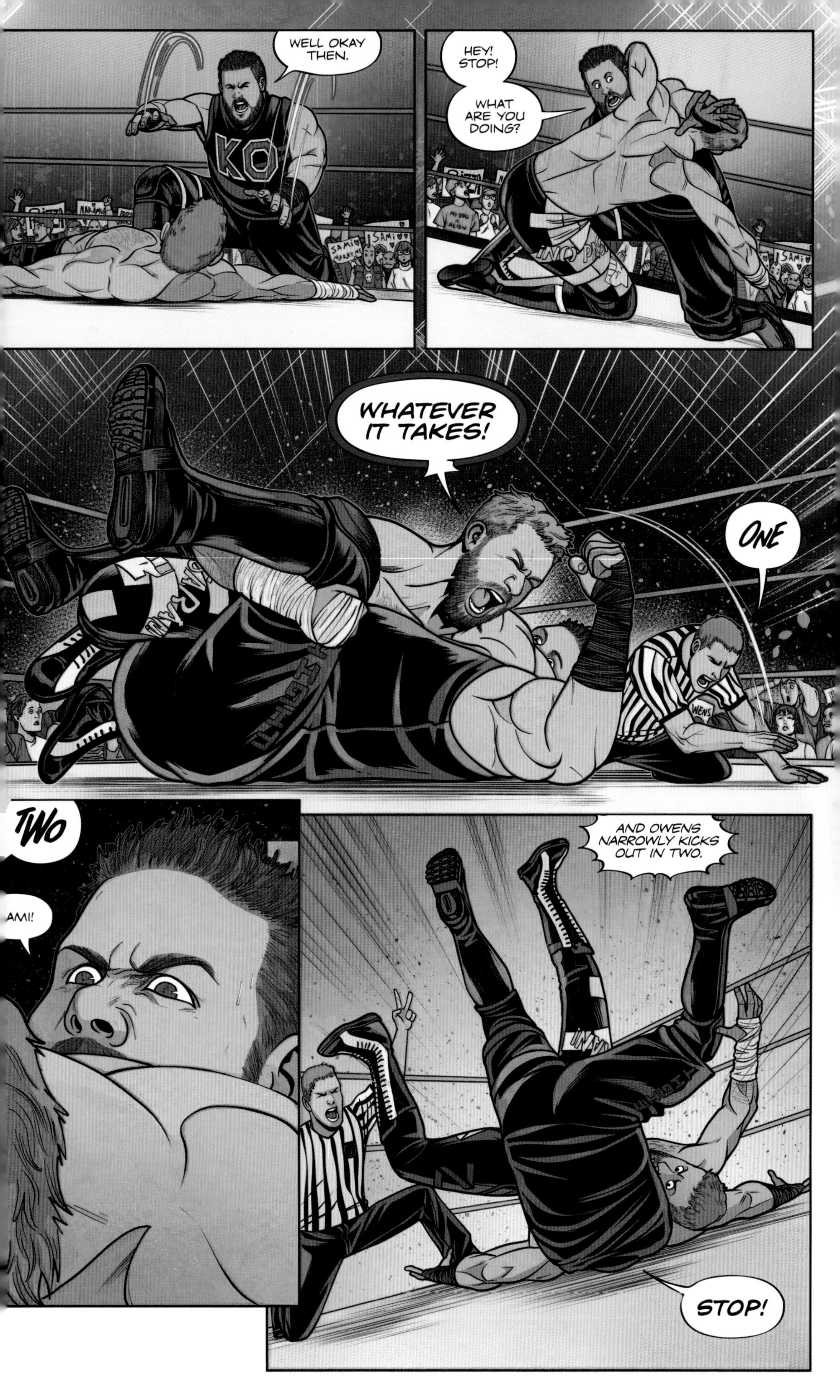
WELL OKAY THEN.
HEY! STOP!
WHAT ARE YOU DOING?
WHATEVER IT TAKES!
ONE
TWO
AMI!
AND OWENS NARROWLY KICKS OUT IN TWO.
STOP!

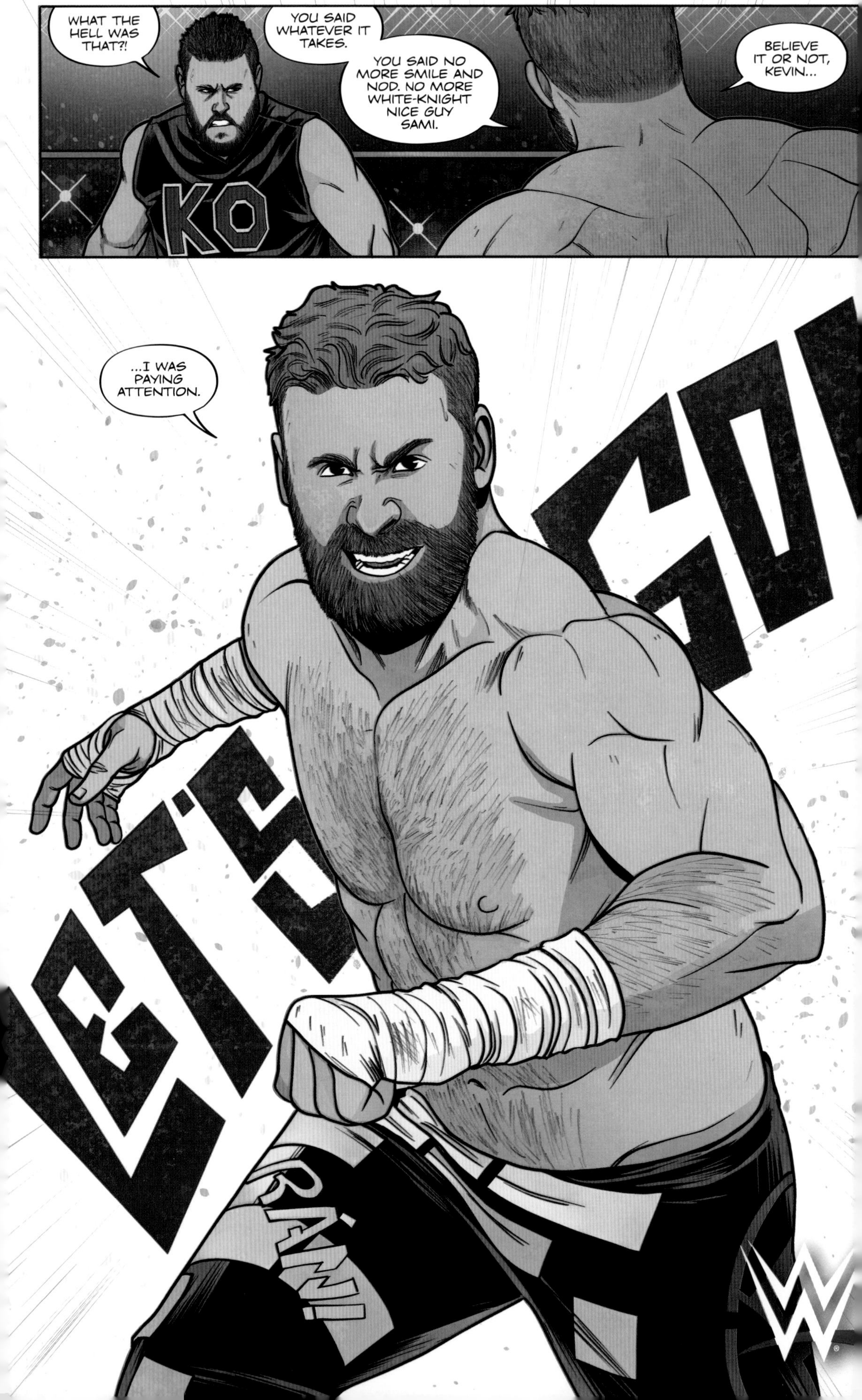
WHAT THE HELL WAS THAT?!
YOU SAID WHATEVER IT TAKES.
YOU SAID NO MORE SMILE AND NOD. NO MORE WHITE-KNIGHT NICE GUY SAMI.
BELIEVE IT OR NOT, KEVIN...
KO
...I WAS PAYING ATTENTION.
LET'S
SAMI

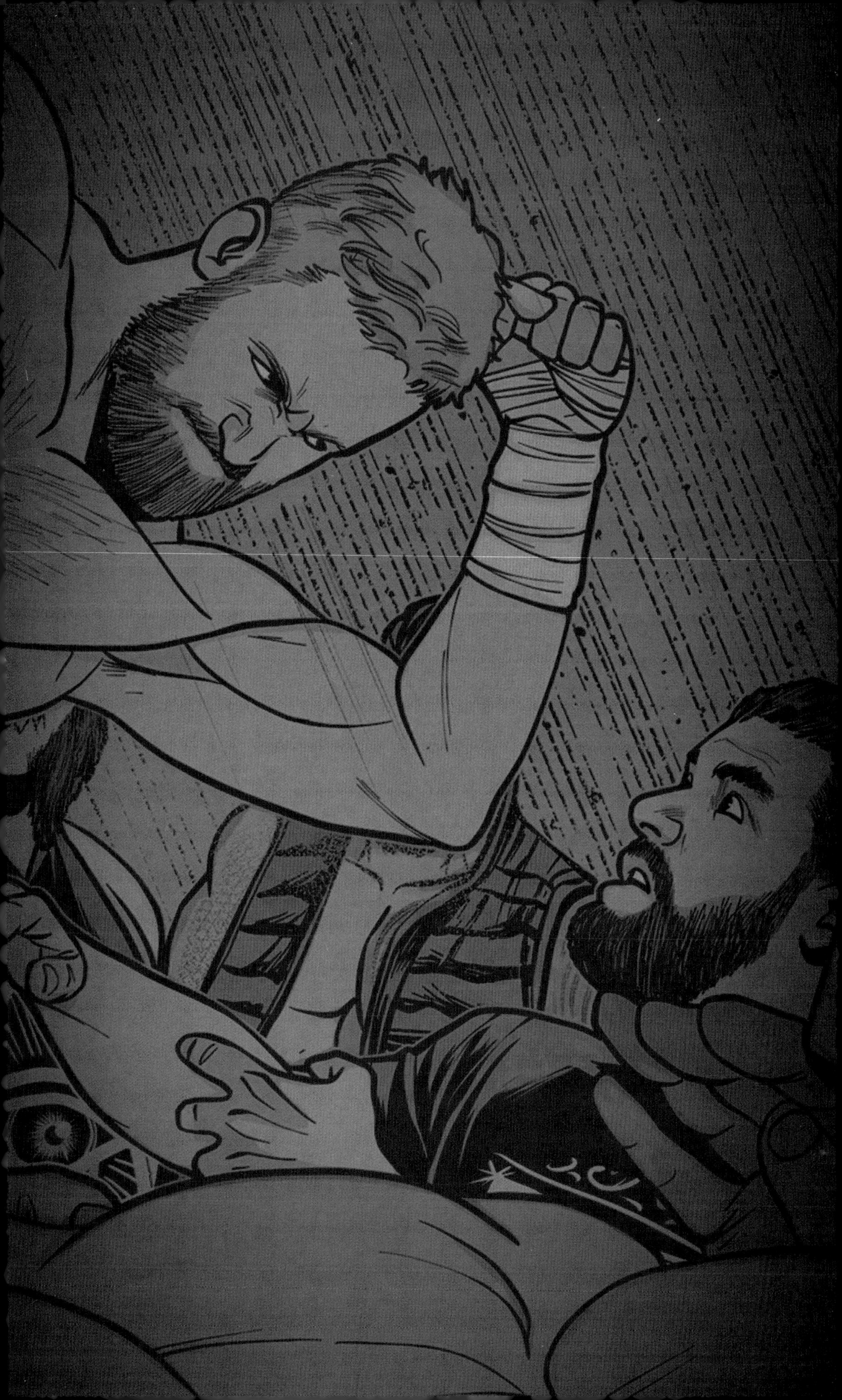

COVER GALLERY

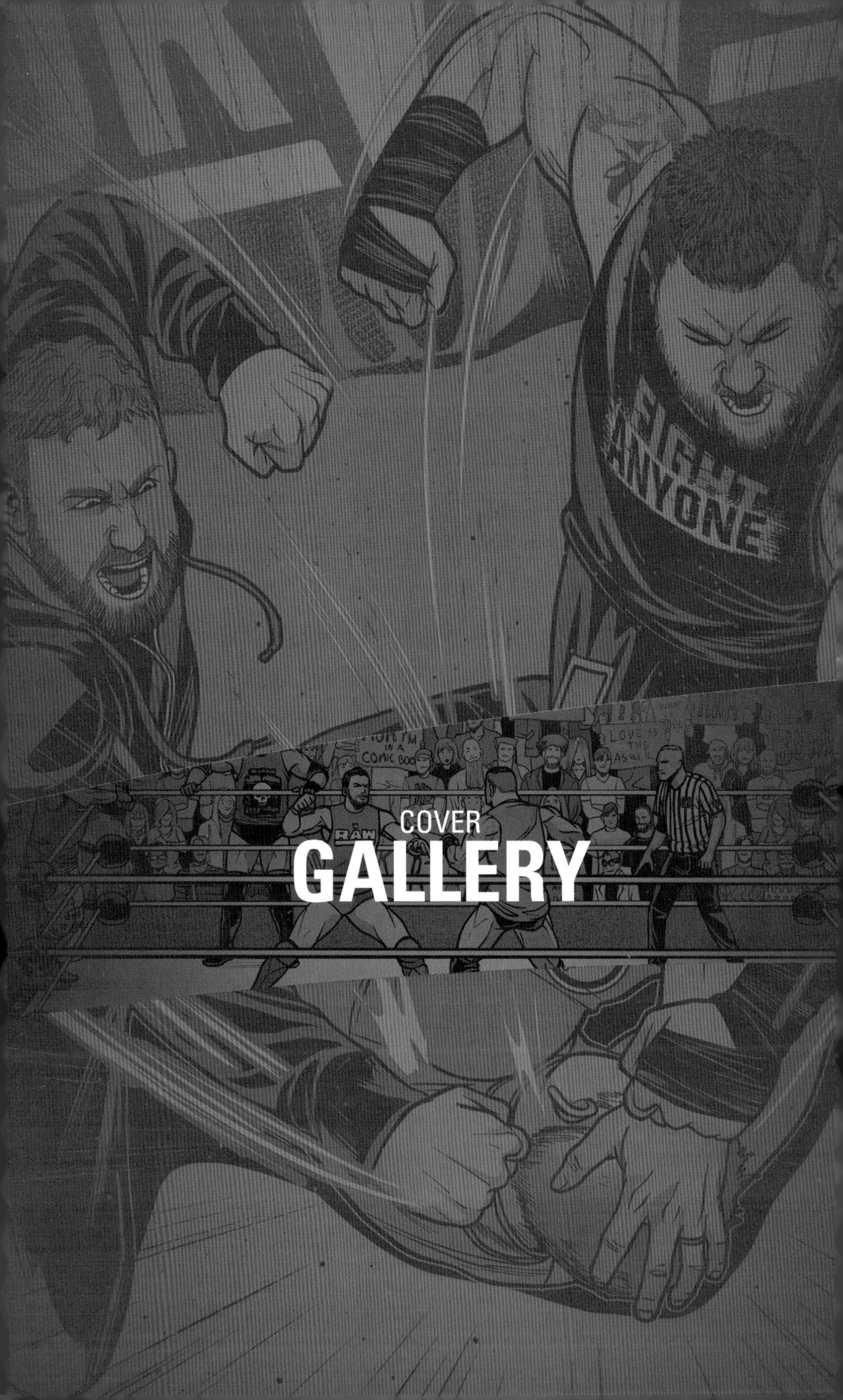
ANYONE
RAW

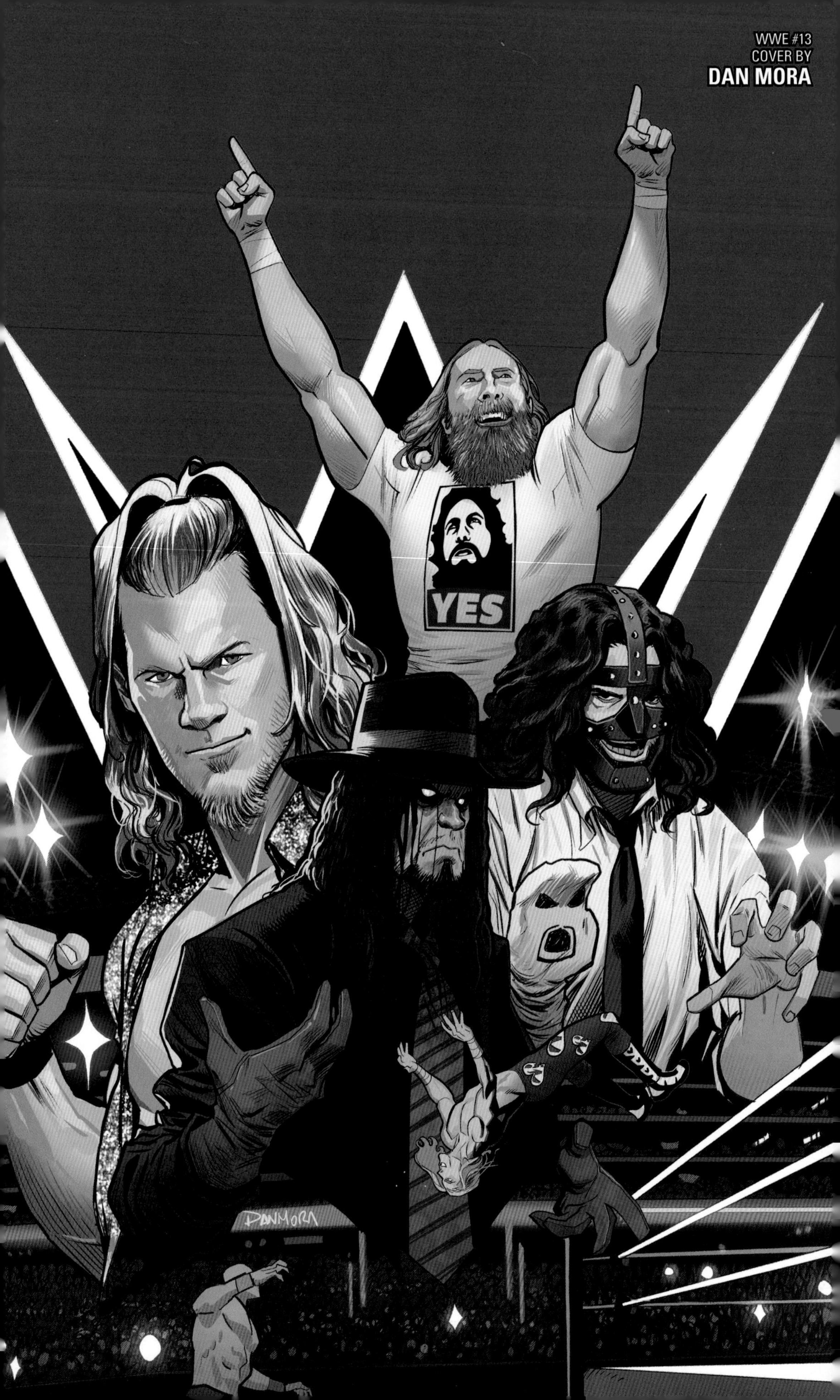
YES
DANMORA

WWE #13
COVER BY
DAN MORA

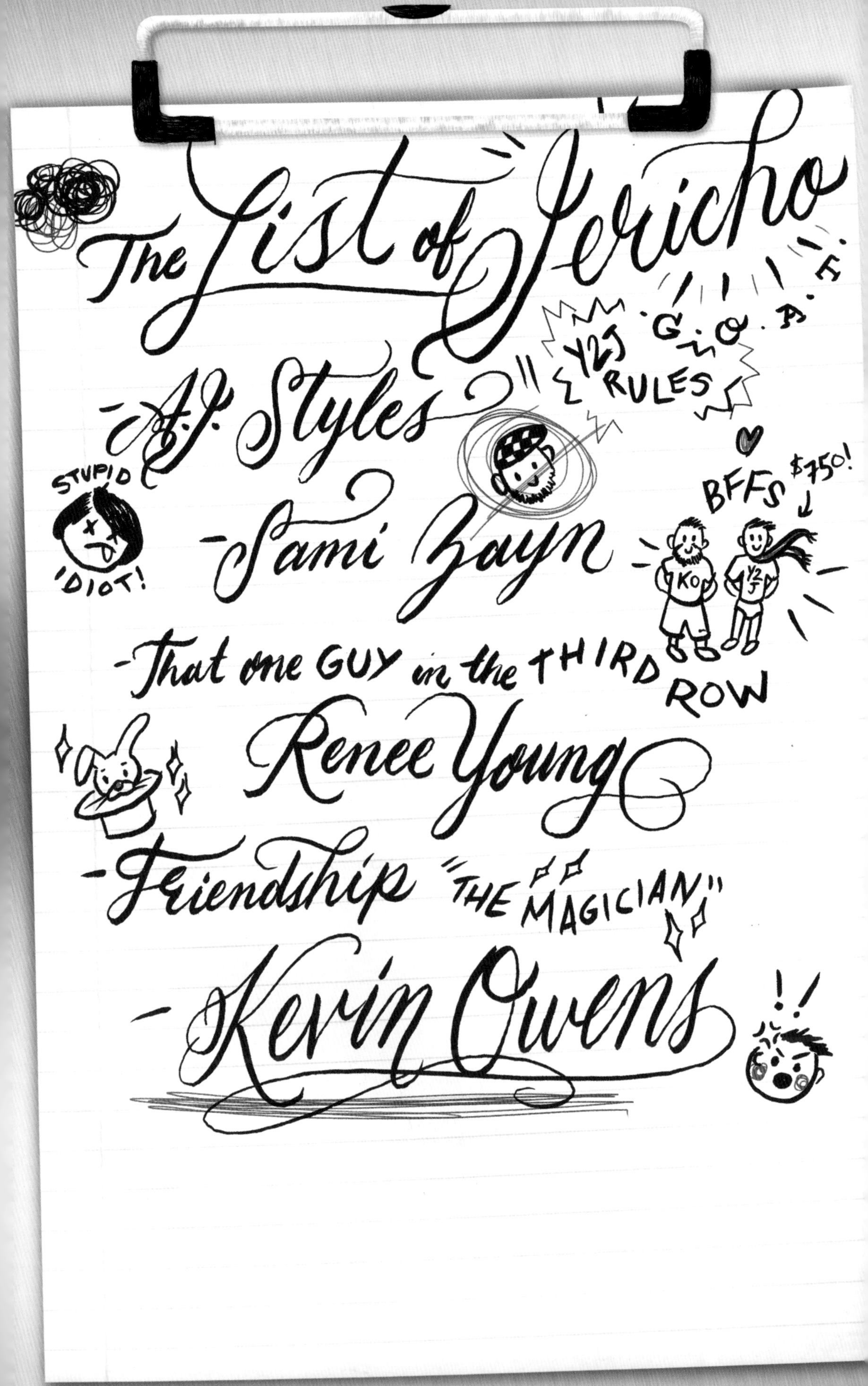

The List of Jericho
G.O.A.T.
Y2J RULES
- A.J. Styles
STUPID
IDIOT!
- Sami Zayn
BFFS
$750!
KO
Y2J
- That one GUY in the THIRD ROW
Renee Young
- Friendship
"THE MAGICIAN"
- Kevin Owens

WWE #13
LIST OF JERICHO COVER BY
ADAM X VASS

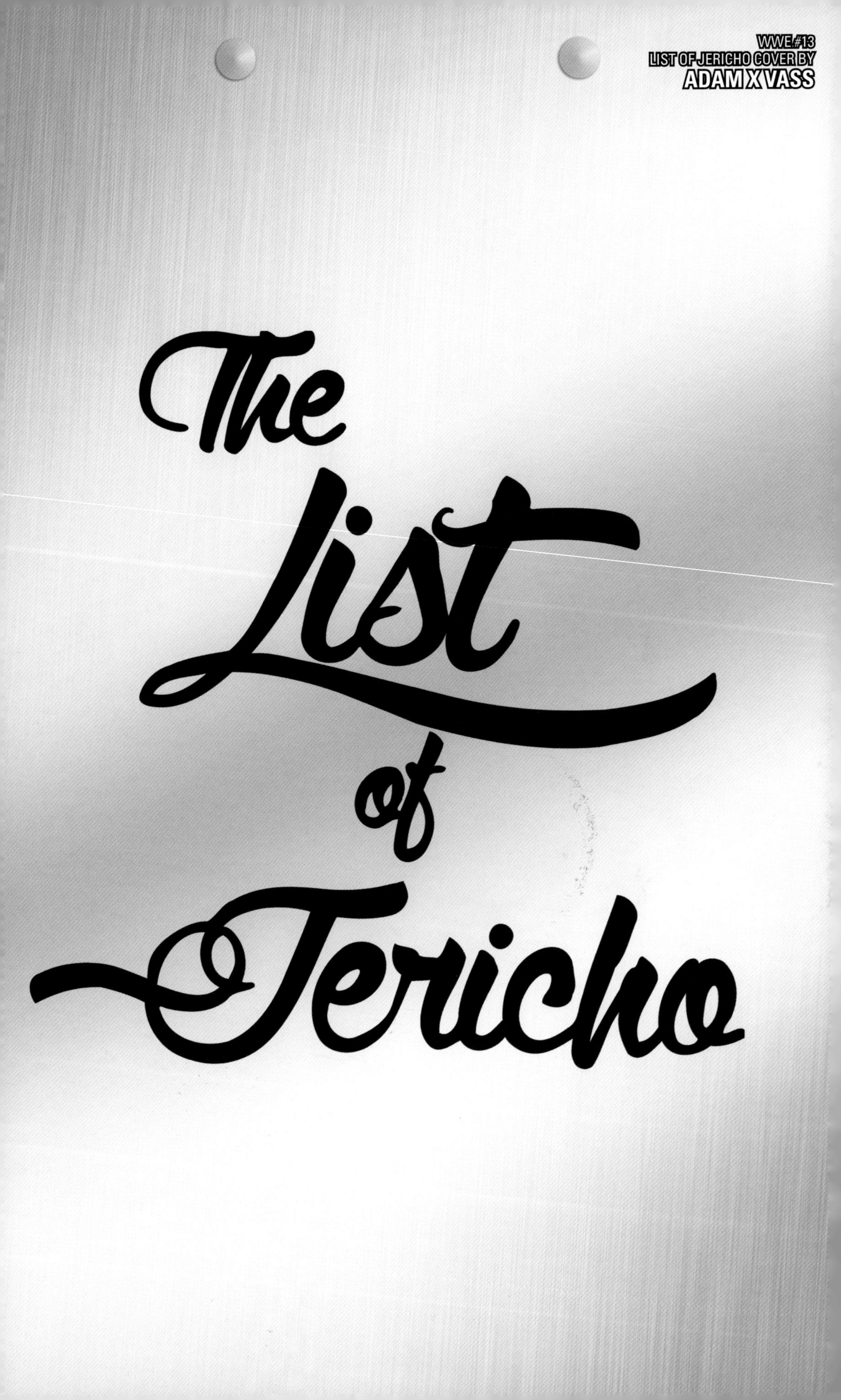
The
List
of
Jericho

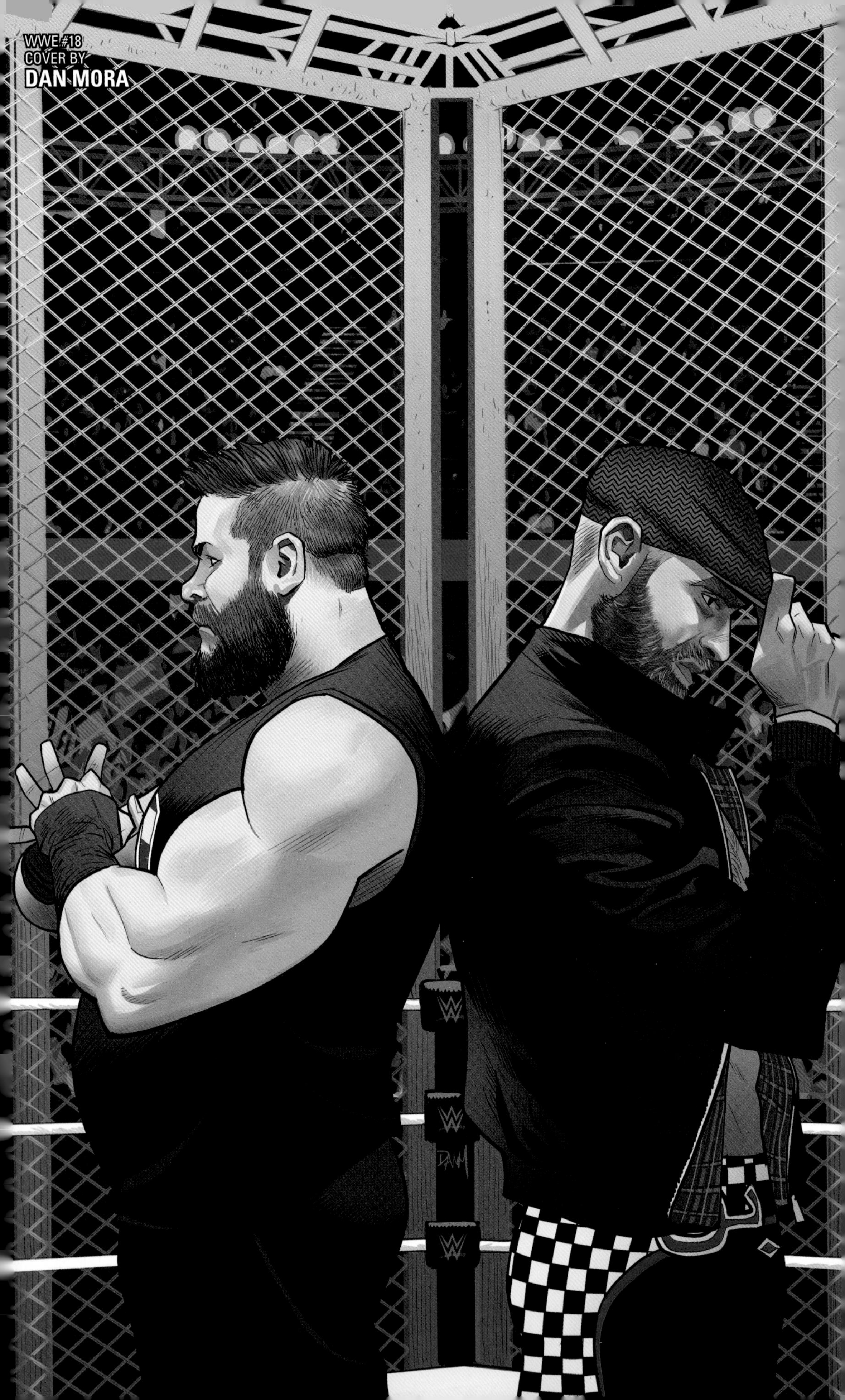

WWE #18
COVER BY
DAN MORA

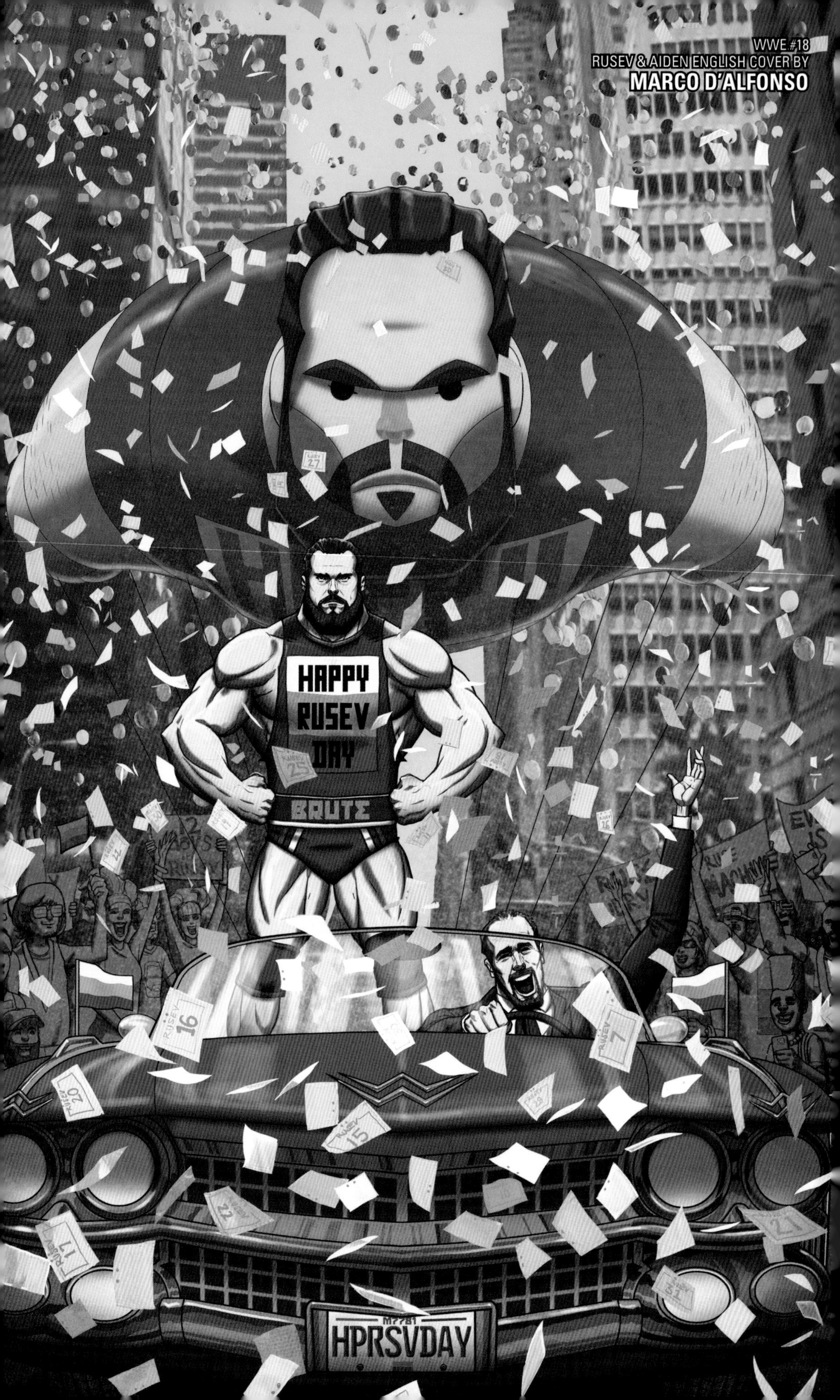
HAPPY
RUSEV
DAY
BRUTE
HPRSVDAY

WWE #18
RUSEV & AIDEN ENGLISH COVER BY
MARCO D'ALFONSO

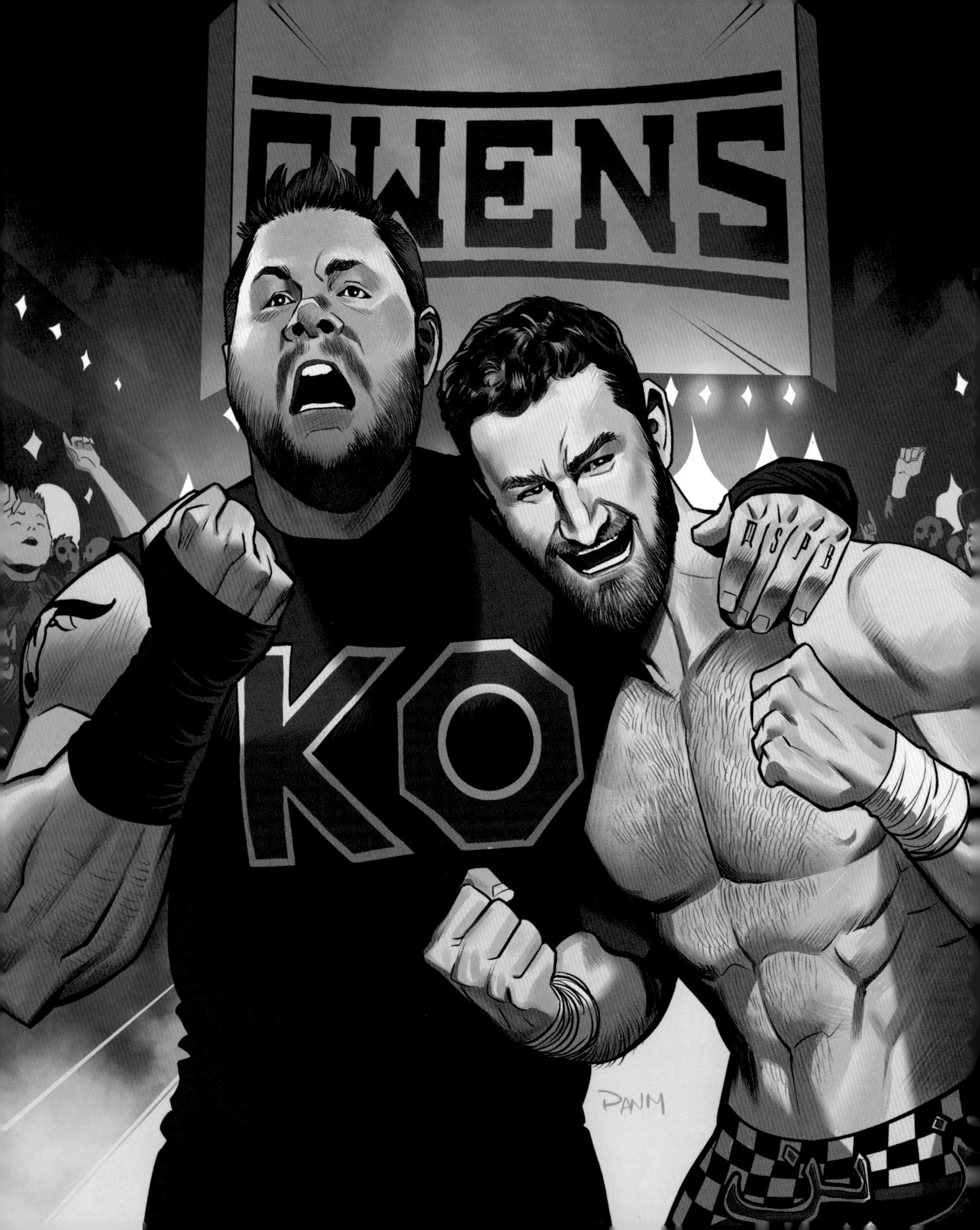
OWENS
KO

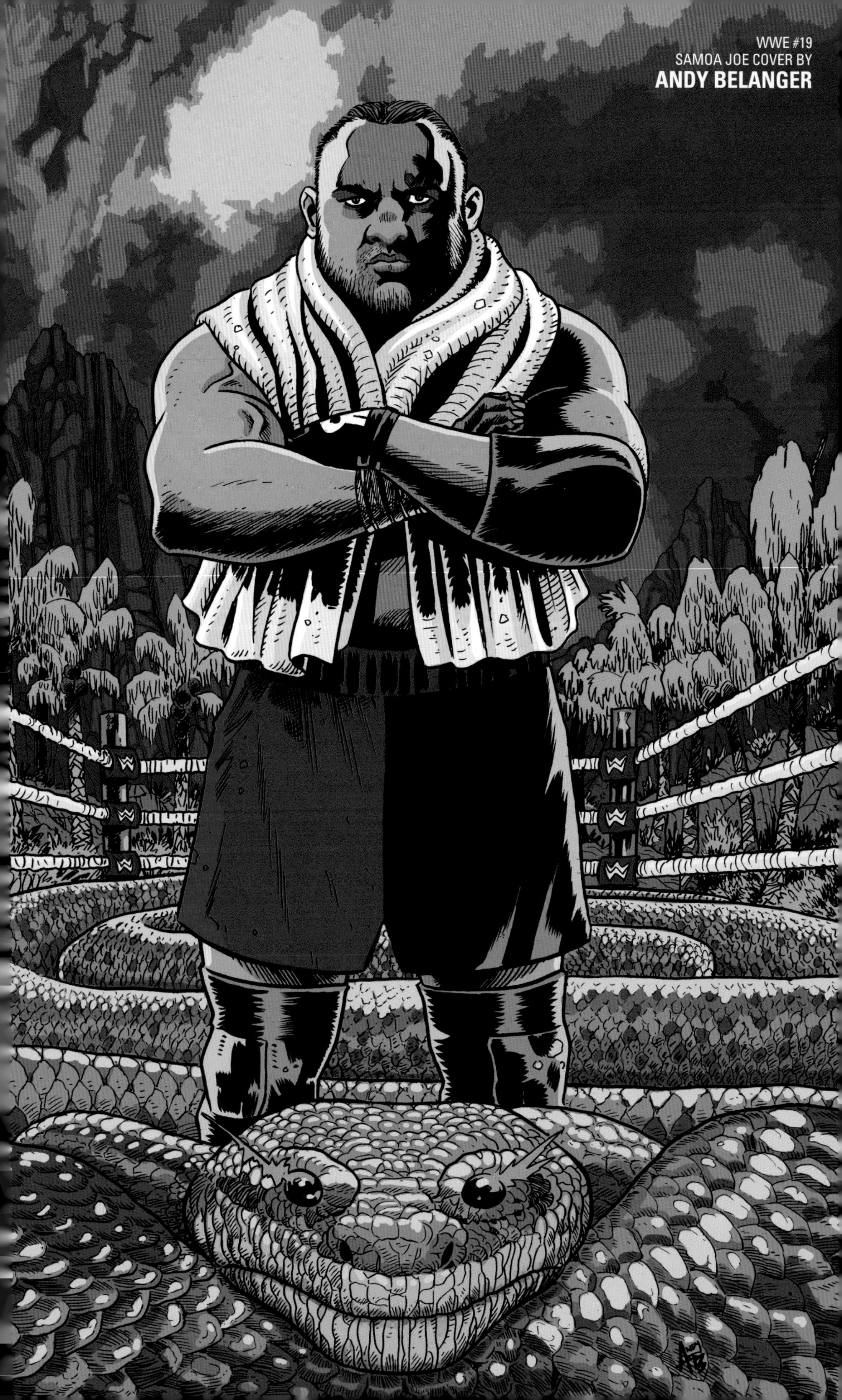

WWE #19
SAMOA JOE COVER BY
ANDY BELANGER

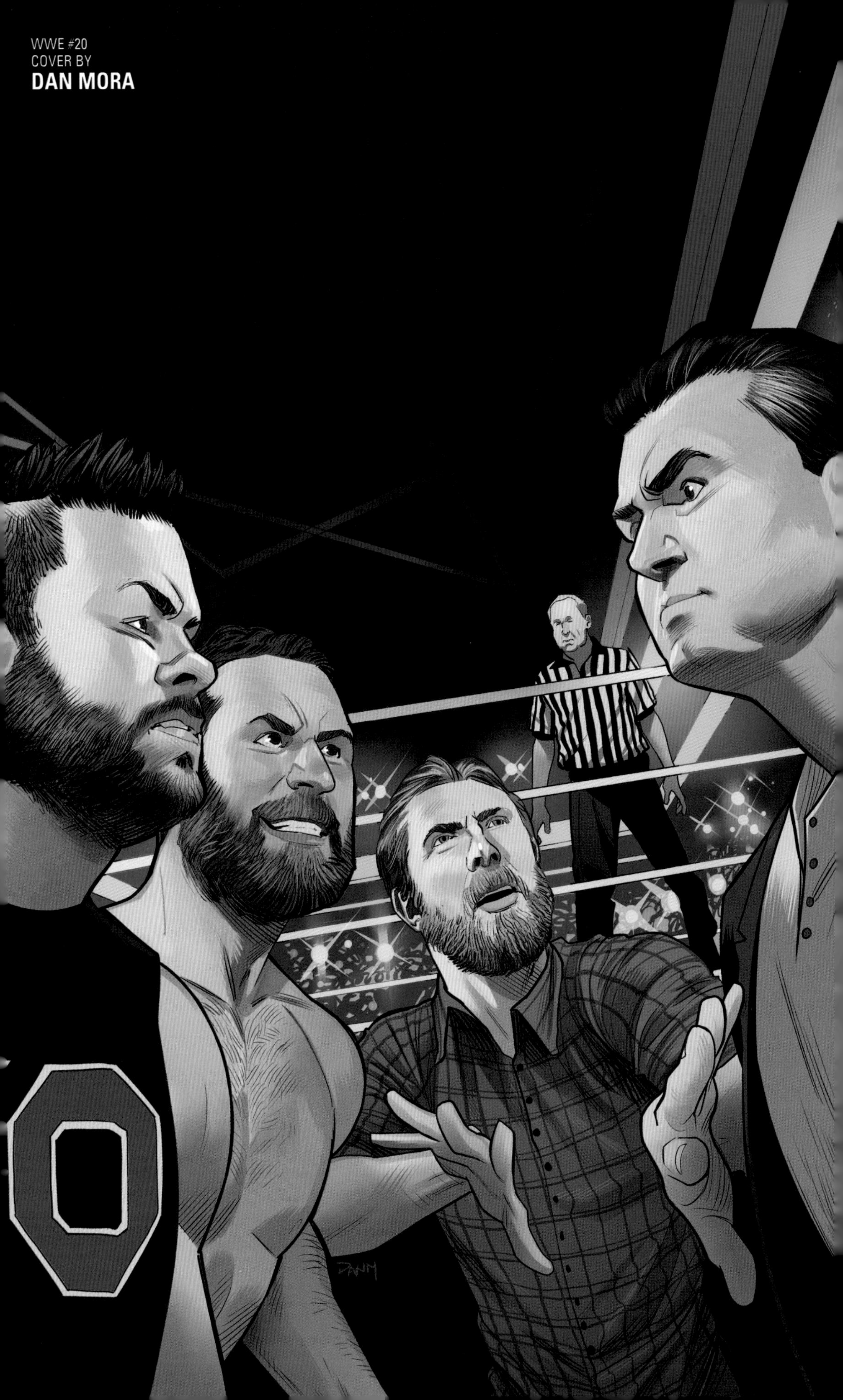

WWE #20
COVER BY
DAN MORA

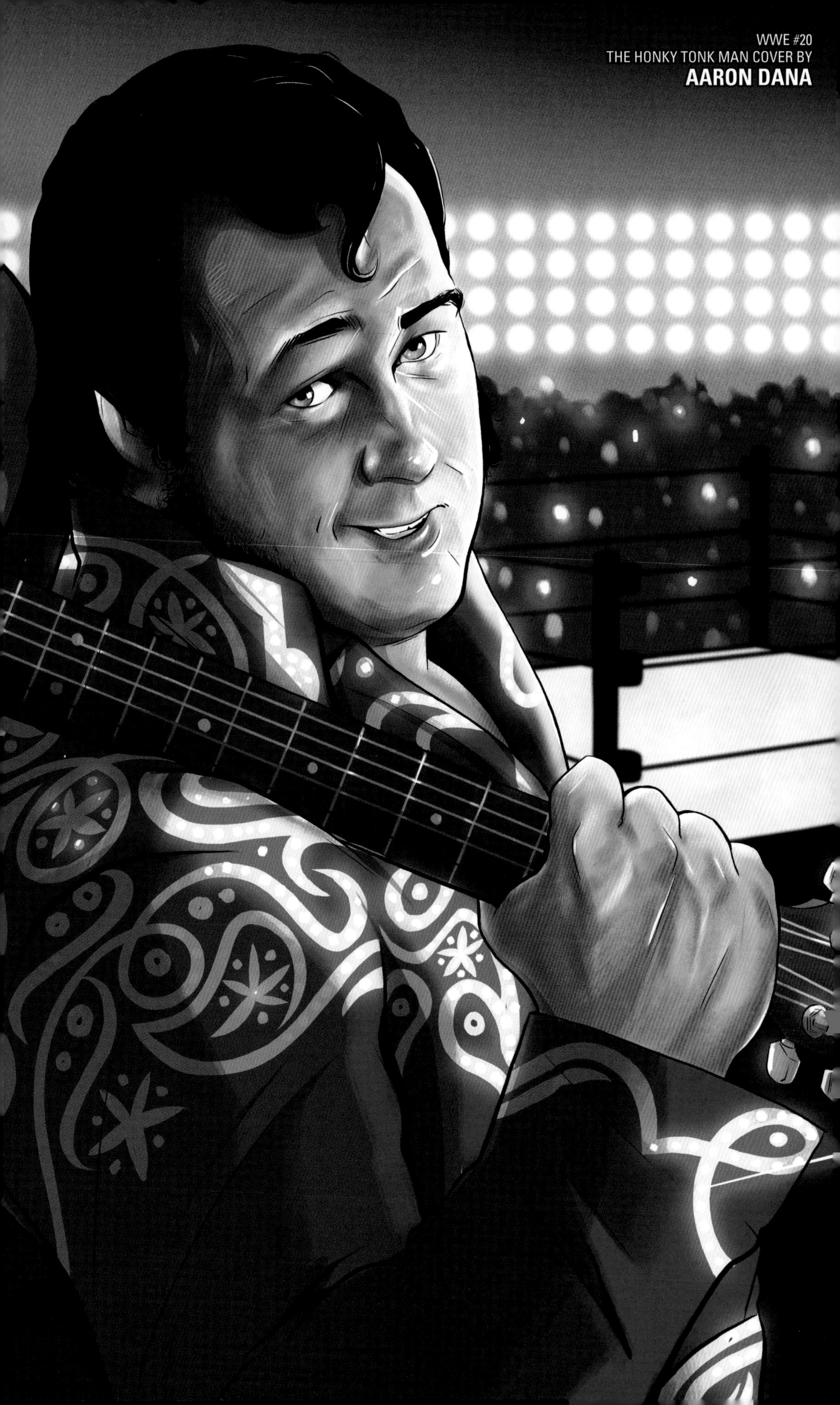

WWE #20
THE HONKY TONK MAN COVER BY
AARON DANA

WWE #13
KURT ANGLE ACTION FIGURE COVER BY
ADAM RICHES

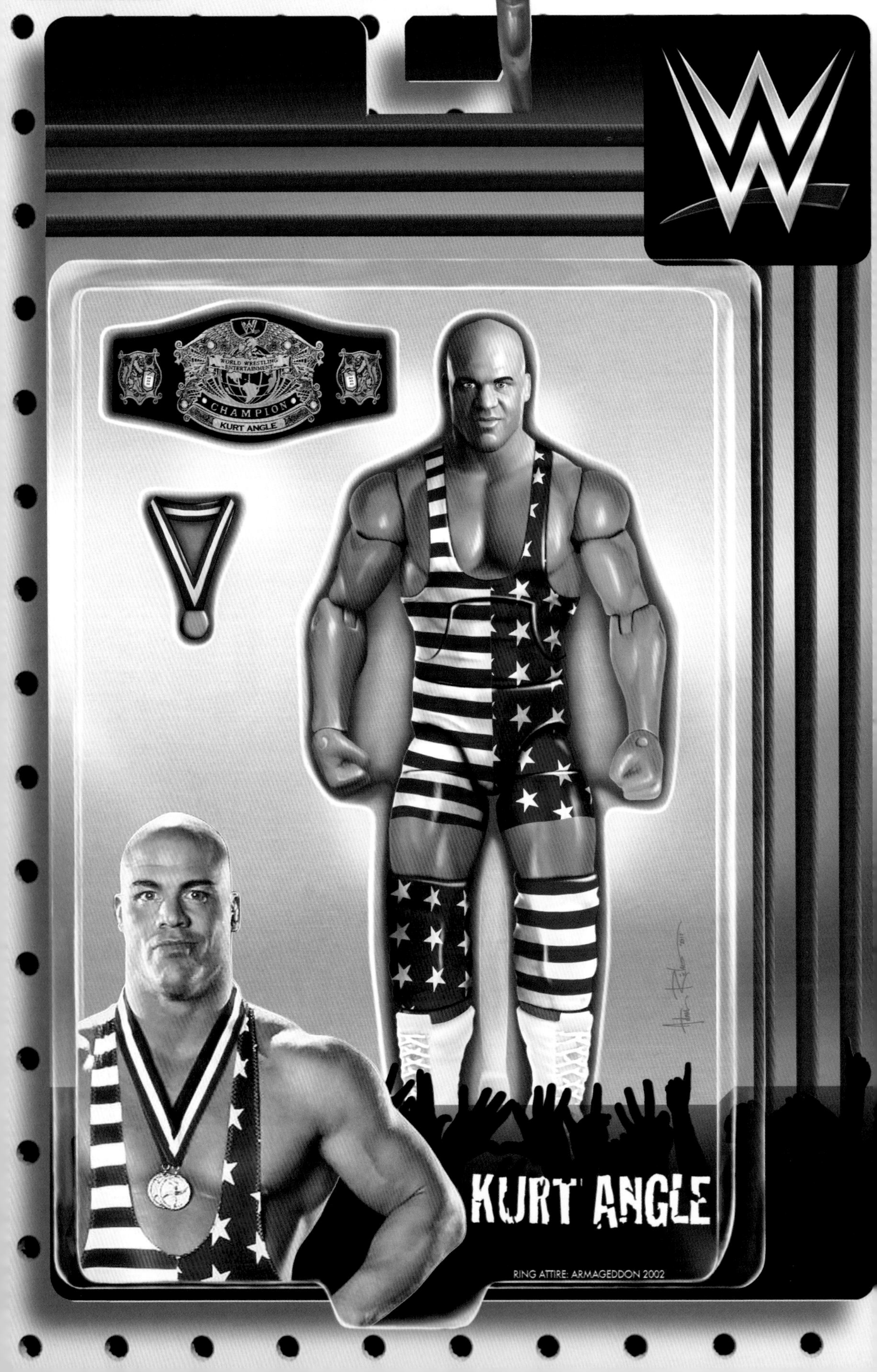

WORLD WRESTLING ENTERTAINMENT
CHAMPION
KURT ANGLE
KURT ANGLE
RING ATTIRE: ARMAGEDDON 2002

WWE #18
ZACK RYDER ACTION FIGURE COVER BY
ADAM RICHES

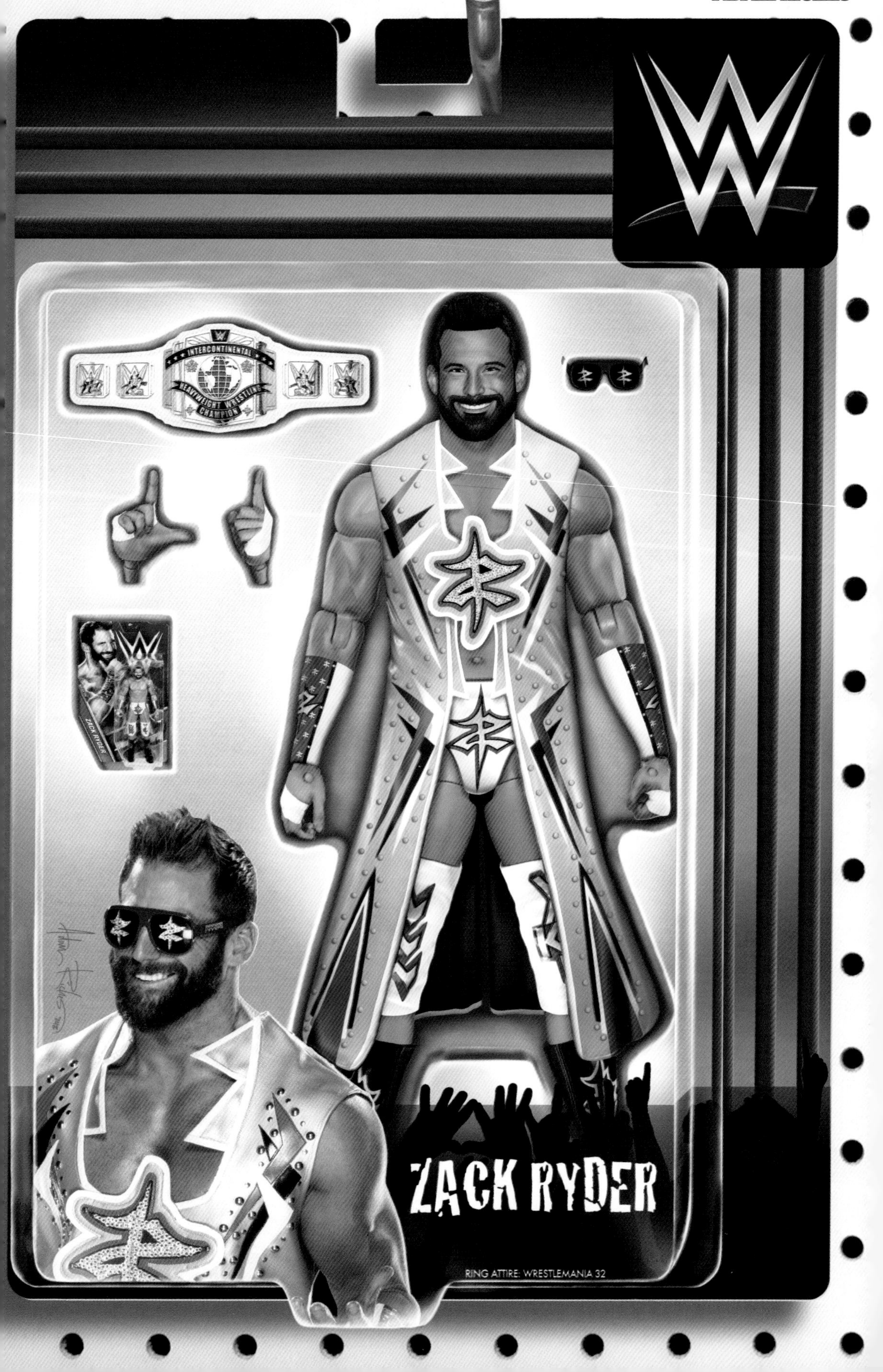
ZACK RYDER
RING ATTIRE: WRESTLEMANIA 32

WWE #19
CARMELLA ACTION FIGURE COVER BY
ADAM RICHES

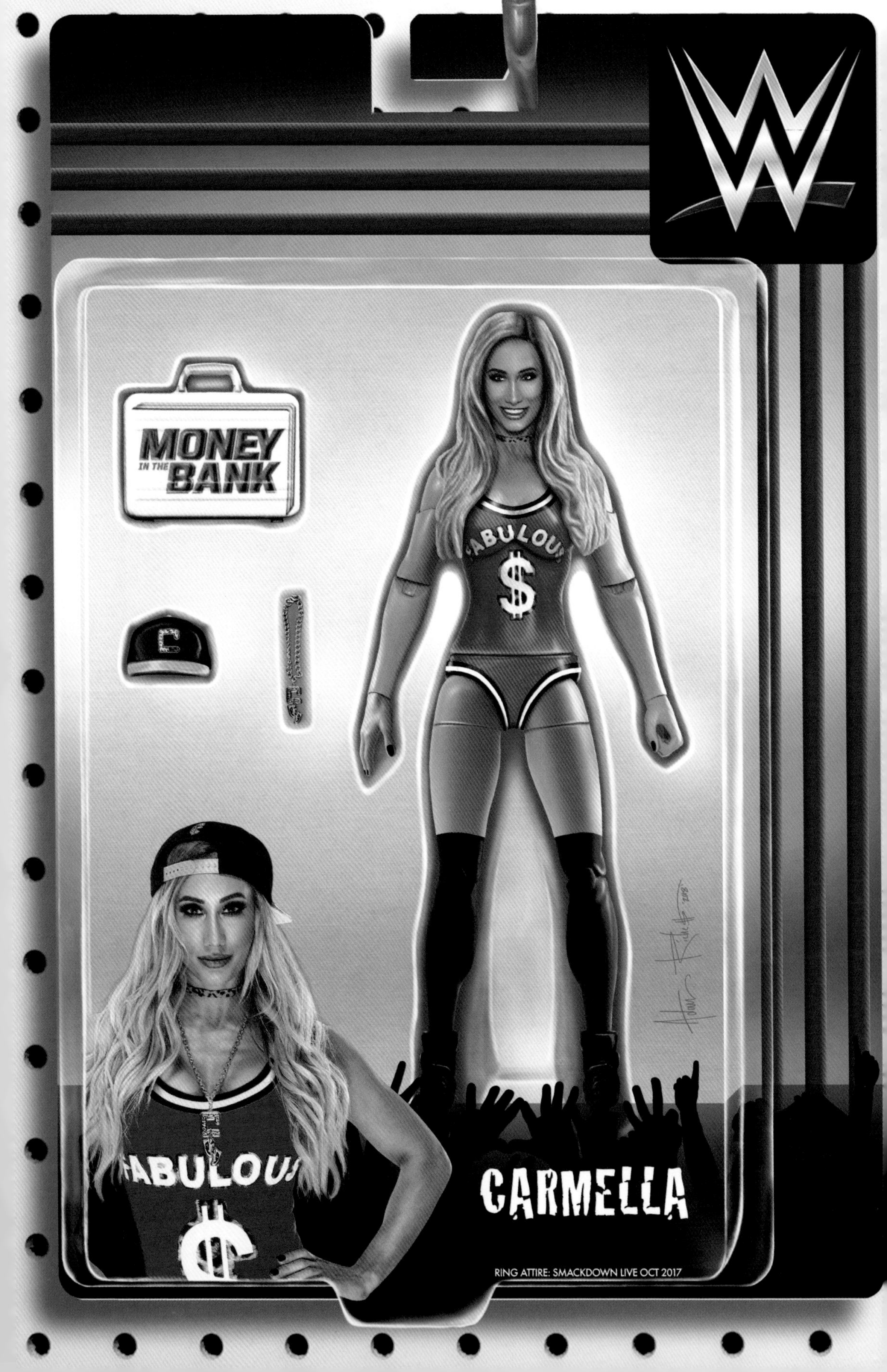
MONEY
IN THE
BANK
CARMELLA
RING ATTIRE: SMACKDOWN LIVE OCT 2017

WWE #20
KING BOOKER ACTION FIGURE COVER BY
ADAM RICHES

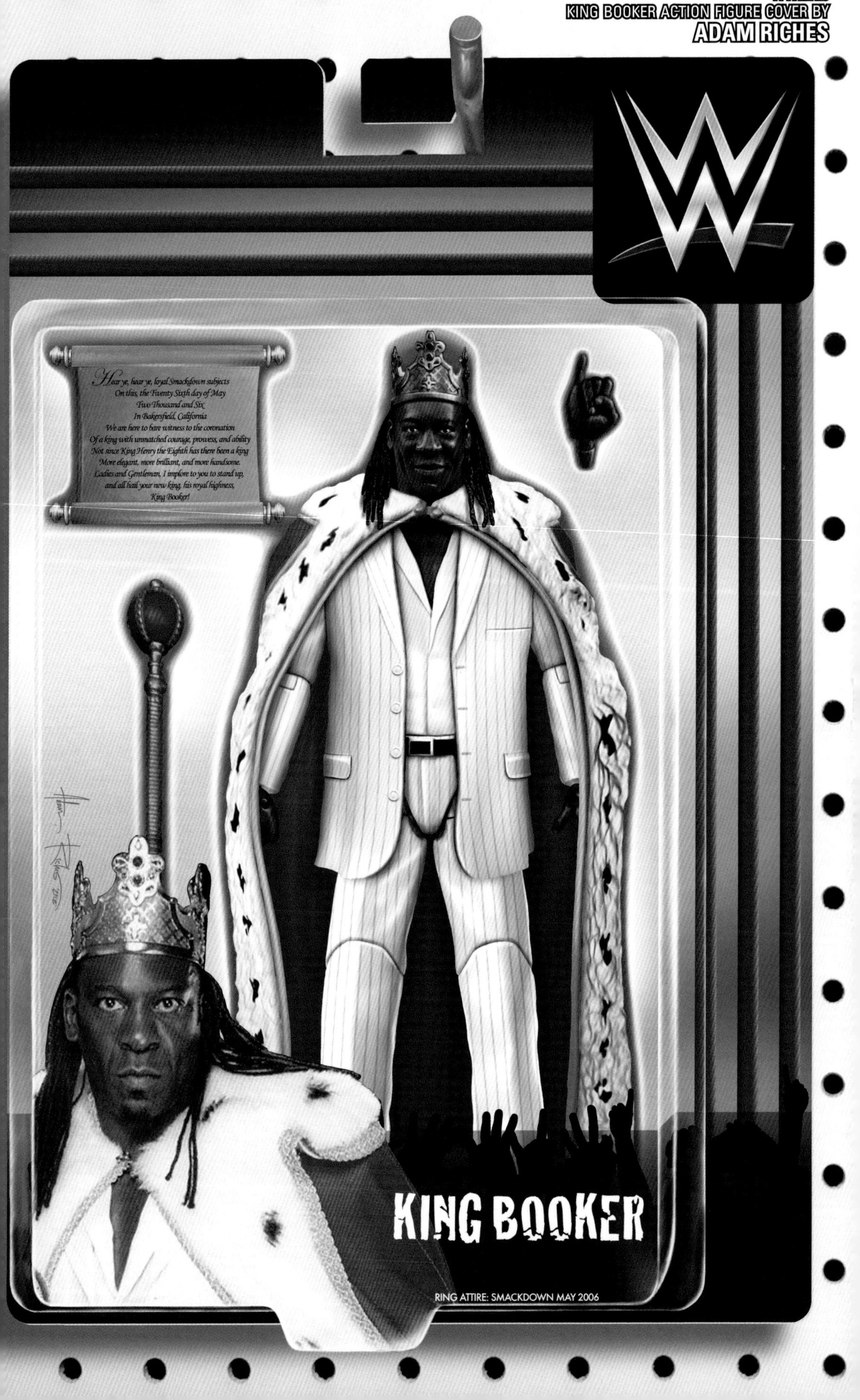
Hear ye, hear ye, loyal Smackdown subjects
On this, the Twenty Sixth day of May
Two Thousand and Six
In Bakersfield, California
We are here to bare witness to the coronation
Of a king with unmatched courage, prowess, and ability
Not since King Henry the Eighth has there been a king
More elegant, more brilliant, and more handsome.
Ladies and Gentleman, I implore to you to stand up,
and all hail your new king, his royal highness,
King Booker!
KING BOOKER
RING ATTIRE: SMACKDOWN MAY 2006

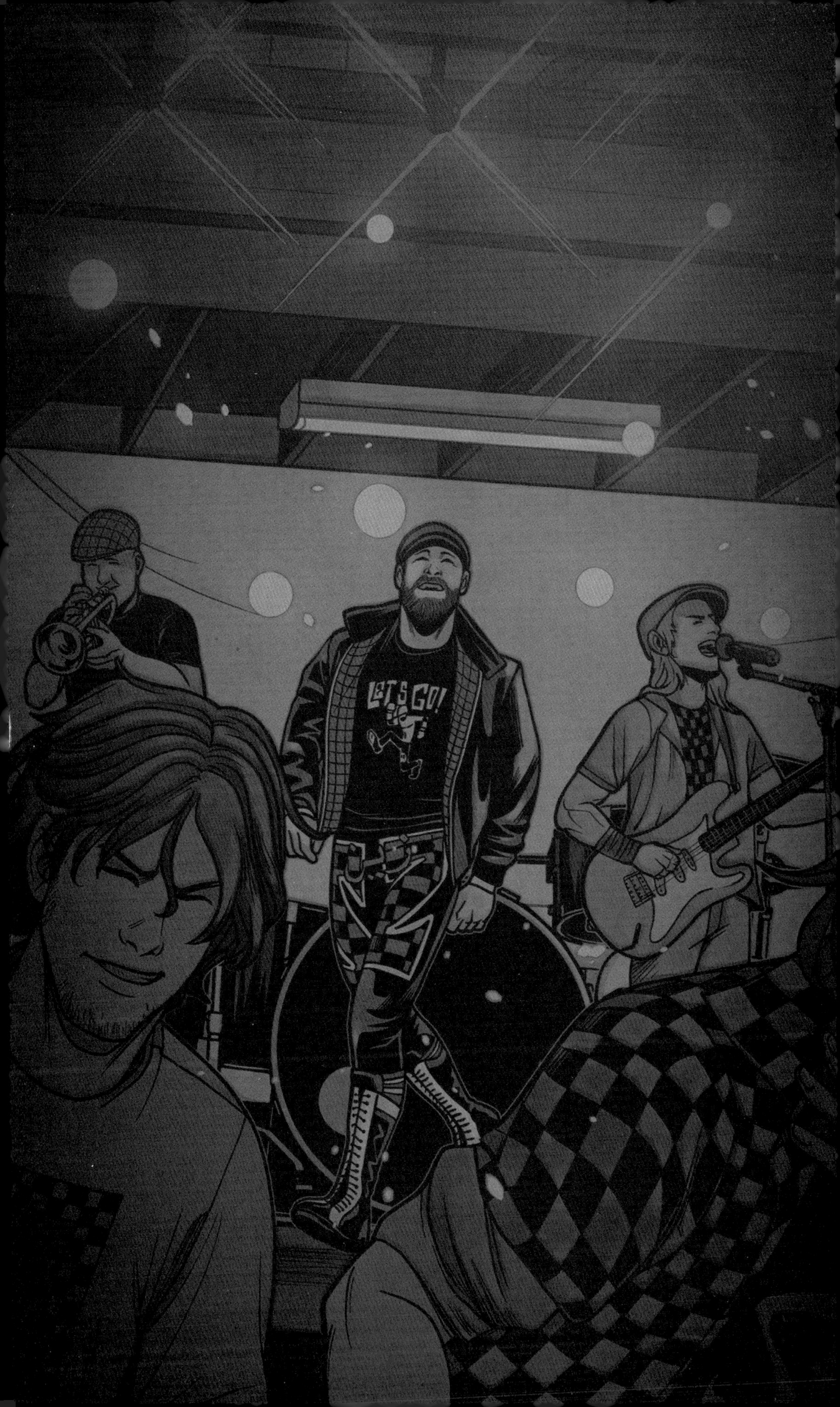
LETS GO!

DISCOVER
VISIONARY CREATORS

THE WOODS
JAMES TYNION IV • MICHAEL DIALYNAS
VOL. 1
THE ARROW

"The Spire is fantastic! My kind of genre free-for-all." —BRIAN K. VAUGHAN (Saga)
THE SPIRE
SIMON SPURRIER
JEFF STOKELY
ANDRÉ MAY

MARK WAID • PETER KRAUSE
IRREDEEMABLE
AFTERWORD BY GRANT MORRISON

J.G. JONES
MARK WAID
STRANGE FRUIT
Foreword by
ELVIS MITCHELL

MICHAEL ALAN NELSON
DAN MORA
GABRIEL CASSATA
HEXED
THE HARLOT & THE THIEF VOLUME ONE

ABNETT & CULBARD
WILD'S END
FIRST LIGHT
"IT'S REALLY GREAT!" JEFF LEMIRE

BOOM! STUDIOS

AVAILABLE AT YOUR LOCAL COMICS SHOP AND BOOKSTORE

To find a comics shop in your area, call 1-888-266-4226

WWW.**BOOM-STUDIOS**.COM

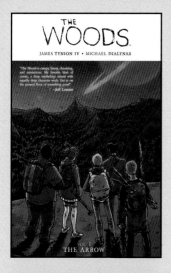

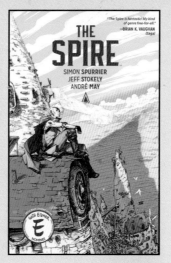

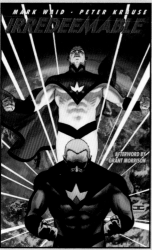

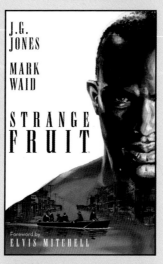

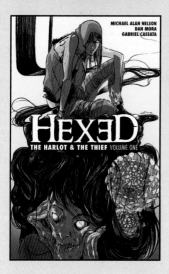

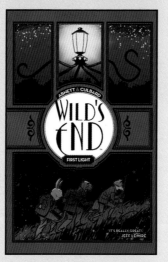

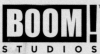

James Tynion IV

The Woods

Volume 1
ISBN: 978-1-60886-454-6 | $9.99 US
Volume 2
ISBN: 978-1-60886-495-9 | $14.99 US
Volume 3
ISBN: 978-1-60886-773-8 | $14.99 US

The Backstagers

Volume 1
ISBN: 978-1-60886-993-0 | $14.99 US

Simon Spurrier

Six-Gun Gorilla

ISBN: 978-1-60886-390-7 | $19.99 US

The Spire

ISBN: 978-1-60886-913-8 | $29.99 US

Weavers

ISBN: 978-1-60886-963-3 | $19.99 US

Mark Waid

Irredeemable

Volume 1
ISBN: 978-1-93450-690-5 | $16.99 US
Volume 2
ISBN: 978-1-60886-000-5 | $16.99 US

Incorruptible

Volume 1
ISBN: 978-1-60886-015-9 | $16.99 US
Volume 2
ISBN: 978-1-60886-028-9 | $16.99 US

Strange Fruit

ISBN: 978-1-60886-872-8 | $24.99 US

Michael Alan Nelson

Hexed The Harlot & The Thief

Volume 1
ISBN: 978-1-60886-718-9 | $14.99 US
Volume 2
ISBN: 978-1-60886-816-2 | $14.99 US

Day Men

Volume 1
ISBN: 978-1-60886-393-8 | $9.99 US
Volume 2
ISBN: 978-1-60886-852-0 | $9.99 US

Dan Abnett

Wild's End

Volume 1: First Light
ISBN: 978-1-60886-735-6 | $19.99 US
Volume 2: The Enemy Within
ISBN: 978-1-60886-877-3 | $19.99 US

Hypernaturals

Volume 1
ISBN: 978-1-60886-298-6 | $16.99 US
Volume 2
ISBN: 978-1-60886-319-8 | $19.99 US

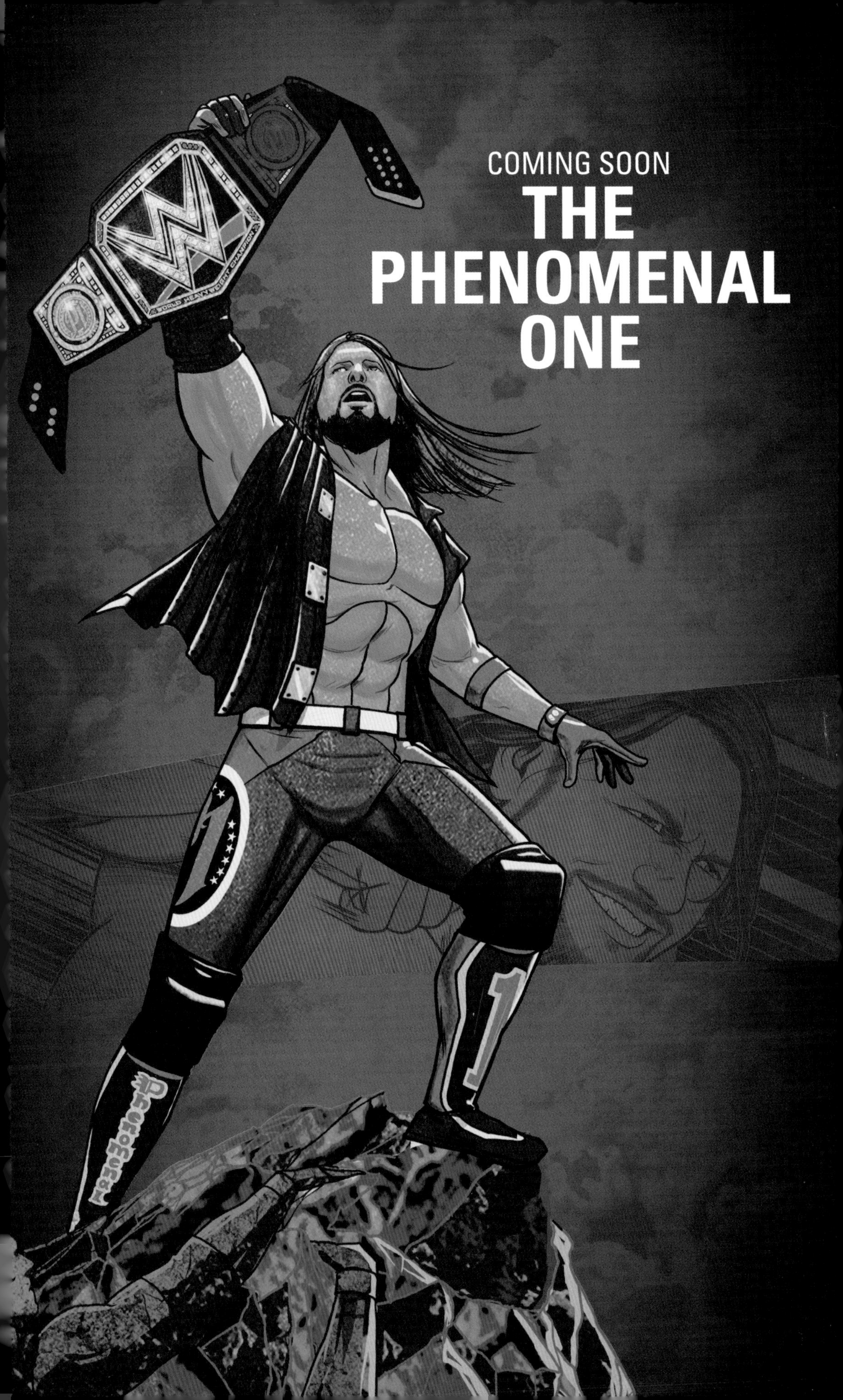
COMING SOON
THE PHENOMENAL ONE